MW00560688

WAY OF THE
BUSHMAN

"Rare ancient wisdom desperately needed in today's world."
ROBBIE HOLZ, COAUTHOR OF
SECRETS OF ABORIGINAL HEALING AND
AUTHOR OF *ABORIGINAL SECRETS OF AWAKENING*

"First and foremost, Bradford Keeney has danced with the San (Bushmen) and met them at a kinesthetic level of understanding that is unparalleled in previous anthropological research. Having met the elder healers on their own terms, Brad developed a deep relationship that brought a new voice and insight to the representation and interpretation of their healing dance. Hillary and Brad have a very special physical and academic skillset and an exceptional dedication to research. This book reveals new depths in the beliefs and practices of San (Bushman) healing that will hopefully be as valuable for the San (Bushmen) as a record and guide in a fast-changing world as it is for the wider world to appreciate these extraordinary people."
CHRIS LOW, ANTHROPOLOGIST AND PHYSICIAN,
AFRICAN STUDIES CENTRE, UNIVERSITY OF OXFORD

"Other anthropologists had not succeeded in pushing through to the deep experience that is the key to Bushman spirituality. With Brad Keeney's acceptance as a healer, hithero closed doors began to open. This work describes in previously unavailable detail how the Bushmen learn the techniques of transition and transformation, how they journey to the spirit realm, and how they climb the ropes of God. As we read the words of these Bushman elders, we can almost feel what it must be like to undertake such journeys."

DAVID LEWIS-WILLIAMS, PH.D., FOUNDER OF
THE ROCK ART RESEARCH INSTITUTE,
UNIVERSITY OF WITWATERSRAND,
JOHANNESBURG, SOUTH AFRICA,
AND AUTHOR OF *DECIPHERING ANCIENT MINDS*

"Bradford and Hillary Keeney have broken through the dusty curtain that often separates anthropologists from the people whose beliefs and practices they want to understand. Instead of writing exclusively about their own impressions, they foreground the teachings of Jul'hoan Bushman elders from northeastern Namibia. Their parallel commentary shows how a form of circular interaction and change-oriented activities have kept the ancient religion and its practitioners alive and successful despite major social upheaval in their community over the past century or more. It is a poignant reminder that the opportunity to share the experiences described with rare insight in this 'bible' may never arise in the same way again."

JANETTE DEACON, PH.D., ARCHAEOLOGIST
AND AUTHORITY ON BUSHMAN ROCK ART

WAY OF THE
BUSHMAN

Spiritual Teachings
and Practices
of the Kalahari Ju|'hoansi

AS TOLD BY THE TRIBAL ELDERS
Translated by Beesa Boo

EDITED WITH COMMENTARY BY
Bradford Keeney, Ph.D., and Hillary Keeney, Ph.D.

Bear & Company
Rochester, Vermont • Toronto, Canada

Bear & Company
One Park Street
Rochester, Vermont 05767
www.BearandCompanyBooks.com

Text stock is SFI certified

Bear & Company is a division of Inner Traditions International

Copyright © 2015 by Bradford Keeney and Hillary Keeney

All rights reserved. No part of this book may be reproduced or utilized in
any form or by any means, electronic or mechanical, including photocopying,
recording, or by any information storage and retrieval system, without permission
in writing from the publisher.

Library of Congress Cataloging-in-Publication Data

Way of the Bushman : spiritual teachings and practices of the Kalahari Ju|'hoansi
/ as told by the tribal Elders ; translated by Beesa Boo ; edited with commentary
by Bradford Keeney, Ph.D., and Hillary Keeney, Ph.D.

    pages cm

  Summary: "The first comprehensive presentation of the core teachings of the
Kalahari Bushmen as told by the Tribal Elders"—Provided by publisher.

  Includes bibliographical references and index.

  ISBN 978-1-59143-205-0 (pbk.) — ISBN 978-1-59143-784-0 (e-book)

  1. San (African people)—Kalahari Desert—Religion. 2. !Kung (African
people)—Kalahari Desert—Religion. 3. San (African people)—Rites and
ceremonies. 4. !Kung (African people)—Rites and ceremonies. 5. Spiritual life.
I. Boo, Beesa, translator. II. Keeney, Bradford, 1951– editor. III. Keeney, Hillary,
editor.

  BL2480.S24W39 2015

  299.6'81—dc23

                                                    2014045915

Printed and bound in the United States by Lake Book Manufacturing, Inc.
The text stock is SFI certified. The Sustainable Forestry Initiative® program
promotes sustainable forest management.

10 9 8 7 6 5 4 3 2 1

Text design by Debbie Glogover and layout by Virginia Scott Bowman
This book was typeset in Garamond Premier Pro with Gill Sans MT Pro, Franklin
Gothic, and Trajan Sans Pro used as display typefaces

To send correspondence to the author of this book, mail a first-class letter to the
author c/o Inner Traditions • Bear & Company, One Park Street, Rochester, VT
05767, and we will forward the communication, or contact the author directly at
www.keeneyinstitute.org.

CONTENTS

PART TWO

The Elders Speak: Remembrances

❊

PRONUNCIATION GUIDE

Throughout this book you will notice unusual punctuation marks in words from the Jul'hoan language of the Kalahari Bushmen. These marks are symbols for the four distinct click sounds and the glottal stop used in this language. According to anthropologist and linguist Megan Biesele, they are pronounced as follows:

| | is a dental click that sounds like *tsk, tsk* and is made by putting the tongue behind the teeth.
≠ is an alveolar click, a soft pop made by putting the tongue behind the ridge that is located behind the front teeth.
! is an alveolar-palatal click, a sharp pop made by drawing the tongue down quickly from the roof of the mouth.
‖ is a lateral click, a clucking sound similar to that made by the English when they urge on a horse.
’ Is a glottal stop, as in the Cockney English pronunciation of *bottle*.

This book also has a "Dictionary of the Jul'hoan Religion" by Beesa Boo and Bradford Keeney that contains definitions and pronunciations of words used by the nlom-kxaosi. Readers can go to

www.keeneyinstitute.org/judictionary.php

to hear an audio recording of Beesa Boo pronouncing these words.

ENTERING THE WORLD
OF THE JUI'HOANSI

Way of the Bushman presents the spiritual teachings and practices of the Jul'hoan Bushmen (or San) of southern Africa. Theirs is a radically ecstatic way of healing, shamanism, and spirituality that dances with the divine. Relying less on belief than on felt experience, the Bushman way is more concerned with being moved by a mysterious, vibratory life force the Bushmen call *nlom*. Their experiences with nlom and the ecstatic transformations it brings forth are awakened and nurtured by an emotionally close relationship with the Sky God of creation.* The Bushman healer and shaman, called a *nlom-kxao,* is a hunter and gatherer of nlom, using it to infuse revitalized life into the everyday. Welcome to the sacred ecstatic way of the Bushman!

This spiritual text is a testament to what may be the earliest form of healing and spirituality. Geneticists and anthropologists have gathered scientific evidence suggesting that the Bushmen of southern Africa comprise the oldest living culture. According to a ten-year

---

*Bushman visionary experience of the sky village may include meeting a family of Gods—a Father God, Mother God, and their sons and daughters.

research study published in the journal *Science* (Tishkoff 2009), the Bushmen have the most genetic diversity in their DNA, establishing them as the people most closely associated with the birth of humanity. This study identifies the Bushmen as directly descended from the original population of early human ancestors who gave rise to all the people who left the continent to populate other parts of the world (Connor 2009). Professor Sarah Tishkoff, a molecular biologist at the University of Pennsylvania, metaphorically suggests that the Bushmen's homeland may be considered the "garden of Eden" where human beings began and that they are the closest people to humanity's biblical progenitors, Adam and Eve.

Other African groups that have a "click" language also have the most genetic diversity in their DNA and genetically are the closest people to the Bushmen, enabling scholars to additionally conclude that the "click" language of the Bushmen is the earliest form of language. With this growing body of evidence indicating that our original ancestry traces back to these former hunter-gatherers, it is important to take another look at Bushman culture, for it holds the beginnings not only of human language but also the earliest ways and means of other important kinds of human expression—from art to dance, music, and religion. The Bushman way brings ancient wisdom and ecstatic spiritual know-how to modern times.

The world's first library does not hold books; it holds drawings painted on stone. In southern Africa we find renderings of healing ceremonies and shamanic experience that resemble those taking place today among the Jul'hoansi. *Way of the Bushman* finally offers these spiritual teachings and healing practices as articulated by the elders themselves. This work is a contribution to the history of religion, anthropology, the healing professions, and all spiritual seekers in search of ancient understanding and transformative practice.

The Bushman elders want the world to know, as fully and accurately as possible, their spiritual and healing ways. In the 1870s Wilhelm Bleek, Lucy Lloyd, and Dorothea Bleek accumulated nearly twelve thousand pages of IXam Bushman interviews conducted in Cape Town, South Africa. David Lewis-Williams, a distinguished rock art scientist, calls these transcriptions the "Old Testament" of Bushman religion, whereas the later insights coming from anthropological work with the Kalahari Bushmen in Namibia and Botswana offer the beginning of a "New Testament" that "fulfills the Old," as Lewis-Williams put it (Keeney 2003b, 164).

The decades of anthropological study and reporting of Bushman life among the Jul'hoansi and other Bushman groups included the work of the Laurence Marshall family starting in the late 1950s. Members of the Marshall Expeditions (also called the Peabody-Harvard Smithsonian Kalahari Expeditions) included Laurence Marshall, Lorna Marshall, John Marshall, Elizabeth Marshall Thomas, Nicholas England, and Robert Gordon. This work was followed by the Harvard Kalahari Research Group (HKRG), whose members included Irven DeVore, Richard Lee, Nicholas Jones, Megan Biesele, Marjorie Shostak, and psychologist Richard Katz (who visited from September–November 1968); the University of New Mexico Kalahari Project, whose members included Robert Hitchcock, Elizabeth Cashdan, Melinda Kelly, and Patricia Draper; and various Japanese researchers, including Jiro Tanaka, Masakazu Osaka, Kazuyoshi Sugawara, and Akira Takada. In addition, other studies were conducted by researchers from around the world, including the recent work by Chris Low, an academic anthropologist and physician from Oxford University. Many anthropologists came and established a body of work that included a depiction of what outside investigators thought was the basic nature of Bushman healing and religion.

What the anthropologists and other visiting scholars did not know, however, is that the Bushmen adjust how they talk about their sacred way to the uninitiated. This calibration of conversation is not due to secrecy but because their religion is held not primarily in words but in familiarity with nlom, the non-subtle kind of spiritual electricity that is at the heart of Bushman healing and spirituality. With nǀom flowing inside the Bushman's shaking and trembling body, all manner of spontaneous, difficult to explain, and seemingly impossible spiritual experiences arise. As a result of the anthropologists' blind spots to experiencing nǀom, what the Bushman elders told the anthropologists was comparable to what they would say to a Bushman child or adolescent who has yet to directly experience the transformative charge of nǀom.

Sometimes this talk was more teasing and playful, and it often confused scholars, leading them to believe that Bushman religion and ceremonial performances emphasized ambiguity and contradiction. Even the contested specification of their general name ("Are they Bushmen or San?"*) hints that any discussion about the way their experiential world is named, interpreted, and understood must be regarded with caution and uncertainty. Attention to the ambiguities in Bushman accounts of their religious life may lead one to dismiss how the Bushmen give importance to a shifting way of experientially being in the world and how this changing dynamic provides an overarching perspective that helps illumine the Bushman way. The "multifarious, inchoate, and amorphous . . . confusing tangle of ideas and beliefs, marked by contradictions, inconsistencies, vagueness, and lack of culture-wide standardization" (Guenther 1999, 126) can be regarded as the way Bushmen value experience that constantly shape-shifts, doing so in a unique experiential realm that ceremonial performance aims to access.

Many scholars have accepted Richard Katz's work on Bushman healing, *Boiling Energy,* as an accurate and credible account. However, all of the Bushman nǀom-kxaosi, or traditional healers, we have worked

---

*The preferred name of the Juǀ'hoansi goes back and forth between "Bushmen" and "San." The name "Bushmen" is used to refer to the people discussed in this book because it was the term preferred by most of the people we interviewed over the years. "San" has a pejorative connotation in Nama, the language from which it comes, though "Bushmen" also has limitations and historical disqualifications. We use the latter term with the hope that it be "gradually 'ennobled'" (Biesele 1993; Biesele and Hitchcock 2011).

with expressed serious concern about Katz's ideas, finding they frequently misrepresent and inappropriately explain their healing and spiritual practices. For example, Katz surprisingly did not give primary importance to the love Bushmen have for the Sky God, which is at the core of Bushman spirituality. Most of Katz's accounts represent the kind of information healers give to adolescents when elders tease them or feel that they are not ready to hear about the truth of their ecstatic healing and spirituality. Unfortunately, the popularity of Katz's book has perpetuated misconceptions about Bushman culture, often repeated by other anthropologists who uncritically accept his work. It is better to see Katz's work as an example of the way Bushmen talk to adolescents or uninitiated outsiders.* Seen this way, it is a valuable contribution to understanding the different manners in which Bushmen discuss their spirituality and healing, depending on the audience.

Several researchers have reported their unsuccessful efforts to experience nlom, especially Katz (1982), who also described how the Bushmen teased him about his constant request to receive it. This has inadvertently led to Bushman spirituality being further distanced from our understanding and accessibility. Some of the Bushman elders remember how anthropologists and outsiders to nlom tried to experience nlom and that one effort alone was enough for most of them to feel so disoriented, out of control, anxious, and frightened that they never tried again. This is the same experience that all Bushmen have

---

*During his first three-month visit to the Bushmen in 1968, Katz asked a strong healer for n/om but was teased: "Don't you think the police will be after me for giving you n/om?" which Katz interpreted as a humorous way of telling him that he "needed time to learn about n/om, more time than I had allocated to spend in the Kalahari" (Katz, Biesele, and St. Denis 1997, 6). When he returned twenty-one years later for his second and last visit, Katz reevaluated his earlier effort to receive n/om: "there was no problem with the police . . . the problem was with me" (Katz, Biesele, and St. Denis 1997, 6). What Katz likely didn't know is that the Bushman mention of "getting in trouble with the police" is a clichéd response that healers often say to naive requests for knowledge about n/om, something we have frequently heard them say to adolescents asking for n/om.

in the beginning, and it makes them initially see nǀom as dangerous and scary. Only the mature nǀom-kxaosi learn how to have a feeling for nǀom, relishing the ecstatic joy it delivers as the most important experience in their life and one to invite again and again.

Bradford Keeney engaged in a different kind of relationship with the Bushmen, for he was regarded as a nǀom-kxao by elders throughout Botswana and Namibia. He participated in Bushman ceremonies for more than two decades and was accepted as a "heart of the spears," someone who has mastered the Bushman healing and spiritual way. David Lewis-Williams, founder of the Rock Art Research Institute, University of the Witwatersrand in Johannesburg, South Africa, described Brad Keeney's unique role as follows:

> After many astounding experiences, the Bushmen accepted Keeney as a "doctor," a nǀom-kxao, one who is believed to possess and control a supernatural essence or power that can be harnessed to heal people with physical and social ills. . . . Other anthropologists had attempted to become nǀom-kxaosi, but they had not succeeded in pushing through to the deeply altered state of consciousness that is the key to Bushman spirituality. At once, hitherto closed doors began to open. Keeney's work describes in previously unavailable detail how the Bushmen learn the techniques of transition and transformation, how they journey to the spirit realm and how they climb the ropes or threads of God. As we read the words of these Bushman elders, we can almost feel what it must be like to undertake such journeys of the mind. (Keeney 2003b, 161)

With Brad's insider status as a member of the Bushman healing and spiritual community, he also served as a Senior Research Fellow at the Rock Art Research Institute in Johannesburg, where he would present his findings to rock art scholars. He came to his fieldwork mentored by renowned anthropologist and interdisciplinary scholar Gregory Bateson, bringing a cybernetic way of seeing that was more interactional, circular, and systemic than the naive presumptions of objectivity held by social scientists and perpetuated by most anthropological and rock art investigators. As Brad's work began to uncover previously unknown information about the Bushmen, he contacted anthropologist Megan Biesele, a former member of the Harvard Kalahari Research Group. She flew to Brad's home to discuss his findings and was startled to hear reports about Bushman spiritual experience that had not been disclosed before. She later went back to the Kalahari and checked with the Bushman elders to see if these reports were accurate and to confirm whether Brad had actually entered the Bushman spiritual universe. She later reported:

> There is no question in the minds of the Bushman healers that Keeney's strength and purposes are coterminous with theirs. I know this from talking myself with some of the Kalahari shamans who danced with him. They affirmed his power as a healer and their enjoyment of dancing with him. His work honors them by taking the details of their healing tradition in an effective way to a wider public, as they requested he do. (Keeney 2005, 183)

INTRODUCING THE BUSHMAN ELDERS

Brad interviewed many of the Bushman elders from Botswana and Namibia between 1991 and 2012.* Members and participants in the Keeney Bushman Expeditions in Botswana and Namibia included Bradford Keeney, Hillary Keeney, Beesa Boo, ≠Oma IHun, Izak Barnard, Hans Vahrmeijer, Patrick Hill, Peter Johnson, Grant Lessard, Kern Nickerson, Frank Filipetti, Tony Labriola, Mark Kundla, Piri Miller, Benjamin Smith, David Lewis-Williams, Geoffrey Blundell, Jeremy Hollmann, Jeffrey Kottler, and Jon Carlson. The collected

*The authors would like to thank their funding sources, which include the University of South Africa, Pretoria, where Brad served as a visiting professor in 1991 and 1992; the Ringing Rocks Foundation, Pennsylvania; University of St. Thomas, St. Paul, Minn.; University of Louisiana; the Kalahari Peoples Fund; and Schoolhouse Originals Foundation.

material from those expeditions has been edited and organized with Hillary Keeney, whom Bushman elders have also acknowledged as a nǀom-kxao and able teacher of the Bushman way. Brad and Hillary were enthusiastically encouraged by the Bushman elders to present these teachings to a world audience, hoping that it would provide needed spiritual medicine for troubled times. They see outsiders as being in dire need of renewed nǀom and believe that without it there is no hope for the kind of spiritually empowered wisdom that can save us from the continual breaking of the relational ropes that hold the world together.

This text is limited to the teachings of the northern Bushmen, called Juǀ'hoansi Bushmen, who largely reside in the northeastern part of Namibia. Note that the Bushmen who historically occupied the central Kalahari of Botswana, where Brad also frequently visited, have been at critical risk due to government action that threatens their way of living, while the southern Bushmen—including those who once occupied the cape of southern Africa, where Bleek did his interviews—are essentially extinct. *Way of the Bushman* presents the teaching of the Juǀ'hoansi Bushmen located in the Nyae Nyae area of northeastern Namibia.

For more than two decades this fieldwork focused on the healing and spiritual practices of both women and men Bushman nǀom-kxaosi. Brad became a member of both the men and women's healing ways and made the first film recording of a Bushman women's healing dance. Keeney's initial reports were published as first-person narratives (Keeney 1999; Keeney 2003b).

One of the historically interesting primary informants in the present work is ǀKunta Boo, an elder Juǀ'hoan Bushman who lives on a farm near Tsumkwe in the Nyae Nyae area of Namibia. ǀKunta has been involved with anthropologists since his youth. He was filmed in the 1950s by John Marshall in the first recording ever made of a Bushman healing dance (*Nǀum Tchai: The Ceremonial Dance of the ǃKung Bushmen,* distributed by Documentary Educational Resources), in which he was shown being initiated as a young nǀom-kxao. Later, he served as a primary informant for Megan Biesele—"the Bushman healer she had known and worked with the longest" (Biesele and Davis-Floyd 1996)—in her study of Juǀ'hoan hunting (Biesele and Barclay 2001), healing (Biesele and Davis-Floyd 1996), and folktales (Biesele 1993).* ǀKunta Boo is regarded as a strong nǀom-kxao (traditional doctor) in his community, and he is renowned throughout the Nyae Nyae area as an extraordinary storyteller.

In addition to ǀKunta Boo, other Bushman elders of equal, if not greater, authority in their communities were interviewed. These elders include N!ae Kxao, Tcoq'a ǀUi, N!ae G≠kau, Ti!'ae ≠Oma, ǀKunta ǀAi!ae, ≠Oma Dahm, ǀUi N!a'an, Tci!xo !Ui, ǀXoan ǀKun, Kaqece ǀKaece, ǀUi Debe, N!ani Gǀaq'o, and Gǀaq'o Kaqece. N!ae Kxao is the wife of ǀKunta Boo and a respected elder woman nǀom-kxao in her community. She and ǀKunta Boo were in their early seventies at the time of this publication.

Of the men healers, the Bushmen generally believed that the strongest and wisest healers were ≠Oma Dahm, Gǀaq'o Kaqece, and ǀKunta ǀAi!ae, though they were not given much interview time by anthropologists, perhaps because they were less likely to speak about spiritual and healing matters. Scholars were especially attracted to ǀKunta Boo because of his storytelling skills and the fact that he enjoys talking. ǀKunta dances the giraffe, elephant, and gǃoah dances; since many Bushmen do not approve of the elephant dance, their elders approached him with caution for fear that he might use the elephant dance against them and make them sick. Though we have no knowledge that he ever did this, the Bushmen were divided about their opinion of him. At the same time he is respected by all Bushmen as a great storyteller and valuable repository of Bushman stories and remembrances about their culture, healing, and spiritual ways. In the future ǀKunta Boo will likely be

---

*Though Megan Biesele and Richard Katz rarely identify their sources, our work has identified many of the nǀom-kxaosi they interviewed. Biesele has confirmed with Brad Keeney that ǀKunta Boo was her main informant.

regarded as important a figure in Bushman culture as Black Elk is to Lakota American Indian history.

≠Oma Dahm was deeply loved by all Bushmen and was one of the strongest healers of his time. He was as "soft," "sharing," and "strong in nǀom" (all necessarily intertwined) as any Bushman nǀom-kxao could ever become. In the more distant village of ǁNhoqʼma, Gǃaqʼo Kaqece was the strongest local nǀom-kxao and, like ǀKunta Boo, he danced all the dances. In his village there was no fear of the elephant dance so the entire community trusted him to be their most important healer. He lived to be approximately eighty years old. Except for ǀKunta Boo, all these men nǀom-kxaosi have passed away; ǀKunta Boo is still alive at the time of this writing (late 2014).

The strongest women healers included Tiǃʼae ≠Oma and Nǃae G≠kau. Tiǃʼae was so strong that many men healers were afraid to receive nǀom from her. Her brother was Nǃxau ≠Toma, the actor who starred in the popular film *The Gods Must Be Crazy*. Tiǃʼae shook stronger than most men and women. After Tiǃʼae passed away in her seventies, Nǃae G≠kau emerged as a strong healer after her husband, ǀKunta ǀAiǃae, passed away. He had been regarded by some as the strongest healer of his community.

The other men and women healers who participated in these interviews are also strong and respected elders but are secondary in ability and knowledge to the principal nǀom-kxaosi named here.

In the first decade of Brad's work with the Bushmen, he primarily danced and healed in the men's way. Later, Brad became a part of the women's way of healing, expressed in the gǃoah dance; he found some of the women to be the strongest Bushman healers. This observation had not been reported by anthropologists, as they have tended to emphasize the men's way of healing in their accounts. Brad became so close to his Bushman friends that a couple of villages asked him to live the rest of his life with them. Several of the Bushman women nǀom-kxaosi, especially Tiǃʼae ≠Oma, Nǃae G≠kau, Tcoqʼa ǀUi, and ǀXoan ǀKun, were especially fond of shaking and sharing nǀom with Brad. Some of the villagers gently teased them about spending so much time trembling and shaking together under a tree in the middle of the village and then dancing all night with the community.

Brad came close to leaving his academic life and joining a village, but other duties and responsibilities called him back. The closeness he cultivated with Bushman elders gave him deeper access to the nature of the way they hold and express ecstatic healing and spirituality.

In 2006, the findings of this long-term fieldwork, which spanned thirty-eight field trips, were reported to the surviving Bushman elders who had participated in the interviews. With translator Beesa Boo, the interviews were digitally recorded and archived. At that time, the Bushman interviewees and translators expressed concerns over the accuracy of the Juǀ'hoan dictionary published by Patrick Dickens (1994). Important words concerning Bushman healing and religious practices were frequently misspelled and definitions were often incorrect. Perusal of the literature reporting studies of the Bushmen over the years not only demonstrates changing names for the groups studied but variations in the spelling of critical words as well. To address this concern, for the purposes of this project a dictionary was made of the words that Juǀ'hoan Bushmen use in religious discourse. Beesa Boo, from Tsumkwe, Namibia, created a list of these words, pronouncing them in both the Juǀ'hoan language and in English. He recorded their definitions in both languages and wrote them in his own handwriting. This dictionary was accepted and approved by our Bushman colleagues. The spellings we use here follow this dictionary and the dictionary itself is included as an appendix. Readers can go to our website to hear an audio recording of Beesa Boo pronouncing each word: www.keeneyinstitute .org/judictionary.php.

Even with this dictionary produced by native speakers, we acknowledge that ongoing research is necessary to advance the best spelling and definition(s) of Juǀ'hoan words. Notable in this effort is the Juǀ'hoan Transcription Group in the Nyae Nyae area of Namibia, initiated by

Megan Biesele, which uses a group translation process to try to achieve conformity in word spellings. Beesa Boo, our translator, is a member of that group, and the Juʼhoan words reported in this book have been checked by him prior to publication. We acknowledge that, like Bushman culture, these spellings may later change after further consideration by the present Juʼhoan transcription group or transcription groups to come.

In 2012, the initial draft of this work was articulated by Brad and Hillary Keeney to ǀKunta Boo, his wife, and other elders, as another round of checking the accuracy of these reports and the way we expressed them. The Bushman elders gave full permission to publish this work and acknowledged that it is not an idiosyncratic perspective on Bushman ways but is representative of how Bushman spiritual and traditional teachings were portrayed by their parents, grandparents, and other elders they have closely known. These elders also requested that we add our own commentary that would help explain Bushman experience to outsiders. The book's main voice belongs to the nǀom-kxaosi elders, with our commentary interspersed. The interview material is presented as one composite voice in Part One of the book, "Core Teachings." Unique accounts of traditions, ceremonies, and healing ways are attributed to specific elders in the second part of the book, "The Elders Speak: Remembrances." We are called Bo and Nǃae by our Bushman colleagues; writing the commentary for this book required our being in both the Bushman world and the world that uses explanatory language, balancing ourselves between our different names and communities of belonging.

KEYS TO APPROACHING THE BUSHMAN TEACHINGS

The Bushman teachings on healing and spirituality may provoke you to reexamine some of your cherished beliefs and practices. The Bushman way is often contrary to commonly accepted beliefs held in today's spiritual, shamanic, and healing orientations. The Bushmen do not value the power of intention, positive thinking, "new thought," contemplative mindfulness, or even most dreams, spiritual insight, interpretations, and magical incantations, for they distrust all language and productions of the mind, seeing it as the means trickster uses to distract us from having a directly felt relationship with God. They steer us away from our habits of emphasizing whatever we *think* and *profess* healing, shamanism, and spirituality to be about. Instead, they invite us to directly feel and relate to its source, the unnamable mystery that surpasses all understanding.

Today's hunger for spiritual understanding may be for something more than another dose of talk. If you hunger for direct spiritual experience, then the Bushmen offer help in finding it, for they care most about getting pierced by nǀom, by the arrows of God's love that enter hearts that are soft and ready enough to receive them. These arrows, thorns, and nails of God's love awaken new spiritual senses and the expression of ecstasy through trembling dance and pulsing song.

There are several key principles to effectively approaching the Bushman way, and it begins with appreciating the nature of the ecstatic experience the Bushmen seek. The Bushmen teach that there is no experience of healing, shamanism, and spirituality without nǀom, the mysterious non-subtle life force that brings these sacred pursuits to life. Little effort is given to defining nǀom in words because it must be experienced to be understood. It is "not subtle" because one knows when it is present: it feels like amplified spiritual electricity imparting an ecstatic vibration to the body that supercharges all experience. Nǀom has little in common with most approaches to energy medicine that we know today. To illustrate, ǀKunta Boo tells how John Marshall, the earliest filmmaker to visit the Bushmen, once took a well-known Chinese energy doctor to the Kalahari. When the Bushmen touched the Chinese doctor he collapsed and fell into a coma. He had never experienced energy like this, nor is it likely that other outside practitioners have either, something substantiated by our own experience with practitioners of various kinds of energy healing systems who have visited the Bushmen.

Bushmen regard nǀom as inseparable from the amplified emotion that arises from a major heart awakening. It may be inspired by relationship with divinity, longing for present or past loved ones, or a felt intimacy with the biological world, including trees, animals, and honeybees. As a Bushman nǀom-kxao is filled with nǀom, it not only makes her want to dance, it excites her to ecstatically tremble and shake, touching others with fluttering hands and vibrant hugs.

Bushman nǀom-kxaosi always share heightened energy with others, placing nǀom in a social loop for its circulation. It is worth noting that the Bushmen do not have the so-called "spiritual accidents" that are often associated with intense energy practices. This is because they do not bottle up and hold the energy inside themselves. There is nothing in the Bushman way akin to an individual practice that sets up a closed circuit. This in itself makes their contribution to energy medicine and energetic spiritual practice significant, because here we find the strongest energy medicine and spiritual voltage available without any concern for misfire or accident. In the Bushman way we return to community healing and the holding and sharing of its revitalizing energy, creating safety and strengthening the spiritual current.

It is easy to misunderstand Bushman spirituality, for it does not primarily teach anything other than the importance of "having a strong rope to God," the passageway for nǀom into the body. When we move into this territory of non-subtle energy we find a whole new set of body automatisms that are automatically released as one grows in relationship with nǀom. These include a powerful pump in the belly that brings forth an ecstatic dance stomp and rhythmic vocal expression. This is where the importance of a special kind of song and altered vocal expressions are critically important. Without this kind of sound making, the energy of nǀom cannot reach its highest peak. All Bushman healers are nǀom singers and dancers. Their spiritual work is not possible without these ecstatic forms of expression being present. However, these necessary expressive forms cannot be consciously willed or purposefully taught. They can only be evoked by the highest inspiration of a felt relationship to the Sky God.

The importance Bushmen give to "loving the Sky God" in their healing and spirituality is often minimized or completely omitted by anthropological accounts, possibly due to the agnosticism or philosophical biases of many of these scholars. Without an acknowledgment of this primary spiritual experience for Bushmen, anything written or stated about their religion lacks appropriate context, meaning, and validity. When a Bushman says he or she has a "rope to God," this is acknowledgment that a relationship with the sacred underlies all ecstatic experience, from healing to visionary travel.

Bradford Keeney was the first outsider the Bushmen knew who experienced their most revered and rare sacred visions, including what they call the receiving of God's ostrich egg. (Part One of this book discusses this divine vision in detail.) This is why the Bushmen fully brought Brad inside conversations concerning Bushman spiritual experience, offering details and teachings previously not discussed with anyone outside Bushman culture. Brad has repeatedly experienced nearly all aspects of Bushman healing, shamanism, and spirituality reported in this book. This is what has enabled this teaching to be shared openly and has provided a bridge between Bushman spirituality and outside ways of viewing it.

Izak Barnard, the founder of Penduka Safaris in South Africa and Botswana, was one of the earliest outsiders to contact some of the Bushman villages. He also opened some of the first trails for vehicles to have access to remote places in the Kalahari. Barnard was himself a crusty and cynical old-time character of the bush and made it no secret that he had little respect for most visitors, especially anthropologists, for he saw how their writing too often projected their own fantasies of a romanticized Bushman life. After numerous trips observing Brad's work, Barnard wrote a legal testament that he wanted to leave for the historical record:

I am the founder of the oldest mobile safari company in southern Africa. I have advised anthropological researchers who came to the Kalahari from Europe, the United States, Argentina, and Japan, and served as a guide for many of them, along with assisting the BBC and National Geographic. . . . Through Bradford Keeney I discovered a new world of old Africa that was not even known to me. I am referring to the spiritual life of the Bushmen. . . . I watched firsthand as Professor Keeney experienced their spiritual universe. Brad missed nothing, and he became one of the Bushman people. He is not regarded as an outsider. (Keeney 2003b, 157)

From an insider's position, Brad found that we must be careful to not assume that other ecstatic dances and healing ways are similar to Bushman ecstatic expression. The Bushmen bring something different for consideration in the way they distinguish whether movements and expression are awakened by nǀom, whether they are inspired by love or power, and whether they are imitative or authentic. The way of the Bushman flows top-down, from the Sky God to the dance ground. Finding a rope that connects you to the Sky God enables you to receive spiritual gifts from song to dance and even guidance in a hunt. When the Sky God or ancestors pull on this rope, a Bushman feels the tugging and moves accordingly. This may help explain some of the Bushmen's uncanny talents. For example, they have been regarded as great guides and trackers, but the Bushman secret is that they are guided by the pulling of their ropes.

Anthropologists and other outside observers have also imposed their own ideas concerning "trance" onto Bushman experience, even calling their healing dance a "trance dance." Similarly, Bushman spiritual experience as well as their renderings of it on ancient rock art have been characterized as comparable to hallucinations brought on by hypnotic trance, hyperventilation, strenuous repetitive (trance-inducing) movement, and sonic entrainment, all concepts derived from non-Bushman theories about the nature of "altered states of consciousness," human experience, and transformation. For a Bushman, a strong rope to God is all that is required to connect directly with God—to lose sight of and connection with this primary distinction results in being steered far away from the kind of experience Bushmen value most.

Nlom-inspired expression occurs spontaneously without conscious choice, intention, or technique. Hence, it is not possible to teach Bushman spirituality by imitation or through systematic method. Memorizing a Bushman nlom song or reproducing a healer's ecstatic sounds will no further lead to an experience of nlom than trying to sound like a lion, flamingo, or hippopotamus will make one a creature of the wild. The same is true for the movements and motions made during healing. When nlom arrives, the selection and sequence of songs, along with the specific movements they inspire, are improvised in the moment and experienced as new even if they have been sung and danced thousands of times before.

Bushman nlom-kxaosi are not concerned with whether their talk is consistent or logically coherent in a way outsiders appreciate. Because experience is dependent upon context, the truth value or consistency of an utterance or description is not only tied to the situation and moment in which it took place but from the influence of how "cooked" by God the speaker is when he experienced it and the degree of nlom involved when he later refers back to the experience.

In the moment of a dance, a healer who is starting to heat his nlom might refer to a bad ancestor, but later as the healer becomes hotter, the same ancestor is no longer bad. The differentiation of "good" and "bad" ancestors by Bushmen refers to the momentary feelings of both observed and observer, as well as the interaction between them, something that anthropologists have largely missed. So all "bad" ancestors are momentarily bad and are also capable of being good, depending upon how they relate to us and how we relate to them. In summary, Bushmen care less about categories that statically evaluate and frame any given moment than they do about the quality and intensity of the nǀom that was present in the past event discussed and the nǀom that arises in the present manner of discussing it.

To the Bushmen, nature is seen as a web of interconnected ropes, strings, and threads. Hunters are connected to eland, kudu, giraffes, and other animals by ropes, and gatherers are connected to the plants they collect by similar ropes. Furthermore, human beings are connected to one another through these ropes. For the Bushmen, the web of nature is literal, and in an awakened state a nǀom-kxao may see the world as a giant spider web. Empowering a rope can send nǀom throughout the entire weave and thereby contribute to the wellness of the whole ecology. Making one's rope to God strong is the most direct way of strengthening all the ropes. In this way a Bushman nǀom-kxao awakens nǀom to heal everything—a sick person, the healer, the whole community, and the entire fabric of nature.

From the Bushman perspective, an immediate experiential encounter with the Sky God is more authoritative than any and all textual understandings and beliefs. The latter are suspect without an accompanying and deeply felt spiritual experience that embodies what is discussed. Here spiritual experience in its most primary form involves an awareness and relationship to luminosity that shines brightest from God's divine ostrich egg. After one sees this luminous egg it never stops inspiring ecstatic experience and expression. Since most cultures do not prepare a person to handle supercharged ecstatic experience, people are not ready to hold on to it when it arrives. They will quickly reach a threshold that no longer allows them to remain awake as more luminosity, energy, and revelation await transmission. The initiate paradoxically passes out or loses consciousness before reaching a fully ecstatic awakening where the oval luminosity is met.

It cannot be emphasized enough that the highest form of Bushman ecstatic healing and spirituality always includes singing nǀom songs. The vibrational impact of nǀom singing is required to heighten and heat nǀom. Bushman healers would see many, if not most, energy practitioners from other cultures as "stuck" in trickster language and mind games. If ecstatic singing is not present, then they would regard that as an indication that the heart has not fully awakened and that nǀom is not sufficiently awakened and heated. There is simply no presence of nor any concept of "subtle energy" in the Kalahari, and mention of such an idea would likely yield gut-wrenching laughter. The Bushmen would likely start teasing one another about "subtle meat," "subtle hunts," or "subtle sex," and with the enjoyed raunchiness of Bushman humor, there would be no end to discussing "subtle shit."

It is also important to note that Bushman ecstatic shaking is more than the physical automatisms that can be brought forth with techniques used in rehabilitative medicine. While this kind of shaking may provide physical therapy and improvement in muscle tone, it has nothing to do with nǀom. Ecstatic shaking that is brought forth by powerful rhythms, wild dance, and nonconventional movement may or may not involve nǀom. For the Bushmen, when shaking arrives spontaneously because of elevated feelings inspired and triggered by nǀom, ecstatic transformation takes place.

The Bushman teachings that follow often took place while the elders were experiencing *thara,* their word for ecstatic shaking. They were ecstatically shaking during the interview because a strong nǀom-kxao is always spiritually awakened—his or her nǀom is heated, causing thara—whenever these topics are discussed. Even the mention of nǀom or the Sky God will initiate thara. Sometimes the interviews turned into singing, a spirited exchange of nǀom, a healing session, or a dance. The Bushman teaching of nǀom holds the nǀom it discusses, ready to pierce the hearts of those ready to receive it. This text aims to embody the ecstatic nǀom energy of which it speaks.

BEING DANCED BY NǀOM

The Bushman healing dance is the main venue for their community experience of ecstatic healing, shamanism, and spirituality. While it has a particular structure and form, it also hosts improvisational variation, guided by the experience of feeling and sharing nǀom. Whether it is named or not, the openness and uncertainty fostered by improvisation helps us become more available to unexpected movement that is spontaneously choreographed by the felt interaction with mystery. However, nǀom takes us past improvisation as it is typically understood in dance and theater contexts. Bushmen propose that they are danced by nǀom. Here the dancer is not improvising but is improvised by nǀom. This is the way of the Bushman—being improvised, moved, danced, sung, and touched by the mystery of nǀom, inseparable from the longing and loving of the Sky God and all of creation.

Bushman nǀom-kxaosi become owners of nǀom (meaning they "own the feeling" for nǀom), and it is the nǀom-kxaosi who share it with others, sending what they call "nails" or "arrows" of transmitted nǀom into those who need healing and transformation. This is typically done through vibratory transmission with touch, movement, or sound that is often absent of words. The Bushmen's most valued form of experience, knowledge, and teaching is somatically held; the movements and sensations of the body in relationship and interaction with others constitute their way of knowing and being. They are a dancing culture. They know through dance, and they dance their ideas, emotions, and laughter as well as their bodies. Their world moves, like the changing seasons, and they move with it, valuing the constant movement and change more than any one static moment.

The typical flow of a Bushman healing dance moves from gathering around a fire, singing nǀom songs and clapping hands in syncopated rhythms, waiting to be spiritually heated and awakened by nǀom, to the ecstatic crescendo of becoming filled with nǀom and sharing it with others. Bushman dancers tremble and shake when charged with nǀom. A virtuous circularity is set in motion where music inspires the dance as dance inspires the music, while at the same time heightened emotion inspires ecstatic expression and ecstasy amplifies even more emotional intensity. As the Bushman nǀom-kxaosi dance around a circle, a greater circulation of nǀom is embodied that, in turn, encircles ancestors and gods. In this sacred place, the Bushmen dance with all their ancestors and gods.

When too much is said about nlom it risks leading the listener and the speaker astray from the inspiration it points toward. Bushmen are familiar with how talk and thought can become a trap leading them away from the very thing they are trying to experience. As the Bushmen say, talk can "bend the ropes." They regard language as the invention of trickster—it is the narrating and interpreting mind that likes to name, categorize, know, and explain. Trickster mind is utilized in certain practical matters, but it is not allowed to interfere with the serious matters of nlom.

At the same time, words can be filled with nlom, and in their utterance both speaker and audience can be surprised, softened, and even struck by nlom. This is the art of ecstatic Bushman storytelling when delivered by a well-seasoned nlom-kxao—hearing such a story is an experience of being danced by nlom. Whether stomping inside the dance circle, telling a story, or following tracks in a hunt, for the Bushmen each important experience of life is first and foremost in relationship with nlom.

As a Bushman dance progresses, the singing and clapping around the fire become louder and more charged with nlom. Everyday talk and laughter give way to enthusiastic singing as the nlom-kxaosi become filled with nlom. When the men nlom-kxaosi dance, nlom makes them shake and bend forward, stomping their feet in the sand. The women nlom-kxaosi stand and sway, trembling intensely like trees. This is when nlom takes over and further guides movement and expression. The nom-kxaosi may be led to lay their trembling hands on someone sitting near the fire, providing healing and revitalization.

There is a "choreography" involved with this dance, but it is unlike that found on any ballroom floor or theatrical stage. Nor is it like a contemporary ecstatic dance gathering where people experiment with free movement, specified rhythmic movement, or spirited improvisation. The Bushman dance arguably is not about dance at all. Nor is it primarily about shaking or ecstatic expression, although these always take place. The whole Bushman way of life is about awakening, receiving, and sharing nlom. It is about being danced by nlom.

To a Bushman nlom-kxao, no right questions lead to understanding their way. Knowledge of the dance cannot be gleaned from conversation and cannot be held by any interpretive means. Its truths can't be seen or heard; they must be corporally felt. There are no official custodians of Bushman knowledge or social institutions for maintaining any contemplative word-bound tradition. Lorna Marshall, in her classic paper "The Medicine Dance of the !Kung Bushmen," makes this conclusion: "The !Kung are not concerned with carefully preserving the knowledge of their past, and they do not teach it systematically to their young..." (Marshall 1969, 351).

Full-bodied experience is most valued by Bushmen. This experience is born and expressed by the movement of their muscles and skin, not from the ruminations of reflective thought. From the Bushman perspective, their sacred knowledge is encoded in the orally preserved songs and muscle memories of kinesthetic movements. Its expression is sparked by a mysterious presence that moves their bodies to perform ecstatic choreographies of healing movement inseparable from heartfelt touch.

To appreciate the groundbreaking contributions of the Bushmen, we must learn to interact in their preferred way and place ourselves on their dance ground rather than encapsulate them inside our categories of classification. Specifically, Bushmen want to see, hear, and feel our bodies move in the way they occupy and move their bodies. To more fully respect the Bushman way requires that we move forward and dare to be danced by nlom.

The nlom-kxao cannot do ecstatic work alone. He or she must meet the ancestral spirits and gods. Here they merge with divine love, as hands tremble and deliver spiritual birth, death, and resurrection. When shared with others who are open to full participation, all are taken into ecstatic communion and union.

In the Kalahari, nlom dances with all of creation. The dancer's body holds all imaginable names along with their inherent contrasts and differences, embracing any and all sides and forms. In this movement, a whirling wind moves the dancer from side to side. Waves of energy express the "back and forth," "here and there," "this and that," and "is and isn't" of human existence. Love and hate are held next to each other, neither side allowed to run away. Altruism and selfishness face off but neither crosses the line. Good and evil stand their ground, greeting one another. In the body of the Bushman dancer the wheel of life and death is turned as spiritual electricity is churned.

Bushman elders vary in their depth of discernment, understanding, and articulation of the ambiguities, paradoxes, and complexities of life. Some see a simple battle between God and trickster while others have a more complex view of the interpenetration of contrasting sides of any distinction, especially that of the Sky God and the Sky God's complementary side, trickster. An individual Bushman nlom-kxao may also alternate between these simple and complex outlooks over the course of a lifetime or within a single conversation. In the Kalahari, a Bushman's body moves and the fluid stories are encouraged to change with each telling. What is stable in the Bushmen's experience is the process of movement itself—nighttime dancing feet, swaying bodies, trembling hands, pumping bellies, bobbing heads, as well as the ever-changing stories, teasing, and jokes that are shared underneath the daytime shade of a camel thorn tree. Their truths are found moving in the constant circulating and changing rhythms, music, movements, and touch of nlom-inspired living.

The Bushmen teach us that understanding the mystery of life is less important than participating in it. They invite us to dance more and talk less. They want us to feel our hearts rather than fill our minds. The Bushman way is more polyphonic, improvisational, playful, and biological than any flat-planed, textually structured world. Their truths mirror the truths of the sky, earth, plants, and animals that surround them. The way of the Bushman can only be understood in the smell of sweat, the experienced warmth of blood flowing out of a hunted animal, the bare handling of roots and earth, and the tender embrace of one another through hearts and hands that flutter. Round and round the dance circle a furrow of sand is dug, reminding us of the cyclical nature of life. Turn and return to the indigenous fires and circles of unspoken mystery. There the ancestors continue teaching.

WE INVITE YOU
TO DANCE WITH GOD

*A Welcome from the Jul'hoan
Bushman Elders*

As the elder teachers of the oldest living culture on earth, the Jul'hoan Bushman (San) people, we hold the most enduring traditional wisdom concerning healing and spiritual experience. This book is a testimony of our ecstatic ways. Beesa Boo has carefully translated our words and we accept the word changes and comments that Brad and Hillary Keeney have made to help others more readily comprehend our teachings. The preparation of this document has taken several decades. We happily share our basic teachings about spirituality and healing with those whose hearts are sincerely open.

It is important that we get these things clear. The strongest healers are almost gone. There are only a few of us left. The young healers don't know everything and often mix things up. The elder healers need to set the record straight about our oldest and most enduring truths. These are urgent and dangerous times and our wisdom is needed to heal the world. We believe it is extremely important for future healers to know the original spiritual teachings. In addition, those who already know, but don't know that they know, will be confirmed and substantiated, and this will make them stronger.

This is the saddest time in our history. It is a very troubled world and we suffer.* However, instead of giving in to being sad we try to make our feelings boil with nlom. Rather than crying, we shake. In this way, we change the sadness of suffering into the reenergizing presence of nlom. We cook our suffering. When it boils, we experience joy in being spiritually wealthy with nlom.

We are not saying that we want to remain materially poor and continue as victims of unfair politics and economies. We are human and have the same needs as everyone else. We, too, have rights and basic needs that must be respected and appropriately addressed. Yet no matter what happens to us with the climate, economy, or politics, we will always have a rope to God. We will always be able to keep our arrows from God clean with ≠hoe djxani, our healing dance. More importantly, we are able to dance with God, and this brings the greatest joy and deepest love. On behalf of all Bushman elders and ancestors, we invite you to this dance.

We are grateful that our words and teachings have been written and preserved for the future. When we hear what has been written we realize that nothing is wrong. As |Kunta Boo says, "Every word we discussed is accurate and I've seen that no word went astray. It is written correctly and everything is right. It's good and I'm very happy. This has been written to describe the way it is. This is the day the truth has been told."

---

*For example, Bushmen of the Central Kalahari Game Reserve in Botswana are being starved and intimidated off their land by government forces, in part motivated by mining interests. (One mine, Ghaghoo, is estimated to hold $3.3 billion dollars in diamonds.) Other mining companies are also exploring and developing commercial projects throughout Bushman-occupied land in both Botswana and Namibia.

PART ONE

CORE TEACHINGS

1

GOD'S DIVINE EGG

We begin with our most important truth: we are able to directly receive God's love, the source of the universal life force or what we call nlom. We are speaking about an awakened and energized love that inspires us to spontaneously tremble and shake in ecstatic bliss, often rendering speech impossible. It is unlike any other kind of love, which is one of the reasons we are hesitant to even name it. This life force is called in and expressed by enthusiastic singing, drumming, and dancing. When our healers feel the intense heat of nlom boil inside of them as a result of the sincere and prayerful singing and dancing, they can deliver God's love directly to a person in the form of an "arrow," "nail," "needle," or "thorn" of nlom. When your heart is pierced by this kind of celebrated relationship with the Sky God,* !Xun!a'an, all manner of spiritual gifts may spring forth, including divine guidance, heightened joy, and the gifts for healing and teaching.

There is no way to adequately describe this transformative experience. It holds the greatest power, yet in its fullest presence it lifts us from any desire to be powerful. It opens our hearts and moves us

---

*The Bushmen refer to the supreme divinity of creation as both "Sky God" and "God." Accordingly, we will use both terms in this text and recognize them as equivalent.

past a desire for power to feeling a big love for everyone and a related-ness to all life. As we become filled with nǀom, we can communicate with God and the ancestors. Finally, this love becomes a pulse of pure vibration, returning us to the source of all creation again and again.

All of this takes place because of "God's ostrich egg," !Xu dsuu-nǃo. This divine ostrich egg is the home of all spiritual gifts from God. The most extraordinary experience for a human being is to encounter this divine egg; such an encounter can thoroughly transform a person when he or she beholds it. Our strongest spiritual teachers and healers have witnessed and interacted with this egg. This is how our most valuable spiritual gifts and teachings are received, including the ability to have direct communication and interaction with God. (See editors' commentary 1.1 on page 8.)

It has been this way for thousands of years—God's ostrich egg has always initiated our leading spiritual teachers and healers. It was true for our grandfathers and grandmothers and for their ancestors, all the way back to the beginning of all Bushmen, the first people on Earth. Only the Sky God decides who will receive the egg and lead others in spiritual matters. If a person has seen God's ostrich egg, he or she is the strongest healer. These are the people you need to speak with to learn anything about our healing and spirituality. We have an old saying about people who become the strongest healers. We like to say that person "has fallen from God's village" or "has fallen from heaven." This is only true for a few people—it is rare to find a strong healer like this.

Practically all of the anthropologists and outsiders we have met do not have an adequate understanding of how we heal and relate to God. They are good friends and have helped us in many ways, but their education didn't prepare them to understand anything about our experience of spirituality, what we call ≠umsi !Xu, our religious beliefs about God and healing.

We celebrate anyone who sees God's egg. The egg usually comes to a recipient when he or she is a young adult, although it can be received

at any time during one's life.* Some have a direct encounter with the
egg while they are awake; most who encounter the egg experience it in
a visionary dream. The experience of God's ostrich egg arrives unan-
nounced; God decides who will receive the egg and when. A person
can neither prepare for it nor choose for it to happen. For instance,
the recipient can be walking around and all of a sudden feel his body
become very lightweight, as if he is not walking but is instead glid-
ing along the surface of the ground. He becomes peacefully confident
and then all of a sudden, without warning, his belly gets hot and he
starts to shake. The internal fire comes slowly up his spine until it gets
to the top of his head. If the recipient is strong and has no fear, this
internal fire will pour out of his head and become a huge egg of light.
It can be as tall as a person as it stands directly in front of him.†

When the strongest recipient stares at this oval shining light, he or
she faces all of the important ancestors and spiritual teachers throughout history.‡ This recipient is not dreaming or hallucinating but is fully
awake. The recipient sees that the egg holds the arrows of nlom, the
ropes to God, all the songs and dances, and everything that is important for living and for healing. He is drawn to look into this egg while
shaking with intense delight, weeping with gratitude, and feeling his
heart expand beyond measure. (See editors' commentary 1.2.) The great
ancestors and spiritual luminaries impart all the knowledge needed
about healing and nlom—the enhanced vital life force. (See editors'
commentary 1.3.) It feels as though this knowledge is poured into his
whole being. This can last for many hours.

---

*The mystical egg is most often experienced between the ages of eighteen and twenty-
five, although God's divine egg can be encountered at any time during one's lifespan.
†This phenomenological account holds generally true for most Bushmen who have
reported this experience.
‡Recognizable images and icons as well as unknown figures are revealed in the vision
of the divine egg. It is an experience that leaves the recipient feeling as though no
important spiritual teacher or teaching has been left out. Afterward it feels as though
the recipient has encountered and been taught by all spiritual teachers since the
beginning of human history.

This meeting with the egg is the highest diploma for a healer. Its arrival and subsequent presence in a recipient's life indicate that person has been chosen by the Sky God to be a powerful spiritual teacher and healer. At this time he or she is given everything that is needed to fulfill a special mission.

This is the way original spirituality started. In the beginning, spirituality was complete and full of nlom; spirituality is always born and reborn out of God's egg. We don't understand why other people around the world don't seem to know about this luminous egg that awakens ecstatic experience. They likely get partial glimpses of its spiritual light but rarely see the whole egg; if they did, they'd be dancing and singing often, full of nlom. Other cultures seem to have lost a relationship and understanding of this pinnacle experience, while we have honored it as the source of all spirituality throughout our entire history. We want to reintroduce this experience so that the entire world can become familiar with how we have been shown the way God's gifts are held and disseminated.

Occasionally outside visitors come and ask us to make them a healer. We have to tell them, "We can't make you this way. Only God can do this. God makes a healer. Only God can give the big egg. Stop asking for what no human being can give without God's permission. Understand that asking for this implies that you know what is best for you. Trust God to decide what is best for you. Those who think they are entitled to be healers likely may be less desirable for God to choose. If God wants this knowledge for you, you will be led to a teacher or given the teaching directly by God."

A healer or teacher will only experience the emergence of God's divine egg once in a lifetime, although the egg may appear later in different form as he or she becomes initiated. The encounter with the egg marks the healer's true spiritual birth date. First, the egg makes the recipient a new person as it is beheld and immerses the recipient in what we regard as the most transformative and exhilarating experience possible for a human being. The recipient feels immediately remade. When the recipient sees the egg, she fully realizes that she is being given all that is needed to be known about how to use her hands and body to deliver n|om and pull out sickness. The recipient knows this without question, although the specific knowledge is held in the more unconscious parts of the recipient's mind, waiting to be expressed until appropriately summoned; the acquired knowledge comes forth into consciousness when it is ready to do so. It takes time to appreciate how much was given when the egg first arrived.

It delights us when a person receives God's divine egg, and it is extremely important to recognize and honor. It means that the recipient is on the best spiritual track and has a direct path to God. Such a person will never look for truth after this experience. Spiritual truth will own the recipient and he will own it; that is, he will own a strong feeling for it. Yes, he will continue to stumble in everyday life and sometimes forget what he is and what was given to him. But the recipient is forever inside this egg and it will make things right and offer guidance and healing, even when the person gets off track in his actions or his thoughts.

Editors' Commentary

1.1. On the significance of the ostrich egg

The Bushmen are not alone in regarding an egg form as a most precious gift from the creator god. Other original cosmologies also consider civilizing gifts for humanity to be received via an egg. The Bushman designation of this divine egg as an ostrich egg reflects its value as a life-giving gift to the human body as well. An ostrich egg is one of the most valuable material treasures for a Bushman. In addition to providing a meal for an entire family, its shell serves as a container for storing water, the most important resource for a Bushman.

1.2. On viewing the egg

This experience brings great clarity, enhanced emotional elevation, and deeper relationship to wisdom than what many characterize as hallucinations, which are too easily subject to fragmentation and are without kinesthetic celebration and heartfelt validity. As well, this experience is contextualized as enhancing love rather than power, as it inspires humility and song rather than ego inflation, carnivalesque experience, and exaggerated display. Again, only the strongest nlom-kxaosi view this egg when fully awake while other strong doctors may see it in a dream. An inexperienced or less developed nlom-kxao may not even know about God's ostrich egg.

1.3. On the enhanced vital life force

We recommend saying "enhanced life force" because many people outside of the Kalahari are more familiar with subtle forms of life energy. The Bushmen relate to non-subtle energy that they call nlom. Nlom can be understood as intensely amplified chi, supercharged kundalini, or extremely concentrated holy ghost power. The practitioners of Asian forms of energy medicine, including a master of chi gong, who experienced Bushman healing work have been overcome by its magnitude and have usually fainted shortly after receiving nlom.

2

GETTING COOKED BY GOD

We dance and sing in order to heat nǀom—to get ourselves spiritually "cooked." Healers put arrows, nails, or needles of nǀom (ǁauhsi) into us. In the old days it was called a "thorn" of nǀom, or *nǃaihsi*. (See editors' commentary 2.1 on page 13.) The needle, nail, or arrow carries nǀom; it is not nǀom but is the holder of nǀom. More precisely, nǀom is inside a special kind of song that is compacted into an arrow or nail, enabling it to be sent in the air from one person to another.

Once a nail is inside of us, it can be heated by singing its song with appropriate enthusiasm and sincerity. When we are calm, as when we are asleep, the nǀom is also asleep. But as we start to sing, the emerging heat wakes us up; if we sing strongly, the nǀom comes to life. When we pick up the song and sing it hard, then the nǀom becomes strong. We know that nǀom is awake when we begin to tremble and shake ecstatically.

The most important job of a healer and spiritual teacher is to help make nails and arrows of nǀom get hot, which requires building our capacity to carry and hold heated nǀom to become very strong, stronger than what most people know is possible. Spiritually cooking our nails is what brings us the health, guidance, inspiration, and direction we constantly need. Appropriately aroused feelings and heated nǀom are necessary to awaken second sight and all the other spiritual senses. Our nails and arrows of nǀom must be heated in order to be awake.

When we hold hot nǀom, we wake up our heart and our spiritual sensitivities. Heating our nǀom helps us burst open so we can see and hear what can be most deeply perceived. When these feelings are not strong, our truest nature is asleep. This is why we say that people whose feelings about nǀom are not aroused are asleep. Without the ecstatic experiences of singing, dancing, and trembling we are asleep—we remain in a trance of spiritual slumber.

When our nǀom-inspired feelings are very strong, we know it because we can't help but shake. For the Bushmen, if a person isn't shaking, his feelings and nǀom aren't strong enough to wake up his spiritual being. His senses can't cross over into a spiritually awakened presence. This shaking comes on you in a natural way whenever you allow your heart to open to God's love. This makes you feel strong enough to transform your being and see things differently.

We must repeatedly put ourselves back into God's pot so we can get cooked. Dancing is how we most often do this. The strongest healers love to dance, shake, get cooked, and receive nǀom. They love nǀom and want to have it cook them as much as possible. These healers want to dance all the time—they need to dance—because they find themselves becoming more true and alive when they're deeply involved in the dance.

When we say we need to dance, we don't mean any kind of dance. We are talking about the body movements that take place when nǀom-filled music awakens our heart and cooks our nails and arrows. (See editors' commentary 2.2.) Without being cooked, all people are guaranteed to get lost and spiritually off track, which then encourages the creation and transmission of dirty nails. For instance, jealousy and anger can create dirty nails. Other people can shoot a dirty nail into us, either purposefully or accidentally. They may be able to do so because they have expertise at shooting harmful arrows, what we call *nǃo'an-nǀom*, throwing a dirty arrow to hurt someone. These people are sometimes called bad doctors or bad witchdoctors. The other way of getting shot by a dirty arrow involves someone we are close to who escalates a hurtful emotion, such as anger. Without any intention of doing so, they can accidentally shoot a dirty arrow.

If we haven't been dancing, our nails of nlom will get dirty. Handling a dirty arrow is a dangerous business. We must never forget to dance in order to stay healthy by continuously making our nails clean. If one has never danced like this, then one has likely been in a deep sleep and one's nails are becoming ever dirtier. Dirty nails make us sick. We must dance to make them clean.

Both men and women need to renew their needles. Both have nlom songs that they sing for cleaning up dirty nails. People need to dance every week, even twice a week, and give nlom massages* to each other. Everything would be healthy and optimally good if this consistently took place. When our nails are clean and strong, we feel a vibrant buzzing and hear an uplifting tonal hum inside of us. There is always music in our heart and head. It seems like someone is singing inside our body. We become filled with song. When we are fully cooked we are a living song and a vessel that carries the vibrations of this sacred song to others through all our action and presence. Whether or not the song is actually heard by anyone else matters less than the fact that its vibrational and transformative presence is always realized and transmitted through everything we do.[†]

The healer is most vulnerable and at the greatest risk when her nails get dirty. Trickster comes twice as fast to healers as to other people. People don't understand the difficulty of a healer's life. As a healer opens his heart and lets God fill him with nails, the people must dance.

---

*A nlom massage refers to someone vibrantly massaging another person while under the influence of heated nlom.

†It is the vibrational aspect of a nlom song that is valued, even more than melody, harmony, rhythm, and lyrics or being in tune and having a beautiful sound. The vibrational quality of the sound cannot be consciously willed or it will feel inauthentic and not deliver nlom. This accounts for why it is not enough to heat one's nlom by memorizing a song. Instead, the song must arise spontaneously from the energized inspiration of nlom.

If there is no dancing and the healer can't be with other healers, then his nails get dirty; since healers have many more nails than other people, it is dangerous when they all get dirty. If the people don't dance, they put their healers in harm's way and then the healers can't help them. The people have to dance to keep the healers strong. When the healers dance, everyone has the best lives, but when the people aren't dancing, they have the hardest lives.*

When a healer stumbles, people shouldn't say, "Hey, look at that healer. He's not a good healer." Instead of laughing at him, they should be saying, "Oh, we're sorry. We haven't been dancing. We made you sick." This is why it's lonely to be a healer, because the people don't always remember or understand the way it works.

Nlom cannot get hot without enthusiastic nlom singing. When the women sing for the men's dance it can be said that the women get cooked first and transmit nlom to the men dancers, who then are able to reciprocate by touching the women and giving them nails in return. Nlom circulates throughout the community, and no one can say whether the singers, drummers, dancers, or healers are the most responsible for waking up nlom and keeping it on the move. Everyone participates in the circulation of nlom. This is why healing must take place inside relationship and community. (See editors' commentary 2.3.)

Editors' Commentary

2.1. On "needles," "nails," "arrows," and "thorns"

Note that all of these names refer to an object that can pierce and cross a boundary. Sometimes when nlom is received it physically feels like being pricked by a needle; or it may instead seem like an electric switch that has suddenly been turned on. Whatever the specific kinesthetic experience, there is a feeling that something from the outside enters one's interior and

---

*In general, the more nlom one has, the more it needs to be circulated and shared via interaction with others.

results in a shift in awareness and experience. The importance of hunting in Bushman life also comes into play in considering this nomenclature. For Bushmen, God can be regarded as hunting human beings, hoping to shoot them with nlom. At the same time, human beings, especially nlom-kxaosi, hunt nlom. More generally, humans hunt God as God hunts them.

With this perspective, the experience of being shot by nlom can be regarded as receiving a connection with God's rope. When this rope is attached to a person, it brings a shock or a pricking or tingling sensation that feels like you have been pierced. Brad once gave an arrow to a young man during a dance; the man immediately felt a stinging sensation, like he had been pricked by a thorn. He started shaking and convulsing and it took hours for him to cool down. Later that night he had a visionary dream in which the Sky God and ancestors attached ropes to his body. From that day forward he was able to feel the ropes pulling him during a dance.

2.2. On nlom inspired ecstatic dance

We must be careful to not assume that all ecstatic dances and movements are similar to Bushman dancing. Without certain kinds of spontaneous movements, including vibratory vocalizations that raise the heart, the Bushman trembling way of healing and transformation is missed. Bushman dancers can differentiate between movements that are inspired by nlom and movements that are imitative or uninspired body automatisms.

2.3. On healing in community

Upon hearing that healers and therapists from other cultures see clients alone in private rooms, Bushmen healers started laughing and commenting that these healers are "crazy" because "it is almost impossible to maintain enough hot nlom to conduct healing without the support of others who are singing and dancing."

3

RECEIVING NǀOM

Nǀom radically awakens us and brings on a whole different way of being in the world. Making the transition from the cool everyday to a hot nǀom universe is smooth for experts but may be disconcerting to novices. The transition often brings with it uncertainty and fear for the less experienced, and this can cause pain by creating resistance to what is trying to take place naturally. The discomfort is not caused by nǀom but by how one interacts with it.

Young people and those learning to be healers often get scared about receiving a nail or arrow of nǀom, fearing that it will be excessively painful. This fear can also be a distraction that blocks an important spiritual and healing opportunity. This does not mean that there will never be any pain for the strongest healers. When a strong healer dances and feels this pain, he will remain happy and know that it will soon turn to joy.

If we fear nǀom, it brings us more pain. If we love nǀom, it delivers joy. (See editors' commentary 3.1 on page 18.) The new and inexperienced healer feels as though he's dying, but the strong healer feels like he's being reborn to once again become his true self. When you're a strong healer, you can't wait to wake up and become your truest self over and over again. New healers are scared and say, "No,

I don't want to die." They haven't learned to not be afraid.

Sometimes a strong healer will bleed from his nose when receiving the medicine of nǀom.* We say we are bursting when this happens. It happens because you are hot with boiling nǀom. When a woman becomes hot with nǀom during a dance, she will sometimes feel a hole in the top of her head, the ǁhannǃang, where nǀom comes out of her body. It is like there is a fire on top of the head that goes down to the tongue.

When nǀom first awakens it tingles; then it gets hotter and opens us. We are not afraid when this happens. It is how we are healed, changed, and awakened. Strong healers welcome dancing hard. We are happy to welcome nǀom.

It is easy for a strong healer to go into ǃaia, our word for becoming spiritually awake. This is like a death and rebirth experience. Our former sleeping everyday self dies and we become our awakened truest form. This is when we truly come to life. Anyone who says we go into "trance" and have a "trance dance" is mistaken. We aren't daydreaming. When we are strong with nǀom, we become more awake; it's easy to existentially die and spiritually wake up, but it may be hard work to return to the everyday way of being. On the other hand, when we are weak with nǀom it's very difficult to existentially die and spiritually awaken, but it's easy to come back to what we were. The strongest healers get cooked easily; for us what is painful is the transition back to our everyday selves. Our bodies need a rest, but our spirit doesn't want to go to sleep. We can have the energy to dance all night, but we can feel dead tired the next day.

---

*A nǀom-kxao who is bent over stomping, what the Bushmen sometimes identify as dancing with the ancestors, has an inner belly pump in motion that brings forth strenuous breathing and guttural sounds. In this situation the nǀom-kxao sometimes snorts as he makes loud rhythmic sounds. This intense action, involving heavy breathing through the nose, can bring on a nosebleed. In addition, it may sound like snoring, which is fascinating given Bleek's early transcriptions of Bushman accounts of healing that frequently mention how a healer "snores" during healing.

It's hard for us to believe that anyone would claim to be a healer or teacher who doesn't know about getting cooked. These are people pretending to be nlom-kxaosi, what we call a *n≠u'uhan*. If your nlom isn't hot, you have nothing that is spiritually important to say! However, if you get very hot, you actually find that you can no longer talk. The more spiritually cooked you are (we are referring to those times when your nlom is very hot), the less you are able to use language. When you are fully cooked in a dance and open your mouth to speak, no words will come out. There will only be unpredictable sounds exploding the air with arrows of nlom. It is worth saying again: when you are in the position of being able to speak the most truth about spiritual matters, no words can come out of your mouth. You can't talk at all. God made it that way. If someone is filled with nlom and loses the ability to talk, then listen carefully. Only then are their sounds true. (See editors' commentary 3.2.)

When we are speechless like this—when we can only make vibratory noises, sounds, and songs—we are better able to communicate with God and the ancestors. This is when we sing very loudly and our singing has a powerful vibration in it. As this vibration is felt in our body, it makes us even stronger.* The medicine of nlom is working best during this time.

Those with spiritual sensitivity can feel our truth when we voice boiling nlom. Only the ancestors and God understand what is being sounded. We can't emphasize enough how loud our singing and sound become while under the influence of nlom. We can't control it. It just comes out of us. This ecstatic loud sound making is a sign of an

---

*Similar to the rising of kundalini up the spine, as nlom rises in the body it may appear that it opens the throat to sing when it arrives at that part of the body. While there may be a truth to this description, it is also accurate that singing in a strong vibratory way helps pull nlom up the body. Again we see a circular interaction, this time in the pushing and pulling of nlom as it rises from the power center of the belly to the love of the heart—it's as though nlom is being both pulled from the top and pushed from the bottom through the body.

awakened healer. If someone is talking calmly and quietly, then they have no nlom. We would never listen to such a person because they are spiritually cold or dead.

As we sing like this, we get even hotter and our head and body feel lighter as our singing gets stronger. As they start to get hot with nlom, inexperienced healers find that they can't stand up and may fall to the ground. As they get stronger with nlom, though, they learn that this is the time they need to stay balanced and not fall. To do so during a dance, their feet must hit the ground in a slow and sure manner that appears as a stomp but in fact feels like their feet will go through the earth. No matter how experienced we are with nlom, it's amazing every time this happens This is when we are dancing the same dance as our ancestors. We say that we are dancing with all our ancestors.

Editors' Commentary

3.1. On resisting nlom or welcoming nlom

A healer's expectation about the experience of nlom contributes to feeding a self-verifying outcome. For example, a vicious cycle ensues as fear of nlom breeds more fear and sets up body resistance that fights the spontaneous movements that nlom inspires; body cramps and other kinds of pain are likely to result. On the other hand, a virtuous circle is brought forth when nlom is desired and its arrival is regarded as the entry into ecstatic joy. In this situation the body does not resist the spontaneous expression that nlom delivers; the more delight one takes in the presence of nlom the easier it is for nlom to heighten and pervade the healer's being in a way that feeds the dancer's escalating joy.

3.2. On nlom and language

As ecstatic experience escalates with the heating of nlom, the ability to use language fades. A Bushman healer whose nlom is boiling is immediately and spontaneously empty of mind, with all cognitive distinctions, naming, and inner discourse quieted. There is only felt experience absent of narrative commentary. This is the most respected and exalted form of human experience in Bushman culture, and it leaves Bushman healers in the position of not giving primary importance to any words that would articulate their experience.

Rather than dismissing this as anti-intellectual or as a primitive kind of religion, it is more accurate to regard Bushmen as recognizing the shapeshifting nature of thought and thereby appropriately not expecting it to remain stable in any form. What is consistently valued is found in the ecstatic joy that fully cooked nlom delivers.

4

THE STATIONS OF N|OM

The initial start up of heating n|om is *gua,* the beginning of !aia, when we feel the power of the fire. During the onset of !aia we become aware of moving toward spiritual experience. We feel our belly tightening as the nails and arrows begin waking up. Our word for this is *g||abesi tuih,* referring to the waking up of our nails in the abdomen.

As we continue waking up we start shaking. Our vision becomes blurry. The world may appear to be whirling. At this time we can float above the dance and feel like we are looking down on it. Though we don't see clearly at this first experiential station of n|om, the place of power, we feel empowered and think that nothing can hurt us.

This first station of being in relationship with n|om is called *n!aroh-||xam.* It is where a n|om-kxao first starts learning about n|om. This n|om-kxao is a beginner, a *n!aroh-ma.* It's like he is in the first grade of n|om school. Beginning healers often encounter a lot of fear at this first n|om station. Any healer who frequently mentions fear of n|om is someone who knows little, because he is just beginning to learn about ecstatic healing and spirituality. When an advanced healer talks to someone who is just beginning to learn about n|om, he will address fear because this meets beginners at the level of school and understanding they are in. Here we again see that a n|om-kxao adjusts the way he talks about n|om given the level of familiarity the other person has with it.

With fear comes the frequent concern that one will die with n|om and constantly be troubled by seeing bad ancestors. This is when young healers want to get out of healing; they don't want to go further because they fear they will die. They don't know that if they go further, their experience, understanding, and way of talking about these concerns will change. So instead they begin singing the kind of song that cools them down or they run away.

The truth is that if a healer sincerely stays with n|om and remains soft with an open mind and heart, he will be wonderfully transformed. His focus on power will disappear and if he has the courage to not run away, he will be reborn into a different feeling. This is when the heart rises.

As we first learn to handle n|om, it is not uncommon to show off the power we feel circulating inside our body. We are testing the truth of what is happening to us. This is when we might stand in the fire or even put our head in the fire. We may even want to demonstrate that we can eat the fire. We may also want to challenge the lions or anybody that's trying to shoot bad arrows. We shout, "Come, I can put you in your place! I can obliterate whatever you think can harm me! I can fight you and win!" We call those who show off or boast about their n|om *n≠u'uhan-kxaosi*.

Once a healer has played with fire there is no need to do it again. It can easily become a temptation to endlessly fool around with power, but it is a waste of time to show off how much power we have. We must let power go in order to receive a different kind of power. This death of the former power gives birth to a new power, one that is fed by love and song rather than display of might. It cares not about any fight, but instead celebrates the joy of being alive.

As we get stronger, we don't find any attraction or curiosity to power. As our nails get hotter, this power transforms into a vast love. We feel our heart becoming more open. We go past power to feeling a big love for everyone. At this n|om station we feel the suffering of others and feel sad for them; we want to help them so much that our heart starts to open even more than we thought was possible. When we feel this way for other people, our fear goes away. This is when our dance turns into the stomping movement of an awakened healer. This movement helps us not fall over as nǀom gets stronger and each stomp on the ground sends more vibrations into the body. When healers stomp together in a dance we say that they are all walking on the same rope, helping each other climb the rope to God.

As we go from the beginning stage of being an owner of nǀom, nǃaroh-ǁxam, to the second station of handling nǀom, *gǃaʼama-nǃausi*, we no longer want power. This is when we don't care about being strong, when we know it's more joyful to experience having a soft and open heart. This is when we feel that we are weak and small in the grand scheme of things. At the same time, this is also when we become stronger and bigger in matters of spiritual presence and relatedness to life. Beginning healers typically spend a lot of time at the first station, as it takes a lot of time to learn how to raise the heart. In the first nǀom station the contradictions and paradoxes of transition must be experienced and understood, including giving up power to receive more power, giving up control as a means of gaining more control, using our voice more and allowing music and auditory vibration to become primary while finding that words are less able to come forth, and becoming emptier in order to become more full of nǀom. This is when it is possible to heal by pulling out the dirty nails of sickness.

A nǀom-kxao at this stage is called a *ǃaaiha*. The strongest and most experienced healers go straight to this second station when heating nǀom—which usually takes place in a dance—because their hearts rise very fast.

The third nǀom station for a nǀom-kxao is where we feel that we can give a nail of nǀom. Here God uses our hands to transmit nails; rather than pulling out dirty nails, we insert new ones. This is how we help someone become a healer or empower another healer. This is a high level of working with nǀom. We call it *thara nǀom*. When a nǀom-kxao advances to this station she is called a *tco-kxao*. When we give new nails it automatically pushes sickness out. It happens at the same time—putting in a clean nail automatically releases a dirty one. This is when a healer experiences no pain—our experience transforms from pain to joy. We have moved from power to love, effortlessly enabling us to address problems and suffering more directly with healing nlom.

Finally, with more heat, this love becomes recognized as a pure vibration. It's difficult to describe this pinnacle experience. Here we actually go past what we conventionally regard as both power and love to feeling ourselves being more accurately described as the pulse of a pure vibration.* When a healer feels the strongest love, her body doesn't feel like it's a material body. It feels more like a cloud or fog of pulsing energy.† This is the best feeling of ecstatic joy. When this transformation happens, we are free of interpretation and narration—there is no longer any importance given to distinguishing what this vital presence is or isn't. Perhaps the most we can say is that it's like becoming a vibrating cloud. This is our best way of depicting it. After power and love, there is a pulsing white cloud. This is when we move toward becoming inseparable from the original luminous egg. We return to the source of all creation and nlom.‡

---

*We can say that power leads to love—the strongest power—which in turn leads to pure vibration, the most powerful love.

†The less we identify our self as constituting a recognizable identity, the more capacity we have to love and be spiritually alive with nlom.

‡Seasoned nlom-kxaosi can move through all these stations during an evening dance, transitioning through the stations in any order or remaining in one stage during most of the dance. A beginning nlom-kxao, however, will only be able to go in and out of the first station during a dance; it typically takes many dances for beginners to move forward into another station of handling nlom. Some nlom-kxao will never become healers and fewer will ever be able to transmit nails. When anthropologists such as Lee, Biesele, and Katz reported that most Bushman men become healers in their lifetime, they failed to differentiate these stages of development. In truth, many men and women become nlom-kxao, owners of the feeling for nlom (n!aroh-llxam), but only a few nlom-kxaosi learn to pull sickness (!hui) and become a pulling doctor or !aaiha. Even fewer are able to transmit nails and arrows, a nlom-kxao who is a tco-kxao. Finally, it is rare for anyone to be a fully cooked nlom-kxao or heart of the spears, a g≠aqba-n!a'an.

When we are full of power at a healing dance—the beginning stage of cooking our nails—we can see if an ancestor is trying to make someone sick. This is when the ancestor looks very ugly as we see the ancestor standing outside the dance circle. But when we move to the experiential station of love, we see only an ancestor who is expressing love. We experience the love they have for the person they are trying to connect with.

As we continue being cooked, we will eventually not see or hear. At this stage there is only vibration and we only experience its pulse. Strictly speaking, when we are fully cooked by n|om we no longer experience ourselves as a separate identity. We go past the senses. We neither see nor are we blind. Nothing is heard, nor is there silence. There is only the pure feeling of n|om that pulses with vibrant life, with no need to sense or know. There is complete absorption in owning the feeling for what is essential in life. Here we only relate to n|om.

N|om also affects what we regard as sensory experience. Heated n|om first helps us acquire new and transformed senses, but as n|om becomes hotter we have less interest in all sensory experience. This is when our hearts fully rise. We move from emphasizing both personal sensation and conceptual (language-mediated) knowing to being swept away by the rhythmic heart of God. Should anything that was formerly disturbing come toward us, we are able to say, "No, I don't need you anymore." It doesn't matter what it is or whether it is judged good or bad. Nothing bothers us for long. We rarely get angry and when we do, we know how to transform it. At the same time, we do not get too giddy with superficial joy. We are present in a different way, changed into being a luminous electrical cloud that pulses love and n|om.

While we say that we go past the senses, we must also say that we sense more fully, doing so in a way that is freer to amplify and unite all the senses into a more whole (and holier) emotion. While we are absent of narrated knowing or internal chitchat, a deeper knowing arises that surpasses the ability of words to convey. Finally, while words and concepts may not have the same kind of value they previously held, they may spontaneously arise in more profound ways, shifting from serving representation to fostering evocation and creation. This domain of experience leads us to the rope to God, the direct pathway to the divine, the feeling that can only be felt when all our senses intensify and combine, flowing into the oceanic love whose infinite waves cross any separation of divine breath, universal heartbeat, and eternal rhythm. This is where experience and knowing are inseparable from the vitality that gives them life.

5

ROPES TO GOD

In the process of becoming the strongest form of healer and spiritual teacher, our first encounter with the egg gets us started, then we often dance and ecstatically tremble for years until we encounter the egg again and see it crack open. This happens in a *kabi,* a sacred dream or vision.* The "owner" of the egg (meaning a person who has received the divine egg and owns the feeling for it) experiences God's ostrich egg floating in front of her in a kabi. If she keeps her focus one-pointedly on that egg and it cracks open, she will soon see God's rope, *!hui,* a luminous cord that connects her to God's village. Most owners of the egg saw the rope in the next dance following the kabi where we witnessed the egg cracking. Once we see the rope in a kabi, things change for us in subsequent dances.

To become fully developed as a spiritual teacher and healer, a person must first be reborn with the sacred egg. Through using its gifts the egg readies the recipient to experience it cracking open. This is when access to the divine rope is received. This rope is an invitation and means to climb directly to God's village.

A kabi is differentiated from a psychological dream (!'un*) and is believed to be sacred, that is, a communication or visitation from the Sky God or ancestors.

One time after dancing, |Kunta Boo saw the !hui, the straight rope to the sky. He walked toward it and went up. "Without any effort I floated up the rope. At the end of the rope, in God's village, my grandfather met me and took me down a road to meet the big Sky God. He touched me with his hands and transmitted nǀom. The nǀom he gave with his touch poured healing wisdom into me. He made me a nǀom-kxao, an owner of nǀom. Then God said, 'You need to go back down.' That's how I was taught."*

These journeys to the Sky God and the ancestors teach us about healing. For example, we learn that when we pull out sickness, it is important to make a certain kind of loud sound. However, we must first change ourselves in order to be able to pull the dirty nail that causes sickness. Our nǀom must be hot enough so that our everyday self is vacated, helping us spiritually awaken and feel reborn, ready to heal others.

There are many kinds of ropes. Some are red and blue or green. We especially want the one that is a brilliant white light. The red and blue ropes can be dangerous. The white ropes are the ones to follow—they take us to the place where life is renewed again and again. |Kunta |Ai!ae remembers hearing about the ropes and the ostrich egg when he was young. "When I was a boy I heard my parents and the older healers talk about the big ostrich egg. When it cracks open into two sides, one side has the red and green ropes.† The other side holds all the white ropes. You will see them as lines going around the egg. The left side has a green line and a red line circling it, while the right side of the cracked

---

*The most common kabi about meeting God (called a cunkuri) follows this general theme: "As we move toward the rope, we start going up it. At the end of the rope an ancestor meets us and takes us to meet God, members of God's family, or other ancestors. There we are given spiritual gifts such as songs, dances, or healing touch and have other kinds of encounters that deliver nǀom. Then God or an ancestor says it is time for us to return and help others in the community. It is so wonderful in the sky village that we sometimes want to stay, but we are told that it is not time for us to live in the village. Our job is to help others with the spiritual gifts we have been given."
†The ostrich egg does not crack apart for someone facing it for the first time. This takes place later in a cunkuri.

egg has the white line around it. This is the source of life. When you face this egg, it will give you its power. It grants you permission to have the ropes in your life."

There are spiritual ropes that look like power lines or telephone lines. They enable the ancestors to send spiritual energy or nlom. The line or rope that goes straight up to the sky is God's rope. We can climb it to visit God's village, use it as a telephone line to transmit and receive messages, or receive spiritual electricity from it. God sends nlom through that wire or rope.

We must be very strong to use this rope—if we are strong enough we can go up it. We have to be strong to go up and even stronger to return. As we use the rope, we must sing to keep our strength. The song must be one given by God. If we get scared we sing this nlom song. Singing it makes everything fine. If we get scared and don't sing, we can easily get into trouble. We must remember to sing. Only then can we ask and trust the ancestors to give us the right way.*

When we are stranded on a rope, we can use the root of the acacia tree. We chew it and spray it from our mouth. At the same time, we ask God for the right way to go. This is how we receive clear direction.

If we are spiritually flying and see a big fire in the sky, called *da'a,* we recognize it as the fire of death. We must not be tempted to move toward it. It may seduce us into thinking that it will make us stronger or that we are already strong enough to handle it, but we must ignore these thoughts. It is important to be on the right path. If we are lucky we will go all the way to the end of the rope. As we travel, we see the stars, but they are blurry because we are flying so fast. If we go all the way, we eventually find a large camel thorn tree standing on sandy ground. This is where God and the original ancestors live.[†]

---

*Intense singing of a nlom song keeps one in a highly ecstatic state where conscious thought is minimized and unable to interfere with the natural automatisms of nlom-inspired movement.

†This experience is one of the most important kabis for a strong nlom-kxao. Again, this type of kabi that is associated with God is called a cunkuri.

God's village in the sky has no sickness and no arguments. It is beautiful and perfect without any strife or combat. A nlom-kxao aims to visit this village and receive the strongest nlom, but to get there our nails must be cooked all the way. We must go past being afraid of nlom and look forward to getting fully cooked.

When one of our healers was on the rope, he was taken to a place where he was served an extraordinary meal on a large table. "After I finished eating, the Sky God showed me the right way. He said, 'You must follow this rope until you reach the place where you are going.'" The healer was basically told to become strong enough to go to the end of the rope. He had been fed nlom and it helped him travel further. At the end of the rope is found the beginning. There we find our original home in God's sky village, looking the same as it always has been since the beginning of the ancestors.

To climb a rope to God, the rope must be thick and strong. The size of the rope that goes up to the sky depends upon the strength of the healer. The strongest healers have a bigger rope while weaker healers might have a very thin thread. Healers want to give each other nails not only to make themselves stronger but also to make their ropes stronger and thicker. You must have a lot of nlom to maintain the strength of this rope.*

A strong healer knows how to make the ropes strong for all kinds of relationships. There are ropes between people; when we give each other nails, we make these ropes stronger. When that rope is strong, we can actually feel the other person tugging and pulling. When it happens for the first time, it definitely surprises us.† It is literally like a rope pulling on our body, usually around our lower belly. When we

---

*The thickest rope's diameter is approximately the size of an elevator cable while the thinnest ones are like thread.

†This feels like an automatism, which happens outside of a person's will, as if something is pulling his or her gut back and forth toward another person. In intimate situations it can also happen with the sexual organs of both men and women, where they feel pulled to a sexual partner by an invisible rope.

make our ropes stronger, it helps strengthen all the ropes in nature. Even the ropes to the animals and plants get stronger. It's a way of making the whole world healthy.* This is how our ecstatic healing way helps make everything strong.

Each healer is given her own rope. She should use it to make all the ropes strong. If there is no healer making the ropes strong, then all the ropes get weak and the world starts to die. The ropes can become so thin that they break. (See editors' commentary 5.1 on page 33.) Living things die when the ropes get spoiled.

We have been told that there are people outside the Kalahari who claim to be healers or spiritual teachers, although say they never saw the egg nor heard about it. Because they do not own the egg, they may be tempted to minimize its importance or suggest that there are other equivalent means of becoming fully spiritually developed. Over thousands of years of directly making our way to God, we recognize that the egg is the biggest gift God gives to human beings. Not receiving it means that one likely has not gone through the whole process of being spiritually cooked and in relationship with God. (See editors' commentary 5.2.)

There is nothing wrong with someone not receiving the egg, because it is not everyone's preordained mission to receive the egg. But when a community or culture has no one with the egg they will easily be led astray and become lost. They will be without adequate guidance. Their ropes will bend and lead them astray.† We have found that there is no other way to initiate, foster, and ordain the strongest possible healers and teachers.

Outsiders to our way with nǀom appear to live in an upside down

---

*Nature is seen as a web of interconnected ropes. Empowering a rope sends nǀom throughout the entire network and thereby contributes to the wellness of the whole ecology.

†Any rope that does not go straight to the sky is assumed to take one away from God and is therefore considered not as reliable.

world. They think they are awake when they are actually asleep, and when they get too excited with spiritual energy they get scared and fall back asleep. We have watched Christian missionaries get excited when they worship in their services, but they are not able to stay awake very long when their n|om gets heated. The people in their church pass out, or what people refer to as being "slain in the spirit." These missionaries are novices to n|om and need to learn to avoid passing out so the n|om can get stronger. Otherwise, they will never get strong enough to find a rope to God and climb to his village. Without fully cooked n|om, you can't wake up all the way. We meet very few people who have ever been fully awake. Most people are always asleep. We're partially teasing, but we're also making a point about the way people are in their spiritual lives.

Over the years we have only trusted spiritual teachers who have faced the egg. This is why trickster (|xuri kxaosi) has not been able to lead us away from the most basic spiritual truths. From the beginning we have had owners of the egg who had a rope—a direct line—to God.* Their job is to help us not get lost. They help other healers get on the best tracks to God.

When someone owns the egg and has a rope to God, we are able to visit such a person with the ropes no matter where he is in the world. (See editors' commentary 5.3.) The egg gives us new eyes and we feel things when we look through them. These strong and enhanced spiritual feelings concerning n|om help us see in a different way. We call this "seeing properly" (kxae≠xaisi). Without this kind of strong feeling we are spiritually blind. When we are opened, our feelings and relationship with n|om intensify enough to wake up our spiritual

---

*Someone filled with n|om may see luminous lines, threads, or ropes going in different directions. One can even see a lattice structure of ropes like a spider's web. However, with sufficient n|om one rope takes prominence over all other ropes—a vertical rope that goes straight to the sky. This is regarded as a rope to God, enabling a journey to God's village in the sky. It may appear as a ladder, staircase, or a road. When told about Jacob's ladder in the Old Testament, Bushman healers regard it as a reference to the rope to God.

seeing, hearing, smelling, tasting, and touch. If we are not opened, we have no idea what any of this means, although trickster may try to convince us that we do. That's when we are not on the right track.

In some ways it's a waste of time to talk to someone who is not open about what it is like to be opened. They will conceptualize and fantasize through the eyes of someone who is spiritually blind and deaf. In other words, they will be pretending. We know this because we can smell inauthenticity, hear the absence of nlom in a song, and see that there is no appropriate shiver in their body. No matter. We will teach anyway, doing so for those who have been opened so they will know they are not alone. We do so for the future of the original spiritual way. As owners of the egg and the ropes, we are bringing back forgotten truths that have been masked or distorted by false teachings and teachers with little or no nlom. The world needs to have teachers and healers who sing, dance, and tremble as God's love flows through their hearts. Otherwise there can only be dead talk that leads everyone away from an awakened life. Words mean nothing unless they are bathed and delivered in nlom. Even the words *love, healing,* and *nlom* and the name of God are not alive unless the person voicing them is alive with the truths these words aim to evoke.

We own something that the entire world needs—a rope to God that is a direct link to the original source of nlom. Through the songs it brings we are able to keep alive our communication with the ancestors and God. This makes our healing and spiritual ways renewed and strong. Without this rope, trickster gets a hold on us and then leads us astray. No one can find the rope to God through words and names. It requires being pierced with nlom and receiving the nlom songs that clean and make us ready to feel God pulling us in the right direction. Love, healing, and nlom are brought into our hearts through this rope to God.

Editors' Commentary

5.1. On breaking the ropes

Consider this lament called "The Broken String," transcribed in the 1800s by Wilhelm Bleek and Lucy Lloyd, about the death of a Cape Town–area Bushman's friend who had been a shaman and rainmaker:

> People were those who
> Broke for me the string.
> Therefore,
> The place became like this to me,
> On account of it,
> Because the string was that which broke for me.
> Therefore,
> The place does not feel to me,
> As the place used to feel to me,
> On account of it.
> For,
> The place feels as if it stood open before me,
> Because the string has broken for me.
> Therefore,
> The place does not feel pleasant to me,
> On account of it.

5.2. On the primary importance of experiencing the ineffable

Again, since most cultures do not have spiritual know-how in handling the most amplified spiritual energy, spiritual practitioners lose consciousness before reaching a high enough state of ecstatic experience where the luminous egg can be seen. The Bushman explanation as to why few cultures report seeing the divine egg would entail questioning whether they have sufficient nlom and whether they are able to hold it when it escalates its intensity.

5.3. On long-distance visitations with
owners of the rope to God

Brad has regularly experienced these visitations for nearly three decades and the Bushman elders have confirmed this. South African botanist Hans Vahrmeijer, a leading authority on the Bushman use of medicinal plants, accompanied Brad on many of his early trips to the Kalahari and wrote: "I observed him [Brad] being taught and trained by [the Bushmen] to such a level over the years that even long-distance communication by way of dreams became a natural reality for him" (Keeney 2003b, 158–59).

6
TRANSMITTING N|OM

With more experience we look forward to receiving a nail and waking up. This is when it feels good. When we are fully cooked, n|om is the greatest experience in the world. It brings the highest joy and satisfaction. We feel like we have found the secret to living when we are fully cooked by God. (See editors' commentary 6.1 on page 41.)

A healer must be fully cooked to transmit an arrow of n|om to another person. There are different ways of transmitting n|om, depending on the people involved and the circumstances. The old healers from the past would sometimes shoot the medicine of n|om into a novice healer with a special kind of bow and arrow. A big healer would first get the bow ready and then lightly shoot an arrow to help send the n|om. The arrow would fall near the person; the n|om subsequently jumps out of the arrow and enters the person becoming a healer.

The strongest healers from the past carried these arrows on their back during a dance. They cooked oryx horn arrows with n|om medicine made from a plant before using them in a dance. They used to dance with the arrows so they could make them hot with n|om. When the arrows were full of n|om, the big healer would pull out an arrow and shoot it toward someone who was trying to become a healer. |Kunta Boo witnessed this method of delivering n|om when he was a boy, but he himself never did it. His grandfather did it often a long time ago. Another old way to send nǀom was to cough up a needle into our hands and then apply it to the person wanting to be a healer.

When we transmit a nail to help someone become a healer or a stronger healer, it feels good to our body. It is like merging our hearts, and it's one of the best feelings in the world. It makes the two of us become one. (See editors' commentary 6.2.)

When putting in a nail or arrow there must be only one kind, the female nail or arrow, which is what we call the strongest possible nail. It is the best one to give to others. It can give birth to more arrows and nails. We send arrows of nǀom with our trembling hands. We can also shoot such an arrow through our eyes or by snapping a finger. In addition, we can make a big clapping sound. These are the typical ways of transmitting arrows of nǀom.

Our healers have always laid their hands on a person to give nǀom. This is how we were taught. When our ancestors shot an arrow with the oryx horn, they also laid their hands on us. Both of these ways of sending nǀom are equally strong. (See editors' commentary 6.3.)

A big healer is able to put her heart against another person's heart so that the shaking vibration of nǀom passes through. This vibratory hug that rests heart upon heart is called ≠ara-khoe and is a very strong experience.* In addition, healers may lie down on each other on the ground. Here one person shakes nǀom into another person's body or we shake together. The belly can shake it into another person's body. We can heal someone this way.

The strongest healers always shoot each other.† They enjoy testing

---

*Bradford Keeney demonstrated the Bushman way of transmitting a vibration into the body, including this heart-to-heart transmission, to renowned osteopath Dr. Robert Fulford, who claimed it was "the key to healing," the "vibrational medicine he had searched for" during his career.

†A Bushman healing dance is therefore as much for the healers as it is for those who are sick. It is an opportunity for healers to make each other stronger with nǀom. Jealousy is rare among nǀom-kxaosi, for the presence of stronger doctors means that all healers will be empowered.

themselves by shooting and sharing arrows of nlom. When they release an arrow they make a loud sound. If a person is weak, he will fall over. The person who shot that arrow then goes over and picks the fallen healer up, placing his hands on him to help cool him down and bring him back. For beginners, the first time they receive a nail of nlom in a dance may bring so much pain that they don't want to go back to a dance. Or if they do, they just sit near the dancers. But when a strong healer feels pain, he just keeps on dancing. The strongest healers quickly go past pain; they have no fear. When the nails enter them, it feels like water. They are hungry and thirsty for nlom. They want to drink and eat it.

When God sends a nail or needle to a healer it carries God's love, a love that is infinite and beyond understanding. Whether shot by a bow or thrown by a hand, an imagined sharp object shoots out of God's heart and pierces the healer, bringing a love that is expressed through song. This is why a needle, nail, or arrow is also referred to as a "nlom song"; needles, arrows, and nails of nlom basically deliver songs from God. These objects are therefore both names of God's songs and descriptions of the means used to deliver God's love. God puts love into a song and squeezes or compacts it into a sharp object so it can be shot into our heart. God only communicates through music because God gives us the kind of love that requires music to express it, delivered through an imagined sharp object capable of emotionally piercing our heart. (See editors' commentary 6.4.) After we are hit with this love-bearing delivery, we are awakened to spontaneously sing its song because we are feeling God's love in an unfettered way.

When someone comes to us and requests knowledge about these things, we really can't say much unless we know that they can sing with nlom and receive the nails and arrows. You can only understand our healing and teaching through receiving nails and arrows and through the singing and dancing that naturally arise from nlom, which are all derived from God's love. While a hint of nlom is possible without these experiences, it pales in comparison to the transformative shifts that love-inspired n|om brings, especially when it involves and emphasizes the highest forms of love that are inseparable from a felt relationship with the divine.

A strong healer may want to challenge another healer to teach him more. Outsiders may think that a strong doctor is showing off, but he is really saying, "There's more for you to learn." When a big healer reports what happened to him, he's not bragging about his self-importance. He's celebrating the n|om and spiritual gifts he was given and is signaling that he's ready to share them. Sometimes a healer says, "Oh, my nails are so strong. It's unbelievable." He's not saying, "I'm special." He is saying, "It's amazing what the big Sky God can do. I am happy to bring some of this n|om to you if you are prepared and ready to receive it."

Healers can test each other and learn more. It is good for a big healer to tell the people "Oh, my nails are very strong" because he wants to help them. He's conveying that God has brought some good nails. It's like a hunter bringing home the meat. When a hunter is successful the community will tease him to bring him down to size. They also do the same to the healers. The healers are teased, but only in a good way. People might say, "Do you think you are something?" The healer might tease back, "I can always fight you." Strong healers feel happy when they are teased and they like to prove their strength. A male healer might go into the bush and chase somebody. The chief will later ask what happened. This is when the healer says, "Because he teased me this way, I wanted to prove that I can frighten him." When the people are teasing the big healer, he responds, "You just go ahead and tease me. You can expect me to scare you when you're out in the bush some day."

The strongest healer constantly teases the people, making them even more respectful and cautious about the dance. The healer may say, "Oh yes, n|om will kill you. It's so painful. If I give you a nail, you will die quickly." They exaggerate in order to tease. As everybody's teasing the healers to lessen the serious nature of their job, the healers simultaneously tease them about their power in order to scare them. This helps keep things balanced.

Of course when the dance starts, things get serious. There is no longer any teasing like this because nlom takes over. If the healer feels strong, he comes inside the dance circle near the fire and stomps the ground. That's when he climbs the ropes. (See editors' commentary 6.5.) In this ecstatic way the world is renewed and reborn.

Both men and women can be reborn in the egg and climb the rope to the sky village. *Thara,* our word for shaking, is as strong for both men and women. Thara takes place when a healer's nails of nlom get hot. Just before nlom fully cooks, we wake up (!aia). This is when we feel that nlom is all around us. As soon as it is very hot, we shake. When we see someone's body jerking, it is a sign that they are waking up. When they are awake, they are fully trembling and shaking.

The strongest !aia immediately takes us into thara. This often happens with the strongest nlom-kxoasi. Here we sing with all our heart because ecstatic singing is required for nlom to get spiritually hot. Without a song, we cannot go far with nlom. Shaking by itself is not the point; if it were we could have a lion chase someone and he would shake with fear and that would accomplish the job. When we heard about white doctors teaching people to shake in order to heal trauma and injury, we recognize that they miss the most important wisdom about healing. They are imitating healing rather than embodying its truth. Unless your heart fully opens and rises, doing so with an ecstatic song, you will never be able to see why shaking is simply a part of a strong healer's experience or that the kind of shaking required must be inspired by a spiritually awakened and singing heart. The shaking we are talking about is not merely a physical exercise. It involves being touched by nlom, specially delivered by the arrows of God's love. This makes us want to sing and dance. (See editors' commentary 6.6.)

If we are shaking as a show for others, but don't have any hot needles, we will eventually wear out. Thara is when we are hot and the nlom in our spine is making us shake. We do not control it. It is effortless and natural trembling, as if spontaneously produced. All of this enables us to become reborn.

Beginning healers spend a lot of time in !aia waiting to go into thara, while the strongest ones go straight into it without first even waking up. Thinking about a dance can get them started. Or thinking about God can be enough. There are some healers who are so strong that even if the singing is from some place far away, simply hearing the song is enough for them to enter thara. The healers will start to shake and get reborn again. .

To have a powerful dance and be a strong doctor, we say *!ka tsau l'an,* that is, our heart must rise. It's easier for a woman's heart to rise and this is why women are often the strongest healers. It is sometimes more difficult for men to raise their heart because men tend to be more competitive and showoff. In addition, women are more responsible for holding the singing and clapping in a dance, and this makes them more ready for nǀom. This is the main secret behind why women are often stronger with nǀom than men. Women are typically easy with ways of the heart and the stronger they sing, the hotter and stronger nǀom becomes. However, this is not always the case. Some women are more interested in power than men and some men are softer than most women. All that matters is that we become soft and reach for the biggest love. When we dance for a long time and sing nǀom songs, all our hearts lift in a good way.*

There is no good versus bad nǀom though some beginning nǀom-kxaosi sometimes get mixed up and talk like this is the case. There is only nǀom, and we have a respect name for it in addition to its main name. Its respect name is *tco.* When we feel nǀom, we use the respect name. It is not wise to say the word *nǀom* out loud in public when we feel nǀom. That's when we say *tco.* Someone who has newly acquired nǀom might boast about having it when he doesn't have much. He might even inappropriately use the respect name when there is no nǀom

---

*As the heart rises, we begin to sing and our body vibrations shift to a higher frequency. There is little gross body movement at this stage, though a surge of large physical movement can be interspersed. There is little effort at this phase of heated nǀom, and no effort is exerted by the nǀom-kxao.

present, trying to make others think he owns n|om. We call this kind of boaster a *n≠u'uhan-kxaosi*. They show off in the dance. Sometimes they pretend to have a lot of n|om when they don't have it. They are not true healers.

There is a special way of exchanging n|om that is very important to the strongest healers. A strong man and woman healer (or any two strong healers) can hold each other and give one another nails of n|om. They will shake together and experience themselves getting stronger. We call this *djxani-!uhsi,* referring to two n|om-kxaosi shaking together. As the exchanged energy increases, it can reach a peak where it feels like our head is shooting off into the stars. When this takes place between two people, either one or both people involved can experience going into the sky. This can happen in a very strong dance or during the day when two healers are shaking as they hug. It's different than climbing a rope. It's like we are shot out of a gun and it feels more amazing than sexual intimacy. This is an extraordinary experience.

Whether we are climbing a rope or being shot into space, we must always follow the right rope. If we go up and do not follow the right path, then it could be a bad thing. When we go straight up to the stars, there is joy and happiness. As we mentioned before, this can also happen when we go straight down the rope. What matters is whether the rope is straight. Going up or down gets us to the same place, as long as the rope does not bend.

Our way relies upon singing and dancing to activate the heating of n|om. Our hope is that we will see the rope and climb it. Going up the rope is part of God's work. N|om makes you feel close to God.

Editors' Commentary

6.1. On life organized by n|om

A life organized by n|om is free from the search for a grand understanding. No one looks for "the answer." It is a life free of interpretation similar to Zen—especially Zenless-Zen, Zen without attachment to narration about itself. It is also improvisational and free of the rigidity caused by overattachment to procedural models, templates, and habit. Yet it is more than Zen and improvisation. It is the continually changing dynamic of hunting nlom and being hunted by nlom, and the dance that helps one climb the rope to God.

6.2. On transmitting nails

When removing a dirty nail most of the work is done by the nlom-kxao with the sick person remaining more passive. Giving a new nail is more interactional, with both the nlom-kxao and the recipient in a vibrational synch where each person's movements inspire and escalate the other person's movements. As this takes place there is a sense of union that is brought about by the harmonic relations of these interacting vibrational movements. The degree of coordination and the union realized varies for each situation. A nlom-kxao will find that transmitting a new nail or arrow may require some effort or it may be effortless, depending on how in synch the body movements of transmitter and recipient are with one another.

6.3. On body contact in Bushman healing

All Bushman healing involves body-to-body contact. This can take place in the everyday or in the dreamtime. The idea of holding one's hands above another person's body to heal makes no sense to a nlom-kxao, because direct physical contact intensifies nlom, which determines the strength of its healing potency. Bushman healing and spirituality promotes non-subtle energy medicine and gives no value to subtle energy work, the latter being seen as the work of someone who does not understand or hold nlom. With heated nlom, it is not conceivable to not touch another person.

6.4. On nlom songs

A song carrying nlom, called a "nlom song," is transferred to a person by a so-called arrow or nail. It is not enough to hear the song. The song must be held and delivered by a sharp object that pierces the heart; then the nail, nlom song, and nlom itself awaken. These three names are all different ways of discussing nlom, each underscoring a different aspect of nlom. "Nails" and "arrows" refer to the transference from one person to another (or animal, plant, ancestor, or gods to humans), "nlom songs" indicate the spontaneous expression brought forth by heated nlom, and "nlom" refers to that which is delivered and the songs it inspires.

6.5. On climbing the ropes to God

It may be more accurate to say that the healer reenacts climbing the rope. The first time one visions the rope to God is a moment that brings intense emotion and nlom to the nlom-kxao. The visionary image is less important than the feeling associated with it, and it is the latter that will be evoked in future dances. When you catch the feeling for the rope it brings forth a stomping motion that enacts climbing the rope. The same applies to soul retrieval—it may only be dramatically witnessed in vision once or possibly a few times; the remembered feeling for it afterward inspires a reenactment of what was experienced, along with the ecstatic movements and sounds. Soul retrieval typically refers to when a nlom-kxao becomes unconscious during a dance because her soul has traveled too far and needs to return or else risk not coming back and dying. Other nlom-kxaosi then attempt to retrieve the lost soul in a variety of ways. Note that soul retrieval does not apply to people who are conscious nor does it necessarily have anything to do with illness. The latter is simply regarded as being caused by dirty nails.

6.6. On thara for healing

Shaking (thara) by itself is nothing according to the Bushmen. The shaking must be inspired by emotionally aroused music and dance that celebrates a love for God. Anything else has little nlom, which is the spiritual medicine and power that is being sought. When videos of ecstatic dancers and other shaking ceremonies performed by various spiritual teachers and communities were shown to these Bushman elders, they replied that "there was little to no nlom" brought forth by their movements. Purposeful shaking fails to heat nlom. It can generate numerous physical and emotional responses, some of them arguably beneficial, but it does not cause the heart to rise. Bushmen regard this kind of shaking as infatuated with power that easily leads people astray, as it advances self-inflation and misses the deeper healing and transformation that heart-inspired shaking delivers. The lack of vibratory touching and singing are sure signs that there is little nlom present in someone who is using purposeful movement. Naive imitation of someone else like a guru, stereotyped movements, and an emphasis upon selected interpretations and explanations are also indicative of the absence of heated nlom.

7

Bushman Healers and Healing

We have helped many anthropologists over the decades. Some of us assisted with the writing of a dictionary by Patrick Dickens. We told visiting researchers various cultural stories that we tell our children. For example, Megan Biesele recorded |Kunta Boo's stories. |Kunta was also a close friend of John Marshall. Though Megan Biesele and John Marshall fought over the years, vehemently disagreeing over what was best for Bushman culture, |Kunta wants everyone to know that he was friends with both of them.

We want people to have the right information about our healing. There are some important things that need to be corrected. What we understand and teach about our healing ways partially comes from the healing we received when we were first taught. When we thought we were dying after receiving our first nails, the elders told us that we were not going to die.* At the time we were still young. |Kunta Boo started getting

---

*As discussed in the preface, most scholars have accepted Richard Katz's work on Bushman healing *Boiling Energy* as an accurate and credible account. However, the Bushman nlom-kxaosi we have worked with expressed concern over how his book too frequently misrepresents their healing and spiritual practices and omits some of their most important considerations. (See editors' commentary 7.1 on page 51.)

thin after n|om was placed in his body. He was told that he would not die. The healers kept giving him more n|om. The same happened to all of us. The people would sing and we would dance and tremble. The ancestors visited us in our dreams and said we were to become healers.

John Marshall and his father arrived around the time this was happening to |Kunta Boo. As |Kunta Boo describes this period of his life, "It was when I was being made a healer. My parents were helping me. They were holding me in the dance and making sure no bad-intentioned ancestor would throw me into the fire and tempt me to prove that I won't burn if I never step away from the flames.* I became married to my wife during all of this. I was becoming a healer, though at that time I was still not open. I was only dancing around. Then one day the big healers came to me and insisted that I had grown enough and that I must now lay my hands on the people. They said they would open my eyes so I would be able to heal.

"Though I didn't think I was very good at healing, the strong doctors would say, 'Here you are. You are laying your hands on people. Why don't you open up your eyes now so you can be a healer?'† They opened me so that I could heal even in darkness. I started pulling out

---

*It is not uncommon for Bushmen to walk or stand in the fire during a dance when they are at the first station of feeling power. Bo [Brad] once stood in the middle of the fire with an old elder, standing there for several moments before dancing in it. In addition, some Bushmen put their face into the fire. The community always pulls out such a dancer knowing that while they won't be hurt at first, prolonged exposure will burn. There is a limited grace period that enables fire standing, walking, dancing, and head immersion.

†This reference to "open up your eyes" has two meanings: first it refers to opening spiritually awakened eyes, or what Bushmen sometimes call "second eyes." It also refers to the initiation dance for a developing healer, in which the initiate wraps his arms around the back of a strong healer and closes his eyes as he is danced around the dance circle. The initiate then holds on to the hands of the strong healer and feels him heal others. At a certain moment in the dance, the stronger healer—the teacher—carefully breaks away from the initiate as the latter continues to doctor others, doing so thinking he is still holding on to the teacher. When he is told to open his eyes, he sees that he has been healing by himself. A strong healer who has taught and initiated numerous healers is said to be someone "who has carried many healers on his back." This experience of being initiated by an elder Bushman healer took place for Bo with the Bushman healer Mautope in Botswana.

sickness in others. I was able to heal. After that they would say to me, 'Let's go together. We'll teach you this way.' They taught me for a long time. Finally, they left me because they knew that I was capable.

"I was taught that whenever I heard that someone is sick, I must go there and help that person. I started going to the sick people and healing them. The next day they got better and they were very happy. The strong healers said to themselves, 'Yes, we taught you and you must keep on doing this.' When someone was sick, there was only one healer who they knew could heal. I was that person.*

"Once there was a baby boy who was declared dead. John Marshall and I went to see what was going on. The baby was about to be buried, but I placed my hands on the baby and he came back to life and got better. That person is still living today. He's now an elder."

Nǀom is an important medicine and a healer must never stop using it. Otherwise a healer might bring himself sickness. It's dangerous for a powerful healer to not use his gift. We can get tired and start to ache and then get sick. The stronger we get the more we must use it with others.

It's very important for us to dance because it makes our nails hot and wakes us up to seeing, hearing, and feeling correctly so we can heal. Even our senses of smell and taste change.† A strong healer can see the insides of a person and find the part of the body that is sick. He lays his hands on the spots where he see sickness, then he pulls it out with his

---

*It is not uncommon for a strong Bushman healer to boast about his healing abilities in the same way that a great hunter will tell you that he is a skilled hunter. This isn't done to inflate his ego, but to accurately report his situation. The same healer or doctor who later loses his skills will then accurately say that he is not as good as he used to be. The feigned humility attributed to Bushman healers (and this applies to some other indigenous practitioners as well) may be an invention or fantasy of the anthropologist or outside interpreter. At the same time, Bushmen laugh at someone who boasts about being a healer who, in fact, is only pretending to be a nǀom-kxao. This person is called a n≠u'uhan.

†Reports on Bushman healers, including Bleek's work, have reported them smelling illness when doctoring.

hands. This pulling is called ≠hoe, meaning to pull out sickness with our hands. (See editors' commentary 7.2.)

When we remove sickness, it can physically hurt as we're getting hotter with nlom and struggling to pull it out. The pulling can hurt when we exert too much effort to heal. This pain can come to any healer, including experienced healers. We can feel a cramping pain or a stabbing sensation in the gut because we pull so hard.

When you feel power and try to consciously force the action of healing, it will hurt. But if you are strong and at the same time allow things to happen spontaneously, you give less importance to the fear. Any talk about fearing nlom involves battling the station of fire; power, by its very definition, points to a struggle, usually one thing trying to win over another. When we release the power or struggle and allow nlom to bring things forth effortlessly, there is no pain. Instead, we meet ecstatic joy.

Singing takes our mind away from being overly concerned about whether we will feel pain and be distracted by any unnecessary focus on willpower that tries to make something happen. As Tcoq'a likes to emphasize, "We must sing hard to stay on the right path. This is the key. Singing with all our heart pulls us to the right rope. It keeps things correct." This kind of strong singing makes a powerful vibration in our body. It increases our thara as it silences the purposeful mind.

With vibratory singing, our nails of nlom are made the hottest; this is when happiness and delight flows over us. Pulling out sickness can feel good if we are strong enough, that is, if we have an abundance of cooked nlom. There are times when we are so strong that even when the pain comes we don't feel it. When we pull out sickness we make a certain sound that we call kau-hariri. It's not the sound of pain, but the sound of letting go of a person's pain. It's the sound of pushing the pain away from us, that is, pushing it out of our body. It's a sound that releases.

Taking out illness requires removing a dirty arrow or nail. There are other ways of taking out the illness besides pulling; these include blowing, spitting, or strongly sniffing through the nose. Sometimes a healer will breathe out an illness and this may cause a nosebleed. The strongest healers, the heart of the spears, do more than pull—they pull and push like a pump, removing dirty nails and giving clean ones at the same time.

The nlom-kxao relates to the world through awakened feelings and enhanced sensory experience. When we're in !aia, we experience the strongest feelings. We cannot say enough that this is not about being in the stupor of trance; it's about waking up and heightening our enhanced feelings. (See editors' commentary 7.3.) Only then can we see properly. When we see the sickness we also feel it. The feeling is stronger than the seeing. When we only see images without feeling we are seeing partially; seeing properly requires kxae≠xaisi, seeing with feelings. We actually see the sickness in the flesh. Sometimes it looks green or white. It can also look like a needle. If it looks black, it is a killing thing.

In the beginning a new healer is always looking for sickness. As he becomes stronger over the years, he doesn't have to look. A strong old healer can heal from far away. He can heal and do spiritual work from a distance. The stronger a healer becomes, the more automatic everything is. We don't have to think and we don't even have to see. We just do what needs to be done and say, "Oh, I already know this. It is my capability."* There is no need to know what is wrong with a person or even understand anything. We simply do what needs to be done. These things happen when they are supposed to take place, not when we desire them.†

When we are doctoring someone we must have a good feeling for

---

*In addition, simply being around strong healers results in transmitted nlom and teaching because their ropes of connection are so strong, provided the learner is soft enough and ready to receive it.

†The fully cooked healer does not first diagnose and then subsequently offer treatment. Action is immediately performed that aims to heal. The nlom-kxao is inspired by nlom to act spontaneously. There is not even the awareness that one is acting in order to accomplish anything. The healing action simply happens with no attachment to naming, narrating, or interpreting what is being done.

the person. We want them to be well so much that we beg their ancestors to help them become better. Recently ≠Oma Dahm was brought to a dance. He was so sick that he could have died at anytime. The healers worked on him and two ancestors came later at night. The father ancestor wanted to take him away and the mother ancestor said to the husband, "You will not take him yet." This happened because of a strong dance. It made |Kunta Boo's nails so strong that he went to sleep afterward and had a kabi in which ≠Oma's ancestral parents came to him. They told him that ≠Oma would live.

When we become very strong we don't even have to look for the sickness. That's when our hands go to the spot automatically. Our hands function independent of our conscious mind. Here God enables us to do the work without any need to critically observe or comment on it. We stop creating a story about what is happening. This is true for the most powerful healers. It's as if God is saying, "Don't think about anything and let me help you do the necessary work." This is when we are all working together—God, the ancestors, and the rest of those who are present become one family. We're united, embracing one another, as a vibration harmoniously links us. This vibration can pass through our hands into another person. When we come back to ourselves, we are delighted to find that anyone who felt that vibratory embrace is healed and tuned. This is as true for the healer as it is for the village, the ancestors, and God.

Although our healers have their own unique experiences, overall they are very similar. They commonly involve the ropes, the Sky God's ostrich egg, nails, arrows, thara, and n|om. We all must awaken ourselves to see properly and aim for the spiritual classrooms through kabis. Most importantly, it should be understood that our love for the Sky God and the music he gives us makes all our spiritual gifts possible.

Editors' Commentary

7.1. On misrepresentation of healing practices

Chris Low, an anthropologist and physician associated with the African Studies Centre, University of Oxford, found some of the same issues. In a letter sent to Brad on March 23, 2009, he wrote, "I have long thought Katz only tickled things. . . . I was so pleased to find your work because my findings differ considerably from those of other anthropologists who have worked with the San and your work both confirms and brings exciting new detail to much that I have found in the wider KhoeSan healing world. I have had some difficult exchanges with anthropologists on many of these matters." Later, in March 22, 2013, Low wrote another letter adding: "It is interesting how much authority is attributed to the earlier anthropological interpretations of San healing and how difficult it becomes to introduce new interpretations despite most of the early work barely penetrating the surface. It is surprising how people are happy to rehash this old material as if it were some absolute truth. Your research is refreshing and innovative. Unlike anyone else you focus specifically and with great dedication on the healing dance and bring enlightening insights from your exceptional psychotherapeutic, shamanic, and healing background."

The skewed conclusions about Bushman healing and spirituality that have been perpetuated by Katz and others include the beginner's view that nlom is only feared because it is dangerous, while essentially ignoring an advanced healer's passionate desire to hunt nlom; nlom is primarily described as painful rather than an experience of ecstatic joy; nlom is depicted as power-oriented rather than being a means of abandoning power for a greater submission to love; the ancestral spirits are characterized as only bringing harm and disease in contrast to their capacity and willingness to help heal; and healing is seen as more battle-oriented as it fights malevolent spirits rather than being aimed at delivering infusions of healing nlom. Most important, the primary importance of a rope to God is minimized or ignored, as is the transformative nature of ecstatic shaking, vibratory song, interactional sharing of physically felt vibrations, the abdominal pump required to pull sickness, and the different levels of expertise in handling nlom, among other omissions.

7.2. On pulling out sickness

When Bushmen refer to "pulling out sickness," this is an experience where the abdomen feels like a pump that is able to pull something out of another person's body. The muscles of the abdomen actually contract and release like a physical pump during this healing process. At the same time the healer also feels any sickness or fatigue pulled out of his own body. When nlom is sufficiently heated, this pumping action is automatic. This is when it is time to pull out sickness. If the pumping action is not taking place or is barely operating in the abdomen, then a nlom-kxao should not attempt pulling sickness. This is when sickness can get stuck in the healer's body. Bushmen regard other healers who do not experience a pumping action in their body as taking unnecessary risks when they work with sickness.

7.3. On shaking and trance

The ground of experience for a Bushman nlom-kxao is shaking. Shaking can induce a kind of trance, what has been called a "kinetic trance" by psychiatrist David Akstein (1992). However, trance in itself may not be particularly relevant to the act of healing. As Marshall (1999, 61) reports with respect to healings that take place outside the dance: "At special curings the healers may or may not go into trance. Trance is not essential to healings; it is not a power in itself and does not increase the healer's power."

8

N!o'an-kaI'ae:
The Changing

Everything alive must constantly change. If a part of our life stops transforming, then we risk taking our life in a wrong direction or getting sick. (See editors' commentary 8.1 on page 58.) Even our emotions must keep changing. If they get stuck, then we get emotionally disturbed and vulnerable to sickness. (See editors' commentary 8.2.)

The experience of thara shakes us up and helps things move and change. The needles, nails, and arrows in our body must constantly change. If we leave them alone and don't dance, they will sit still. That's when the nails get dirty and stick together in a ball. When we dance and make our nails hot with nIom, it loosens them and makes them able to move. In this way they are kept clean and vibrant.

IKunta Boo explains, "There is something acting on everything to change. We call this force of change *n!o'an-kaI'ae*. This is the most important Bushman word. It is the force that is making everything move." N!o'an-kaI'ae is the secret of creation and transformation. (See editors' commentary 8.3.) This force is responsible for the creation of all things. It changes everything to become good or bad. This force even created the big Sky God, but it also makes this god change. It is behind all kinds of changes, from the weather to our emotions, healing, and the divine mysteries. It is even behind bad events like throwing a dirty arrow at a person to harm or kill him. Both sickness and healing are brought forth through this same force of change. It brings about all forms of renewal. One day we can feel close to death while on another day we feel radiantly alive. This also applies to the people we love. One day we can be quite upset with a person we love while the next day we are very delighted and pleased with that very same person.

Most sickness comes from anger and jealousy with their accompanying dirty arrows. Anger is the dirtiest arrow. It can make us sick. When people are angry they create a liquid called *ju!kag!ua* that is able to make another person sick. Anger brings this liquid to the heart, which can be sent to others as a means of attacking them. This liquid from an angry person is bad. When we say angry things this liquid can shoot out and enter another's heart. It makes their heart have a liquid on it. Whether before, during, or after a dance, healers may announce if there is a person who is angry. The strong healer will put water in his mouth and then spray it on the angry person. He will spray the chest, back, and forehead in order to get rid of this fluid.

Jealousy is also a bad arrow. All bad feelings are the work of trickster. We have to use the power of change to transform what is bad, even using trickster to change what trickster made bad. The same power that changes a person's emotion from love to anger can also change the anger back to love. The changing does not differentiate between good and evil. It is the force that creates both as well as what can be created to address, challenge, perpetuate, or diminish either of them. Good can become transformed or turned toward evil as easily as evil can be transformed into good.*

Outsiders usually don't understand us because they don't recog-

---

*Like many other shamanic cultures, Bushman healers understand the workings of both positive and negative spiritual practices, recognizing them as using the same underlying force to influence an outcome. Here good medicine is held inside love while bad-intentioned power fuels the workings of harmful witchcraft.

nize the nature of this changing that underlies all our experience. This explains why they are often confused by our presumed inconsistent descriptions of our ancestors. They don't take into account that the ancestors are always changing their feelings too; their moods and intentions are always changing. We have to be careful. While they love us, they can also become upset that we are not with them.

The ancestors, or g‖aoansi, are in relationship with us in the same ways we as living people are in relationship with one another. For instance, though a husband and wife can love each other, they also can get angry and upset. When they are angry they might accidentally throw dirty arrows. The g‖aoansi are the same. They love us, but they can get angry, jealous, selfish, or sad and carelessly throw some dirty arrows. These arrows of sickness are called g‖aoansi tchi. After a husband and wife have an argument and get angry, they should dance as soon as possible to clean the arrows that were made dirty. The same is true for the g‖aoansi. They, too, must keep dancing. This is why they want us to dance together.

Even the big Sky God holds an aspect of trickster that is always changing: there is one big God whose lesser aspect has many different moods, changes, and appearances. It's complicated to talk about this because the trickster forms sound as though they are different and not from the same source. We speak as if there are two gods, a big one and a small one, when there is only one god. There's one God with two aspects—one is stable (big Sky God) and the other constantly changes (small trickster god).*

God can transform into a trickster that can continue changing into any identity. (See editor's commentary on 8.4.) Tricksters, or ǀxuri kxaosi—

---

*Less is said about the Sky God than the trickster god, and that can give the impression to outsiders that the trickster aspect of God, especially its malevolent qualities, is more prevalent. Less is said about the Sky God because whatever is spoken or articulated in words is already in the hands of trickster talk. Therefore talking about the Sky God should be either avoided or used sparingly so as to not hold God in a trickster form. Communication about the Sky God is primarily expressed and better served by dance and song.

whether embodied by God, an ancestor, or a living person—change all the time through *thuru*. Like a snake, we can shed our skin and slide into another form. Our spirit can leave the body and go somewhere else, including inside another animal; thuru can change us into any animal or form. (See editors' commentary 8.5.) In the past some Bushmen would turn themselves into a lion. As a lion we are capable of all kinds of things, including an enhanced skill for killing. A special thread or rope is used for lion thuru. The name of this rope for becoming a lion is *tso*.

We can also see our grandfather or grandmother, or any other ancestor, and feel like we are stepping into that person. In this way we become our ancestor. We can do this with anything or anyone if we "own the feeling" for it.* When the missionaries talk about Jesus, we know that the words are less important than having a rope or strong feeling for him. If we make our rope strong enough, we can step into him. We can even step into God. At times, God has wings like an eagle. We can fly with God. This kind of eagle is a source of power that healers can use to pull out illness.

Beginning healers, called *n!aoah-ma*, can become easily seduced and distracted by powerful experiences like thuru.† A Bushman who uses thuru is acting like the trickster form of God. While interesting and sometimes useful, this is not the most important use of nlom. It should only be used to protect our family or village, but even then, we must be careful. It is easily a distraction and can get us caught in power traps rather than keeping us focused on the more important hunt and quest for love.

While we own the feeling for occupying the identity of these forms, we lose connection to our truest essence—a formless vibration whose momentarily occupied forms are less important than the vital life force

---

*When we own the feeling for the other, we feel so strongly about it that we become less separate from it, and with sufficient intensity, we feel we have stepped into being it.
†Beginning healers are not limited to young adults. Older adults may also begin the process of becoming a nlom-kxao. Sometimes a person more fully becomes a healer after the death of their spouse. This usually occurs when the ancestral spirit of their spouse starts teaching and giving them nails during kabis.

or n!om that gives rise to these transitions and possibilities. When trickster shifts our shape, we say that he has given us ropes that are not straight. They bend and cannot take you to God's village, where the strongest and purest n!om resides.

The rest of the world seems to not know this truth about the nature of change. (See editors' commentary 8.6.) This makes them vulnerable to being made sick or disturbed by their own thoughts, especially when they don't change to dance with the changing world. They think that every time they see one form, that's what it permanently is—whether it's one side of trickster or one aspect of a person. When they see something change unexpectedly, they are confused and troubled. They don't understand that this is the way the underlying dynamic of change works with all things in life. People can go crazy or become ill when they try to stop this changing. To interfere with this natural changing makes things worse. These same people are also scared of thara because they are fearful of the changes it can produce. When we are in thara, we are awake and living inside the world of creation. The Sky God is always in thara, that is, always shaking with n!om. Everything changes in order to keep creation alive.

We, too, are like the double aspect of God and are more complex than any evaluation that determines whether one form is either good or bad. As long as we keep changing we feed life and are replenished.* We dance and shake to help transform everything, including cleaning our nails and arrows of n!om. To heal, we must enter the changing. This is our most important understanding of healing.

To keep healthy, healers must help the feelings keep changing.† We heat up our nails and shake to help things move. This is how we are

---

*Similarly, cybernetician Heinz von Foerster advised, "To know yourself, change!"

†Bushman medicine arguably presented the first form of psychosomatic medicine. However, rather than propose that bad feelings be eradicated, Bushmen recognize them as naturally occurring events. Preventive health care involves using n!om to clean dirty arrows whenever they arise. Rather than reducing stress and attempting to stay in certain states of consciousness, they allow life to happen more naturally while paying attention to when they need to dance, knowing that if they forget, the ancestors or gods will remind them.

from other cultures in the world. We assume other people are
:y can't see the changing circles—when all you see is a line, you
.at one end is right and the other end wrong. We see circles that
keep ⌣anging. As Tcoq'a puts it, "We are dancers for the circle."

We are sharing the wisdom of our strongest healers, the nǀom-kxaosi
who have seen God's ostrich egg. Though few are still alive, this work
was encouraged and directed by the remaining hearts of the spears, our
strongest healers. It is important that we leave this information for the
future. If someone sees the egg and has no one to explain what happened, she may be led to this book so she can understand and accept her
mission. For those who have not seen the egg, parts of this book may
not make sense. However, if they are soft and their heart is open, it will
be possible for them to feel the truths we present. This book is itself
another kind of gift from the sacred ostrich egg. It holds the important
arrows, nails, ropes, and wisdom and can be seen by those whose hearts
have been awakened to see properly.

Editors' Commentary

8.1. On systemic and circular change in Bushman culture

We find a complementarity in these changing relations where stability is
created and maintained by change. This is the heart of circular causality
postulated by the science of cybernetics. Its implications for understanding
everyday life are profound. For example, health no longer can be regarded
as the absence of illness, which implies an either/or dualism and conflict
between them. Instead, illness exercises the healing capacity of a system
and helps assure overall health. We get sick as a means of maintaining
health. This cybernetic or systemic understanding is implicit in the way
Bushmen see their ancestors as making them sick as a means of getting
them to dance themselves back into health, thereby keeping themselves
strong and healthy.

8.2. On emotional change

In the same way that keeping balanced while standing in a boat requires rocking back and forth, any stable system must have oscillations that swing between different states, identities, experiences, and the like. For a marriage to remain stable, some interspersed bickering and conflict is required. This exercises the relationship's capacity to self-correct, that is, successfully handle differences, enabling them to be resolved rather than break apart the marriage.

8.3. On change in the Bushman dance

The early finding of systemic therapy that any change in a pattern of inter-action can lead to other changes is worth examining in this light. For example, changing a couple's dining habits can change their sex life if the pattern of interaction that holds each activity is transformed. With a Bushman dance, changing one's relationship with present experience sets in motion self-correcting means for altering whatever has been stuck, maladaptive, or non-resourceful in one's life, from physical illness to conflicts among marital, family, and community relations.

8.4. On trickster and the relationship between stability and change

In general, all living forms, and this includes ancestral spirits and gods, are regarded as having complementary aspects of both stability and change. While there exists a stable identity where certain things never change, there is also the possibility for change that can take place at any moment. Without spelling it out in a philosophical treatise, Bushmen have an implicit understanding of a non-dualistic relationship of change and stability. In the case of God, there is not a good god versus a bad god, though it is recognized that talk can be structured to give this impression. Instead, there is a singular all-encompassing god of creation, the Sky God, who maintains stability as the ever-loving paternal persona in the sky, while at the same time the whole of this god includes a trickster or changing form that can be either good or bad, depending on the situation at hand. In this interdependent relationship of stability and change, the whole identity of God is created, maintained, and changed. Stability takes place through processes of change, a notion later formalized in the science of cybernetics that defines the organization of stable systems through constant processes of self-corrective change. For the Bushmen, God is complex, and the same complexity of non-dualistic, interactive complementarity holds for all living things, from the gods to humans and animals.

8.5. On thuru

In thuru, there is an imagined crossing of a familiar boundary regarding what constitutes one's shape and form. As one goes through thuru, the skin feels like it is being altered, either through slipping out of one form into another or being stretched and reconfigured with newfound plasticity. This is true for the face as well as the rest of the body. The production of sounds by the vocal cords is also influenced and altered. In general, it literally feels like a transformation similar to those depicted in Hollywood fantasy movies concerning human to animal transformation.

8.6. On circular relationship and the nature of change

A noncircular view of relationship rests upon lineal causal thinking that requires dualisms that value one side of a distinction over another. Life is a battle against death, health tries to conquer sickness, wealth defeats poverty, victory conquers defeat, and light extinguishes dark. From the counter perspective of a world seen as always changing, each side of a distinction is regarded as a moment in a more encompassing cycle of change. Light has its period that is followed by dark and on and on as the cycle keeps turning through these changes. From the larger perspective of time, these opposites are complementary. From the process view of their interaction, each side of a distinction arises out of the other. Light creates dark so that light can be reborn, health creates sickness so that health can be better maintained, and life requires death in order to contribute to the life of the overall ecology. Here the "changing" transforms opposites into being more of the same recycling of their interdependency and cooperative co-creation.

9

FIRST AND SECOND CREATION

Anything can be transformed as it is embraced by the energy of change that underlies primary creation.

In the beginning there were no names. At first there was no speech. The animals and our original ancestors were happy at that time because they did not have to be concerned about names and differentiating this from that. It didn't matter whether beings were able to share or were selfish during that time; since everything always changed, one's potentially selfish behavior would be interrupted by a transformation into generous sharing. People would become good to each other at the first instant of jealousy and anger—whatever they did led to another change so that the opposite would soon present itself. The result was that every creature ended up being changed into all possible forms including the form of each creature because they were all changing equally. It was a world with nothing but changing forms. It was always changing.

There were only animals and our original ancestors in first creation; there were no plants or trees. The elements of first creation were not originally named. Second creation was about the naming. When God started to name the different animals he created the plants; he began with grass. As the Father Sky God made a name, he would immediately create an opposite for the named living thing. Once the animals were named, the trees appeared and they, too, started changing—one tree would become many trees. That's when things started to grow on Earth. The Sky God was essentially creating more living things as he was dispensing names for the animals. The Father God just pointed at the animals and gave them their names, and then their opposites were created and named to go along with them. (See editors' commentary 9.1 on page 69.) Each animal had a plant created to provide it food. The eland was paired with a bush that is like an aloe. It was for the eland to eat. The giraffe had the camel thorn tree. Humans were given the roots of the plants, the water roots, and sweet potatoes. The g!oah tree was also made for human beings—only humans received that plant.

Some animals were told to hunt other animals. This was true for the lion and the people. Our original ancestors were only eating the animals in first creation. Our ancestors and the animals would change back and forth between being the hunter and the hunted. All this changed when plants and trees arrived during the naming.

As things were changing back and forth during the naming, something would get its name and it would stop changing right at that moment. The moment God made a name, the animal stopped changing. The hooves of one animal might be found on another animal at the moment of naming and it would therefore end up with that mixed form. This happened to the horse and eland. These two animals were talking to each other and the horse said tha the wasn't supposed to be the one who chased after other animals and complained about their divided hooves. The horse wanted the eland's hooves so they exchanged hooves. The horse said, "Now I have to try out your hooves and run with them." The eland said, "No, you should have nothing to do with that. Please give me back my hooves." The horse refused. He ran away. He tried them and they suited him very well. The eland was confused. He took the hooves from the horse and wore them and went into the grassland to eat its plants. Since that time people like to use the horse to chase the eland and kill it.

This is how these things were created. If the horse and eland had been named a little later, they might have kept their original hooves.

Second creation was called the "great turning around" or *Manisi n!a'an-n!a'an*. It also could have been called the "great stopping." Giving anything a name is like saying, "Stop changing. You must stop and assume the form that is now named." (See editors' commentary 9.2.) The constant morphing of animals ended when trickster assigned names to particular forms. However, the biggest trick of all was making humans think that the changing had really stopped. In fact, it only appears to have stopped because trickster changed the nature of changing itself. While naming freezes a form, its name can be renamed and in so doing another change emerges. Here names also can morph as can their associated forms, each lingering for a while until the next transformation is called forth. For example, "fall" indicates the stable presence of the fall season, but "winter" arises as part of a more encompassing process of change. Here changing forms and shifting names advance around a cycle of names and forms.

But things are not as simple as they might seem. Because second creation with all its names is actually held inside first creation, we keep getting confused and tricked whenever a shift or transformation takes place because we forget we have never left first creation.* While we name our stable identity and distinguish ourselves from others, our interaction with life brings on shifts and transformations that subsequently result in changed names and forms. At the highest level of reality, the

---

*Paradoxically, once first creation was named it was no longer first creation; it was assumed to be held inside second creation. It is this framing that stopped the world and made us blind to the greater truth that first creation is actually holding second creation. The power of and possibility for healing and transformation require recontextualizing second creation as being a part of the greater whole of first creation, rather than being stuck in the illusory state brought about by second creation holding first creation. The latter, of course, is a fiction, a trick perpetuated by trickster. We are always inside first creation, but when we act like we are not, we resist the changes needed to keep us vibrantly alive. Of course, this is sometimes beneficial, but not all the time. Life requires repeated movement across first and second creation, the alternation of that which is contextualizing the other.

Sky God hosts both second and first creation and goes back and forth between its participation in each—it has both a shifting form and a stable identity. (See editors' commentary 9.3.)

The original ancestors are called *g‖aoan≠'angsi*. The beginning father ancestor was G≠kao Na'an. He had a human body with a giraffe's head. This was the first ancestor and he was always in thara.

It is said that the first song was the song of the grass. The ones who started thara danced the grass dance, called ‖'ai djxani. The giraffe-headed ancestors sang the song of the grass as they danced with the drum. Ancient rock paintings show the ropes to God;* some show the ancestors with giraffe heads. They are not dancers becoming giraffes— these are the original ancestors. Some rock art shows the eland people; again, these are ancestors. We don't see these original ancestors in a dance; they only show up in a kabi. Some rock art scientists think these pictures are what we experience in a dance. This is not our experience. (See editors' commentary 9.4.) We do not become these creatures. They are images of the original ancestors.†

The original father, G≠kao Na'an, and original mother, Gauh-!o, gave birth to the people. Their children did not have giraffe heads. They were human beings. The first ancestors changed all the time. They would change themselves into different animals, doing so everywhere they went. The father, G≠kao Na'an, was the one directing these changing forms.

There were some interesting changes among the animals, as with the horse and eland. As we said, a long time ago the horse and eland were changing back and forth. The eland's hoofs used to belong to the horse, but the horse today has the hooves of the eland on it.

---

*See these rock art images in Keeney, *Ropes to God*, 2003.
†Rock art images of therianthropes (humans morphed with animal features) are better regarded as depictions of ancient ancestors than representations of shamans or healers changing in a dance. At the same time, a nlom-kxao could own the feeling for an original ancestor and step into it through thuru, although this typically does not happen.

The original father and mother made the people with the eland heads. They were from the west. The people with the eland heads were called *n!angsi*. The eland people had hooves that made a special sound. They became healers. This is the reason why when a healer has foam on his mouth we call it eland foam. The eland people were able to become lions and kill others. Or they could become snakes and bite their enemy. They were able to turn into a bad-intentioned healer. The eland-headed people don't, however, have any influence on us today. They also don't try to affect the g‖aoansi. They remain in the original village of the Sky God and first ancestors and don't pay attention to the rest of the world.

The first wise healer was our original father. He was always a good healer. The eland-headed people started as good healers, but the great naming brought forth the first bad healers, differentiating them from the good ones. Then there were both good and bad healers. When things were always changing in the beginning of creation, everything was healthy. There was no sickness or death. It was only when things were named and differentiated that sickness began.

When we go into thara we experientially enter first creation. When we initially enter first creation we experience a constant whirling. This is called *!kabi*. Once we enter first creation we need to walk on the right rope or we can be pulled to the side and start changing into an animal or follow the wrong feelings and desires.

In first creation, change is always potentially problematic as it makes every moment unpredictable and subject to an unexpected and undesired turn of events. For instance, a husband might come home one week with meat to feed the family. The next week he might be told to bring the meat home again, but this time he becomes a lion and eats the family. That's how first creation becomes too dangerous. It enables a wife to turn into a lioness and eat the husband.

We must pay attention to how things are stopped after any reentry into second creation, whether it's birth, a hunt, a dance, a kabi, or any other important life event. For instance, when a person is born she soon transitions from first to second creation the moment a name is given. This is why the weather at the moment of birth is so important. She then immediately stops changing and enters second creation. Perhaps, like the eland and the horse, she might have been stopped at a dangerous time. If she enters second creation and is stopped during good weather, she has good luck. The worst weather condition to be born into involves strong winds and cold temperatures, along with lightning. This unfortunate occurrence will determine less beneficent luck for a person throughout her life. However, that person can go to a healer who can help make her luckier if she was born at an unlucky time. The healer can clean us and change the influence bad weather had on us at birth. When we are spiritually cleaned, the dangerous essence is removed.*

Thara comes from the power that is changing things in first creation. The ropes, a part of first creation, are the trails or paths that can carry us back and forth between first and second creation. We meet God, are visited by the ancestors, find the animals, cross into first creation, and reenter second creation by traveling on the ropes. We have to be careful when we enter first creation. There are some things we should avoid doing. For example, some healers use trickster's bad ropes and tie themselves up before they go to sleep enabling them to ride the hyenas during the night. We don't do that. It is something that some neighboring healers who aren't Bushmen might do. They would not physically turn into hyenas but would ride them in a vision in order to access their power. The hyenas don't lift our hearts. They are dangerous to ride and fill us with the seductions of power. We need to choose better ropes so that we are taken to those things that are good for our lives.

*The moment of birth marks entry into the named world, or second creation, and here the changing is stopped as it was for all living creatures that entered the naming. Whatever qualities of the weather that were present at birth are associated with the newborn and are stopped, or become "fixed." A nlom-kxao can only change these qualities by taking the person back into the changing, into first creation, where the qualities of a different weather condition can be linked to the person when he or she reenters the world of second creation following the healing ceremony—a kind of rebirth with n!ao, the spirit of weather conditions at birth.

Oklas, a healer we all knew from Tsumkwe, got caught on a bad rope and became stuck in the first n|om station of power. He forgot to raise his heart. He left the path we were on and went to follow a different rope. As a result, his mouth was spiritually sewn so he could not say a word; bad healers from another tribe sewed his mouth shut through the use of dark magic. Then they killed him with bad medicine—they harvested a poisonous root from the bush, made it into a powder that they put on a mirror, then handed him the mirror and purposefully dropped it so it broke. When Oklas picked up the pieces, he touched the poison powder with his fingers. It entered his body and killed him.

The first n|om station, n!aroh-||xam, lies in the west of the spiritual universe. This is where bad things can happen. One of the reasons that the Bushmen insult the hunter and tease the healer is to help them not get too serious; being overly serious makes us more susceptible to the temptations of power. Teasing protects a healer or hunter from being a showoff and getting stuck in the first station. If a man in second creation is a hunter, he will remain a hunter. But if he enters first creation, he can actually become the hunted meat. Seriously thinking that we are powerful is dangerous if we stay stuck in the first fire. It interferes with raising our heart.

While a n|om-kxao must cross the boundary between first and second creation, it has risks and can be dangerous. If we take a bad rope, we can be harmed. First creation and second creation are crossed at the intersection of the horizontal and vertical ropes. When we are on a horizontal rope we easily shift our form and may become like another animal. The rope to God, however, is a vertical rope. When we're on the vertical rope, we do not change into another animal. It takes us to the true Sky God who is not influenced by trickster.* When our heart

---

*There is no strict either/or duality here, for a n|om-kxao will sometimes use the horizontal ropes, experience thuru, and receive help from tricksters. Doing so, however, is risky and must be done with caution. Strong healers develop a wisdom that helps them know when it is appropriate to use the horizontal ropes and learn what to do if they get into trouble while they are on one.

rises, we are climbing the vertical rope to God. We are in the second station of nlom, g!a'ama-n!ausi. Here love remains steadfast. Our heart lifts us. If our heart gets big enough, it lifts us to God. It is important that we enter first creation by climbing the rope to God. All other ways are dangerous.

Our ancestors may also help us go up the vertical rope. Because we have such good memories of loving our ancestors, this love helps us follow the straight rope. As always, we should go straight up and avoid moving to the sides.

There was an old blind healer who said that when he danced hard his heart climbed the rope. That's when he loved everyone, including "the man who stole his wife," as he used to say.* When we teach that the rope must be straight, it's the same as saying we must move with a loving heart. Similarly, any mention of our soul going to God means that our heart allows its love for God to carry us to God's village, the most important place in first creation.

We move along a bad rope by the desire to be powerful. We want to avoid being pulled toward the fire in the sky. After a strong dance, a healer might awaken and have the experience of floating above the ground. An ancestor can say, "Now I will take you very far." That's when we fly way past the sky into the stars and see a giant fire. We will feel like the fire is pulling us toward it, but the ancestor's voice warns, "Just keep moving and don't go there. Keep going straight." If we stay on the straight line we will finally end up in a place where there's just sand and a tree. The tree is called $n\neq ah$ and it is the camel thorn tree in God's village. This is how God shows us the way to his home. If we do not have God in our heart to guide us there, we will move toward the big fire, then we will fall and die.

Ignorance comes from being selfish and greedy and sets us on a bad rope. This kind of ignorance is called !xaua-khoe and it is the opposite

---

*We met a missionary who said that the Bushmen have a natural understanding of the Biblical counsel to love an enemy, seeing it as their spontaneous and effortless nature when they are cooked with nlom.

of love. The straight healer is on a straight rope every time. If we go all the way up we find God's village with the special camel thorn tree.

We become lost and sick inside second creation for this is where trickster convinces us that trickster names and talk are more real than the nlom felt in Sky God's expressed love. This is when we must step into first creation, where the names drop away and we are changed, transformed, healed, and energized with the changing, pulsing force of nlom. When we return to second creation we begin all over, ready to participate in life until we get stuck again and need to dance ourselves into first creation. As always, the best entry into the healing nlom of first creation follows and climbs the straight rope to God's village. There we find the greatest nlom and heartfelt joy that fills us with ecstatic song and dance.

Editors' Commentary

9.1. On creating stable realities

Here we find an implicit understanding and use of George Spencer-Brown's *Laws of Form,* where distinction and indication, along with its recursion, are regarded as the means of constructing a stable reality. See Keeney, Keeney, and Chenail's "Recursive Frame Analysis" (2015) for further exemplification of this calculus of indications.

9.2. On stasis, change, and healing

Bushman nlom-kxaosi have a tacit understanding that the granting of names distances us from lived experience. The consequence of framing experience (Bateson 1972; Goffman 1974; Keeney, Keeney, and Chenail 2015) is that it renders static what is actually an ongoing process of change. The quieting of naming, interpretation, and narrativity, on the other hand, helps restore the immediacy of our presence inside a changing stream of events. The Bushmen seem to recognize that vitality and experiential intimacy can be restored by reentering a domain in which experience is left unframed, or at least is allowed to change without a need for names that impose any framed stability or stasis. Their way of specifying this is in terms of a movement from second to first creation. As Jul'hoan nlom-kxaosi say, healing arises when "we enter first creation."

9.3. On the changing nature of Bushman experience

Bushmen value experience that constantly changes but does so in a unique phenomenological domain that ceremonial performance aims to access. The changing nature of Bushman experience and their unstable discourse about it points to the value of transformative change in both their experiential and discursive domains, contextualized as the ongoing interaction between first creation and second creation. Within this perspective, each form of creation shifts in being a context for the other, creating what on the surface appears as ambiguity and contradiction but upon deeper analysis reveals an awareness and sensitivity to paradox, contextual shifting, recursive process, and complexity.

9.4. On Bushman rock art and shamanic experience

The shamanistic hypothesis of rock art advanced by David Lewis-Williams directs us to first consider what is physiologically going on with the shaman, and second, to give serious attention to the ethnographic reports of Bushman nlom-kxaosi about their shamanic experience. Our work builds upon this general premise of the Lewis-Williams orientation and extends it to consider more than retinal, optic nerve, and brain physiology by taking into account other biological phenomenon associated with ecstatic body experience. When observing a Bushman healing dance we do not see them as comparable to subjects being given traditional trance inductions or patients in hospital beds taking psychotropic drugs. What we emphasize are shaking bodies and ecstatic performance. It is the biology of shaking that must be addressed as much as the neurophysiology of hallucination and altered perception.

We should note that using the term *hallucination* rather than *second eyes* or *seeing properly* (kxae≠xaisi), to use a Bushman metaphor, already tells us as much about the community of observers as the observed.

The first term, more associated with mental disease rather than creative expression, is potentially problematic and demeaning. The issue partially dissipates if we turn to more systemic definitions of human experience (Maturana and Varela 1992), which argue that, from the perspective of the closed organization of the neurological system, there is no neurological difference between a hallucination and any other perception.

As far as the entoptics go (the dots, lines, and wiggles that are experienced in the visual field), they are seen throughout the world in a variety of states of consciousness, including light trance and daydreaming. Seeing lines and dots and wiggles in rock art is as much supportive evidence that they were not drawn by shamans as it can be considered evidence that they are characteristic of shamanic experience (Thurston 1991). Among Bushman nlom-kxaosi, we find that entoptics are not the most important aspect of their experience (and may have no relevance). Beginning trainees learning how to enter enhanced awareness are the ones most likely to see entoptics. The threads, lines, and ropes seen by shamans do not look like entoptics. They are more clearly defined and more akin to an iconic image (more elaborated and culturally identifiable images such as birds, elands, and people). The "realness" and "immediacy" of an image are as important a consideration as its complexity when trying to determine whether it is entoptic or not, a point also made by Lewis-Williams and Dowson.

It is necessary to take into account the whole multileveled contextual maze that holds Bushman ecstatic experience. This includes arousing music and rhythms, visitations of a mythological place and time, cultural stories about the original ancestors, a variety of visionary experiences that take place while aroused and calm, and most of all, the body's shaking, quaking, and trembling. In addition, we must note that the nlom-kxao's shaking body is not separated from other bodies. Vibratory movement is shared and passed on to other nonshaking bodies and combined with the shaking of other bodies. Bushman nlom-kxaosi hold one another and shake, tremble, and vibrate together, increasing the ecstatic arousal of all who are shaken.

With all these considerations in mind, we propose that rock art is more than a representation of a nlom-kxao's inner vision. It is an expression inseparable from the relationships realized through ecstatic body experience, connected to what was seen in dream and imagined in myth. It may include entoptics and construals (though we believe these are rare and probably unimportant), unconscious or conscious influences of gender, family, hunt, and place, and a deep longing for a fully felt presence of the sacred, while synesthetically seen and heard.

Rock art interpretation provides a mirror for seeing the epistemology of rock art scientists and, at its best, has become part of the dance itself where the shifting imaginations of the scientists dialogue with the shifting forms on the rock. When the ropes of relationship connect the scientists with the nlom-kxaosi of past and present, there is an acknowledgment of aesthetic expression derived from shaking bodies where the arrows shot into the hunted animals recycle as arrows of sickness and arrows of healing and arrows of inspiration, going in and out of bodies and imagination, enacting a never-ending dance of death and rebirth.

Should not we assume that there were as many reasons for creating the art as there are interpretations made by present-day scholars? At least one ancient artist must have listened to several nlom-kxaosi talk about their shamanic experiences in the dance, as well as heard various elders tell the cultural stories and myths, had a dream or kabi that brought something new to the mix, been regularly shaken in the dance, and then allowed his hands to create something that is related to all that had been cognitively and somatically absorbed. Perhaps, such artists, too, went into an enhanced awareness as they did their creative work, and surprised themselves as their unconscious had more of an opportunity for uninhibited expression. In conclusion, the interpretation of rock art should assume that there were as many different reasons and inspirations to paint as there are different reasons and inspirations among today's nlom-kxaosi in the Kalahari, as well as different motivations for the rock art scientists themselves.

10

MEETING THE ANCESTORS

Most people do not understand our relationship with the ancestors, or gǁaoansi, who have passed on. When anthropologists talk to a beginning healer, they typically hear how the healer is scared of the ancestors. They also hear reports about how often the healers keep seeing the gǁaoansi and how they must fight them. A strong healer will likely not tell anthropologists much or else tease them, warning them how dangerous it is to even talk about these things.

During a dance we might feel that the ancestors are nearby. When we let our nǀom heat, rise, and peak, we can see them. The second our nǀom is heated, we are able to see the ancestors in a flash. Because new and inexperienced healers are filled with fear, they see bad ancestors all the time. Those ancestors love fear. The bad ancestors love fear and anger; it attracts them. When we get past wanting to fight these ancestors, they just go away. This is why it is important to move from the experiential station of power to the station of love. They run away from love.

The strongest healer will tease the younger healers and say things like, "What do you mean? I don't see any gǁaoansi. They don't bother me. They're scared of me because I'm so strong."

The gǁaoansi, our ancestral spirits, are just like us in that their

73

emotions change all the time. All beings—dead and alive—live with changing emotions and are capable of either purposefully or accidentally sending a dirty arrow.

When the ancestors occasionally make us sick, it's usually because they are trying to help us. When we forget to spiritually wake ourselves up they might bring sickness to remind us that we need to dance. In a way it's like they are trying to scare us in order to make us strong. Of course it's not always like this; sometimes an ancestor might miss us so much that he wants us to be with him. That's when an ancestor is acting selfishly. We have to be careful that the ancestor's love doesn't hurt us. While the ancestors are capable of becoming jealous, angry, or missing us too much, most of the time they love us and want us to live a long life.*

There are also ancestors who were jealous or mean when they were alive, and they may remain that way once they pass on to the ancestral home in the sky. For the most part, the ancestors who loved us on Earth will always love us, and this binds the relational world together throughout all of time.

If our nails are strong and clean, the tricksters, whether a trickster ancestor or a trickster god, will stay away. When our nails get dirty, they come toward us. This is why it's dangerous for people not to dance. This is when trickster is able to make us sick or cause us to do bad things.

When the ancestors have a bad feeling and try to hurt us, we can see them for only a second. An ancestor can look like a regular person; we can see them with our eyes closed. Once in a while, though it is a rare experience, a healer might wake up and see a bad ancestor sitting on him. It's scary and looks frightening. The ancestor might be sitting on our belly and we feel like it is making us disappear. We may feel like our flesh is dissolving. That's when we have to wake up our n|om and

*The changing relations and emotions in the spiritual world are similar to those in community life.

deal with it. Some of us have placed our hands on our body at such a time and found that our hands went through our belly as if we were made of a cloud. An ancestor can make our body seem as if it is dissolving away. These things can happen to healers, especially when they are learning.

When we are hot with n|om, any g||aoansi who formerly wanted to attack are now cautious. They don't come at us because our body has turned to light. When the ancestors see a body shaking at the highest and purest vibrations, they don't know we are there. They simply think there's a light that's watching them. They are awestruck by the light and they stand behind something to hide from it.

As our n|om becomes more cooked, we are able to alter our feelings and see the ancestors differently. When we then communicate with the ancestors, we shift to conveying something like, "I know you really love your daughter but you're being selfish. You need to listen to a bigger love and not to your selfish desire." When the ancestors hear us feeling their love it helps them wake up and say, "Oh, I need to not be so selfish. I need to have more love for my family." We see and interact with their loving side as we look at them through our love.

When we are fully cooked and look at an ancestor, we can heal and tune them as well. If we look at an ancestor who is emotionally missing a daughter and trying to make her sick, we can communicate with our feelings, as if saying, "Stop that. She wants to live longer. We want her here now. You must wait for her." If the feeling in our heart descends and we get angry with the ancestors, we will see them through our anger. This is when they look very ugly. In actuality, we're really not seeing them as much as we are seeing their bad wishes. We see the ugliness of their feelings and selfishness. However, we notice this through the ugliness of our anger. Here we are actually seeing bad feelings on both sides of the relationship—in us and in them.

When ancestors act like trickster, they can also take us to our death. If someone is looking at us and it looks like an ostrich is staring, it is trickster. He is easily identified by the nature of his eyes. We watch someone's eyes and know what a person is and whether to trust them. (See editors' commentary 10.1 below.)

When we pass to the spirit world, we won't become a trickster if our heart is big enough and holds enough love. It's only when our heart is closed or hard or too trickster-oriented that we become malevolent or ambiguous. We need to dance a lot so that our hearts become good— that way when we pass over we'll continue being good. Otherwise the future will be very difficult. If we don't heat our nails, we are like someone without life and love. The trickster ancestors will notice this and come close to cause sickness and death.

Editors' Commentary

10.1. On Bushman knowing through the sensate body

Bushmen value their body sensations more than mental calculations and logical arguments when making decisions and evaluations. Body sensations are regarded as giving information about the interactions of their ropes, while mental calculations and argument are regarded as the possible distraction of trickster, something to be cautious about. This is not a strict dichotomy between body and mind. Trickster talk can sometimes be valuable, for trickster can be good or bad. It is simply less reliable than the pulling of ropes that are experienced as body sensations and emotions. Stated differently, the ropes are metaphors for relational interaction and, as such, provide more relevant communication for here-and-now, situational presence. Trickster discourse, on the other hand, can get caught inside the interactions of abstractions and can easily become dissociated from the web of relationships, where life is lived and experienced.

11

KABIS AND
THE CLASSROOMS

The gods and ancestors visit us in experientially intense dreams. The ancestors may come to check on us and make sure we are well. Such a visionary dream, or kabi, is always filled with nǀom. Seeing the ancestors we love in a kabi nearly always makes us cry with happiness because we have been missing them and feeling a heavy heart.* They also watch us and weep as their hearts are touched as well. This crying is very strong. It makes our ropes stronger.

Most kabi dreams make us cry. They also usually make us intensely shake because they have so much nǀom. We sometimes have a kabi of seeing a strong healer inside the egg. That's when we know that person is coming. We see ourselves dancing together inside God's ostrich egg. Before Bo arrived here, ǀKunta Boo had a kabi and saw the rope. The rope went to the ostrich egg and was filled with ancestors who were

---

*Bushmen arguably do not go through the so-called stages of grief after losing a loved family member, for they value longing and heartbreak as a means of empowering their rope to the ancestors. When we asked an elder woman nǀom-kxao what the secret to the Bushmen's closeness to God was, she replied. "The tears we shed for our lost loved ones."

singing and dancing. We were with each other and danced all night with Bo. This showed |Kunta Boo the dance that would soon take place in the village and who would be attending. Most of the healers have had kabis of a strong healer who is inside the egg.

We can also meet God and receive nails in a kabi. Those nails are the strongest. *Cunkuri* is the name for the special kabi that involves meeting God.

God can also show us the camel thorn tree in a kabi. This tree in his village is the original source of n|om. It is where the water of n|om comes from. We are delighted when God wakes us up in the night and tells us to turn our head slightly, usually to the right, though sometimes to the left.* All of a sudden we feel something shift and see that we are in the sky looking down at our body. God and the ancestors then say, "You must travel and pay attention to everything." We immediately go up in the sky and speed through the stars. "Go all the way," we hear them say. Finally, we land where there's sand and a camel thorn tree. That's a very special kabi. We wake up shaking and singing. In this kabi, we are taken to the source of n|om.

If a healer gets on a bad rope, God has a place where he may be sent in a kabi. There he will be fixed and made better. It's like a hospital. Once trickster got a hold of |Kunta Boo. "The people thought I was dead. Trickster had taken me toward the direction of the fire. God said, 'Wait—let me see that child. Who are you? Who is doing this?' I was taken to the Sky God's home and fed there. Then he returned me to the people. The people were burying a hole for my body and they were surprised when my soul returned and I woke up. They cried, 'Although he was dead, now he is here shaking and moving!'

"I told everyone where I went and that I found the old father God. He took me and repaired me at his home. After repairing me, he took

---

*Literally, they are sometimes awakened in the night by a voice that suggests that they slightly turn their head or make some kind of shift of body position. When they do so, they experience slipping out of their corporeal body and imagine their consciousness traveling through the cosmos.

me back to the place where the trickster got me to take a different direction. I was taught things. After that my dancing changed. I started shaking more strongly. This was many years ago."

Some healers have a kabi where they see a big hole underneath the ground. It's a place with a lot of water. It's not real water—it's a kind of spirit water that smells sour because it is urine from God. This is a very special medicine that gives us some of the strongest nails we can ever receive. We can bathe in it, drink it, or have it poured over us. Only the strong healers are able to visit this place, not the new healers. A heart of the spears will experience this water numerous times. It gives him maximal strength while using God's spiritual gifts.

The dance both makes us clean and prepares us to be ready to meet the ancestors and God. A strong dance can make a healer so clean and soft that she later receives a kabi. An ancestor can come and wake us up, asking why we are sleeping and then give us new nails. When we receive nails in a kabi it is called l'an-jukonaqnisi. We can also give other people nails in a kabi—this is how healers help others when they are asleep. A healer's job can take place when awake and asleep. Whenever our nails are hot and nlom is circulating through us, we are able to do spiritual and healing work.

All of this is possible because of the vibrant love that comes through the special nlom songs. Nlom music is the source of our healing and spiritual power. The greatest gift from God is a nlom song, because with it any spiritual experience can happen and any spiritual gift can be received. (See editors' commentary 11.1 on page 83.)

When we go into thara, we clean and ready ourselves to meet the gods and the ancestors. When we laugh, we are also shaking ourselves clean in order to be healthy and to prepare ourselves for the ancestors.* There are two kinds of laughing. Sometimes we laugh because we are

---

*Laughing not only brings on body trembling and shaking, it shakes up habits of construing and explaining the world, as it favors unexpected twists of meaning and surprising reframes of experience.

happy and this helps make our body clean. It is good for our health. Then there are times when we begin laughing and we feel like we can laugh forever. That is when the ancestors are making us laugh. We can get this kind of laughter when we get hot with nlom. When we can't stop laughing, everybody starts laughing and it easily gets crazy. (See editors' commentary 11.2.) We call this laughter g‖auan-n‖hai. Here we feel like we are laughing with an ancestor—the ancestor is laughing and makes us laugh.

The dance prepares a healer to have a special kabi to meet an ancestor. At the end of a dance some outside observers might think, "Oh, the dance is over and the healer's work is done." In fact, the healer may have only become ready to meet the ancestors, who will come to check on him and possibly teach more things.

Whenever we have a kabi we say that this is how we go to school.* We go up the rope in order to attend school, receive a spiritual lesson, and receive a !Xu tci, a gift from God. There is only one classroom in the sky. There are many other classrooms located elsewhere, and some are dangerous and must be avoided. Other classrooms have good lessons waiting for us, but we must be very careful about traveling to any classroom that is not in God's sky village.

There is a long loopy rope that can take you deep into a waterhole. That is a strange and dangerous place to go; we usually do not go there. The waterhole is filled with tricksters. They want us to drink its water, but it will kill us if we are not careful. If a healer is strong enough, he will refuse to go there no matter how hard they try to trick him. He

---

*Bushmen do not teach their healing and spiritual ways in a formal or institutionalized way. There are no community classes held on spirituality, nor are the children told much about the experiences of nlom-kxaosi. Instead, the most important teaching takes place in visionary classrooms and ecstatic experience. Other healers won't talk to a person about these matters until they hear that the person has attended a spiritual classroom. This is one of the reasons that outsiders hear very little about Bushman spirituality if they have not themselves had such an experience.

will tell them they are trying to trick him and that he will not go to that place and die.

The tricksters in the waterhole may lie and say, "Oh, we are good, we love you and we will teach you good things." That's when we must tell them, "You go your own way. I'm on the rope that goes straight up."

We can learn to dance in most of the classrooms, though some places give us specialized teaching. There is a classroom where you can learn to dig for the roots. N!ae Kxao went there. As she describes it, "There I was given a song to sing when I look for roots. In another classroom I learned how to cut someone in order to make a treatment for medicine.* I went to another class to learn how to get a tortoise shell and put a medicine powder in it that I use in the dance. Most of the women go to a classroom where our ancestral mothers show us how to make a special apron or bag with special bead designs. When we go there we see our mother putting beads on some hide. We watch closely and then we ask our mother if she can put some beads on our skirt or purse. That's when our mother hands us the beads and shows us how to make it. This is a very special kabi. Our ancestral mother or grandmother, aunt, or sister can show us the design we are to make. They also show us how to make the beads and designs for our necklaces. It's wonderful.

"My mother held the bag I am carrying. This took place in a kabi that occurred a long time ago. I asked her, 'Please can I have that?' After she said yes, she showed me how to make it. When I woke up the next day, I made the bag just like my mother showed me. That's what it means to receive a special gift from a kabi.

"Everything I make is given to me in a kabi. Sometimes my mother or another ancestor will just hold up a skin that has a bead design on it. I recently made a skin with beads that my mother gave me. She was

---

*Bushman healing sometimes includes making a cut in the skin with a knife and then mixing a medicine plant powder into the blood.

wearing it in the kabi. Then she showed me the design and taught me how to make it for myself. When ancestors show us something it's very beautiful and we want to make it. It's our traditional way of living. All women, not just our healers, experience these kabis."

A healer might announce that someone has experienced a kabi and proceed to use a medicine powder to draw something related to that experience on that person.* The healer does this because it was shown to her in her own kabi. The community will then start singing and dancing. The healer might also blow the medicine powder on the person.† In a kabi we find the classrooms where we learn things and are told what to do. When we're on the right rope and we're told to do things, we must follow this instruction.

Once our village had many people who had a kabi at the same time. We all experienced ourselves dancing with Bo. In our dream we were awake, dancing all night with him, but we were actually asleep having a kabi. The next morning when the sun arose, we all woke up and told each other, "Bo was with us, dancing with us till the sun came up." All of us dreamed this. We saw him all night and that's when we knew, "Bo is coming. He will be here soon." And he was.‡

Some of us also have had the kabi of dreaming we were pregnant with a drum inside our belly. It starts beating a rhythm and then we give birth to the drum. That's when we start singing in our sleep. We wake up singing very loudly. It's a very strong kabi that we have after the g!oah dance—the leaf dance. The g!oah dance, our woman's dance, puts the drum in us. The drum is always there even if we are asleep. It's in our tummy. We were happy when Bo had this kabi. The ancestors gave him the drum.

---

*The nlom-kxao will dip her finger into the powder as if it were ink and then use her finger to draw upon the person's body.

†The breath of the nlom-kxao holds nlom that can be regarded as helping awaken the plant's medicine powder.

‡Community members will often have kabis of a strong healer who is on his way to visit them for a healing dance. Many nlom-kxaosi experienced kabis of Brad before he arrived for a visit.

The people from the past come to show us the places where we can learn what we need to fulfill our lives. These are God's classrooms. We especially value the classroom in the Sky God's village. We wake up shaking and singing because the sky people give us their nǀom. When we go up to the sky people, they teach us and then they take us back to do our work. The main purpose of these journeys is to bring back love, healing, and vitality for others. We help make the world and all its relationships healthy and strong when we deliver these spiritual gifts. The Bushman way to God asks us to be stewards of creation as we serve empowering all the ropes to God. We live to share nǀom rather than hoard it. We find the greatest life when the most powerful love is made available to everyone.

Editors' Commentary

11.1. On nǀom songs, songs from spirit

The same is true for many other old medicine ways, from shamanism to Native American healing practices, as long as they emphasize the vibratory deliverance of a song. The melodic line and lyrics are less important than the awakened voice that delivers a vibration. Whereas Bushman culture has always emphasized this essential vibratory aspect of a holy song, it sometimes is forgotten in other less ecstatic cultures where handing down memorized songs rather than evoking spirit-filled singing takes precedence. For ecstatic healing traditions, a potential candidate for becoming a healer is prepared to directly receive a holy song from the numinous. Without such a song there simply can be no healer. A song from spirit is the spiritual diploma, license, and entry key to ecstatic healing. It can be argued that the core shared experience in training within shamanic healing traditions is receiving and then performing a song that awakens ecstatic conduct and vibratory expression. Rather than listening to entrained rhythm, it is making musical sound received from spirit that opens the channel for healing. Percussion facilitates riding or moving with the song, and ultimately climbing the rope to God.

11.2. On ecstatic laughter

This kind of ecstatic laughter is known to many religions around the world and has been popularized as "holy ghost laughing" in Christian evangelical church services. Whereas diverse religions may similarly identify this phenomenon as a sign of a sacred presence, the Bushmen give less importance to explaining or talking about it. This is true for all Bushman spiritual experience—words are only judged by whether they feed or short circuit the evocation of nlom.

12

ALL OF CREATION DANCES

In the beginning every creature danced like we dance. Everything dances in the changing of first creation. Today the ancestors will come to us if there is a strong dance—the ancestors are happy when they dance with us. They will re-create the world as it was in the beginning. As we dance the world keeps re-creating itself, for the healing and renewal of life.

The strongest dances today are the eland, giraffe, and g!oah dances. The eland dance at a puberty rite is especially strong. We might dance the eland dance, *n!ang djxani,* the whole day and night. We can receive the power to heal at such a dance. While the strongest Bushman nlom-kxao automatically acquires the ability to heal when he receives the ostrich egg, other Bushmen learn healing in a dance. There they are taught by other healers and receive strong nails from them. The eland dance is a good place to both empower existent healers and contribute to making a new healer.

Keep in mind that all dances are able to be strong ones. The strength of a dance depends on the vigor and enthusiasm of the singing. It is the quality of the music that most determines whether our nails get hot. Sometimes it takes men longer to get into the dance and they will give excuses like, "I don't know how to dance" or they will be saying to each other, "I don't feel like dancing." What they need to do is sing with the women. The stronger everyone sings, the more n|om will heat and be available for transformative healing.

The women are always the most important participants in a dance because their singing is required to lift everyone to the highest place. The men need the women to help wake them up. Some of the men also sing with the women. This really helps n|om cook. When we all sing strongly, the singing becomes a big communally shared vibration and this makes everyone's nails become very hot.

We can't get our nails of n|om as hot as we need them to be unless our voice is shaking and singing. Dancing is not enough. Shaking the body is not enough. We must also sing in a heated way in order for our heart to rise. It doesn't matter if we think we don't know the song, because when we get hot enough with n|om, God makes our voice sing something—the sound just comes through us. When we are extremely hot, our singing can get so loud that it almost knocks us out. That's when we own the song and are singing it most correctly.

Proper singing is the secret to heating the nails. Only this kind of singing and dancing makes us the happiest. When the people sing harder everyone gets hotter. If a new song comes out of a n|om-kxao, the women will pick up on it—we follow whatever songs the Sky God sends.

The dance steps are different for each station of handling n|om. As healers progress through the stations, we get hotter and our movements alter. The same is true for the singers and those who are clapping. For the healers, energized singing and clapping helps them feel like n|om is lifting their feet; gu-tsau means to be lifted up by the clapping.

In the beginning of a dance the healer must exert effort in order to dance, but when the dance gets hot with n|om, the singing and clapping effortlessly move the dancer. Sometimes they make our steps very fast. We can get so happy and ecstatically charged in a dance that we straighten out our arms behind us as we move. Or we can get so hot with nǀom that we can stand up on our toes and dance.* The nǀom lifts us up and we feel like we are flying. When the percussive sound gets particularly loud during a dance, our soul can travel.

When a healer's nails become sufficiently hot, we initiate a pumping in our belly that then begins to move spontaneously—this motion enables us to pull out sickness. The pumping action reaches its fullest strength only when the healer is powerfully singing during its action.

At this time we can also hold another person, usually wrapping our arms around her, and together we climb the rope. It feels like the rope comes through our head and goes right through the rest of our body. The feeling alternates between being pulled upward toward the sky and downward toward the earth. Our bodies pump up and down as we climb the rope, producing a noise in our throat as we climb that sounds like a drum. ǁ*Xoan* is the name of this heavy breathing sound that we make when we climb the rope to God.† It feels like fire is coming out of our mouth; it is so hot that it dries up our throat. We feel tight in the belly and can become very hot.

When all of this is taking place, we say that we are standing or climbing on the rope to God, *nǃuan-tso.* The strongest healers love to stand and climb on the rope. They own the rope. Our life is never the same once we own the rope. It takes over everything we do. We are pulled by it and led to where we need to be and guided in what we need to say and do.

There is a limit to the amount of heated nǀom that anyone can handle, including our strongest healers. This is why a dance involves cycles of heating and cooling—we need water to cool us down when we get too hot with nǀom. After we hit a peak, we cool down and then proceed to heat ourselves up again. Around and around this cycle goes,

---

*Both of these movements—arms behind back and standing on toes during a dance— are depicted in ancient Bushman rock art images.
†This sound, which can bring forth spontaneous rhythms, is hypothesized to be the source of signature African rhythms that were later set to drums when percussion instruments were created.

repeating itself throughout a nǀom healing dance. As long as we stay on a good rope, we will be spontaneously heated and cooled in the right way.

The women's gǃoah dance and the men's giraffe dance (≠oah djxani) are equal in their healing powers.* Outside observers who believe that there's more healing in the men's dance need to be corrected and know that the women heal just as much in their dances. (See editors' commentary 12.1 on page 93.) Though the men's and women's dances may begin differently, when they get hot enough and a dancer is fully into thara, the dances look more similar. One significant difference is that the men's dance takes a while to get cooking, whereas the women go straight for the fullest thara.†

The difference between a giraffe dance and gǃoah dance is that when we're in thara for the gǃoah dance, the shaking goes up and down the whole body, whereas in the giraffe dance, we concentrate the shaking in the belly and push it up and down. What makes the giraffe dance unique is how it bends us over as we get a pumping movement inside our belly. We talk about this as an "internal pump." It comes to life when the fire of nǀom is inside us. We have to make an up-and-down motion inside our belly to pump the nǀom fire out. This is when nǀom is

_____

*The giraffe dance is primarily for men, while the gǃoah dance is primarily for women; however, a few men, especially the strongest nǀom-kxaosi, also dance gǃoah with the women.

†The men's giraffe dance aims to heat the nǀom in the abdomen and bring forth a stomping dance that accompanies a guttural pump-like motion, whereas activation of the women's nǀom nails tends to initiate trembling in the legs that ascends to the area around the cervical vertebrae. When both dances are at their peak, both men and women healers experience alternating whole body shaking (from feet to head) and pumping (in the belly). The healing actions associated with the dances look different when the dance begins, but become more similar as the dance intensifies and the healers are fully cooked. According to the Bushmen we know, most healing dances performed for outsiders, including anthropologists, seldom progress toward the most heated forms of healing, so it is uncertain whether or how often outsiders have seen the true intensity of healing in a Bushmen dance, whether a men's dance or a women's dance.

breathing us and flows all throughout the body. Sounds come out of our mouth like a drum. Our belly feels like it is full of boiling water and we may not know our whereabouts. The foam of an eland may come out of our nose and mouth. If we are strong, this can happen while we are dancing in the same place—our feet just stomp back and forth as we get hotter and hotter. We may have to cool down to come back again. This is when we should drink a lot of water to cool off.

Women and men rarely bleed from their nose during a dance. Tcoq'a was taught that "If a nosebleed happens during a dance, it usually means that the healer has too much nǃom. He must be cooled down. If a healer has foam in the mouth, however, it is a gift from God. It's from the eland. This means the healer is successfully going into first creation. When this happens the healing energy is passing through the healer, and as it goes through the mouth, healing music and sounds come forth. This is the time when we see most properly."

There is an interesting thing that sometimes happens with the men in a giraffe dance. If a healer becomes very hot in the giraffe dance, he might suddenly start shaking his whole body like he is in a gǃoah dance. The pumping movement that goes up and down our belly and spine takes place in the giraffe dance. In the gǃoah and elephant dances, we let the shaking disperse throughout our whole body.* However, strong doctors may go back and forth between these two ways of having nǃom move and circulate through them. This is when a strong healer can be seen stomping his feet up and down and all of a sudden his whole body starts trembling as he shifts to standing in place.

Bushman healers have differing opinions about the elephant dance, or ǃxo djxani. Some healers believe the elephant dance is harmful and

---

*The body shaking and movements of the elephant dance are similar to those of the gǃoah dance. The dances differ in that their songs and inspiration come from different sources: the gǃoah plant—which is thought to be a more direct connection to the Sky God—versus an elephant. The former is said to deliver nails of nǃom while the latter serves arrows from the elephant (though some healers call them nails as well). Elephant arrows are the longest arrows of nǃom, the length of an arrow being determined by the animal's size.

should be avoided. Others healers, such as |Kunta Boo, have no problem with dancing it. From |Kunta Boo's perspective, "Some people are scared of the elephant dance because the elephant needles hurt too much. They fear they might be killed. People actually fear all the dances because all the needles are strong. If you dance hard you will become used to the needles and they won't hurt you. In the elephant dance, we shoot an arrow through a long horn. It makes people scared to see that horn. Whenever the horn comes out, the singing becomes very intense and the dancers get more serious. The use of a horn in the elephant dance is similar to the way my grandfather shot oryx arrows in the earlier dances. A person can hold the horn while dancing with it. When the arrow is shot and falls near someone, its n|om jumps into that person."

You don't need to see God's divine egg in order to receive the giraffe dance or any other kind of dance. You can own a dance without being an owner of the egg. The dance, along with its song, can come to you. Everything about the dance concerns opening ourselves to catching the hearts of others. We catch the heart of the different animals we sing about and we catch the hearts of each other. Because God has given us all the songs and dances, they must be used to catch the heart of creation.

In first creation every animal has its own healer. When we dance and are trying to catch the feeling of a giraffe, eland, or another animal, at the same time the animals are dancing around their own fire, trying to catch the feeling of a human n|om-kxao. All the healers and animals are trying to catch each other's hearts at the same time. When Beh was walking home, she actually saw the giraffe that caught her. That special giraffe was like a n|om-kxao for the giraffe. It caught her like she caught it.

As we dance the giraffe dance and enter first creation, there are giraffes around their fire that are also dancing. This is when our mothers, grandmothers, and all our family are dancing in the sky, along with the giraffes from first creation. When the whole of creation dances, it feels like the ancestors and the giraffes are within us. All the changing is happening inside our hearts. At one moment we dance inside the Sky God while in another moment we dance inside our grandfathers. Later we may dance inside the heart of the giraffe. The dance keeps changing who holds our heart as we dance on the rope to God.

It is the dancing that brings a giraffe near a village. Our movements bring the giraffe, while the giraffe's dancing brings the people to the giraffe. Each thinks the other one was brought by their dancing. It's really the rope bringing both of them together. The rope is attached to the abdomen of the giraffe; on all animals the rope is tied to the spine, near the intestines. That is the part of the giraffe where the best meat is found. It also is where the meat's liquid and fat are located. In the old times we used that liquid to wash our bodies. The rope connecting the animal's spine to our spine pulls each of us, bringing us closer as our n|om activates the pulling.

In the eland dance, as the rope between a person and eland gets stronger, it pulls the two together so that their hearts become one. In the g!oah dance, the rope to the g!oah tree pulls on our heart as we move like we are the tree. We feel the wind blowing around us. This is how the g!oah dance makes us feel as its n|om medicine comes in and wakes us up.

When women experience a strong kabi they often see the ways that the ancestral women dance. It makes us shake with great fervor. It is possible to see the original g!oah tree in a kabi. That is a life-changing experience. In the past, we would sew the g!oah leaves together and put them around our waist to dance with; the leaves would tremble as we would shake. We saw this when we were children. |Xoan remembers seeing her parents dance with the leaves. "When they danced they told us they were making us ready to become the future. Or they'd say, 'I'm putting you into the past and the future in order to make your body stronger.'" Anything we do to foster strengthening the rope to the g!oah plant readies us for possibly meeting the plant in a kabi.

One night, when Tcoq'a's grandmother was a little girl, she was sleeping next to her mother when the ancestors and the Sky God came to her. They said that she must stand up and heal her mother because her mother was very sick. They told her, "You must not let your mother die. You must do something to save her."* During that night she was crying and started to shake. She spontaneously began dancing the g!oah dance. The ancestors and God gave it to her. That is how the g!oah dance came to our village.

Though the g!oah dance is for all the strong women dancers, the strongest men can also receive it. Bo owns the g!oah dance, as does |Kunta Boo. When an owner of the dance dances g!oah, it's like water is poured on us and we dance very hard. We dance like we are floating high above the people. We sweat with n!om and when other weaker and less experienced healers cannot stand up, we are there helping them.

Our women like when Bo visits us because the women n!om-kxaosi want to dance with him every night. Most of the men today don't want to dance as much because they are a little lazy. The men sometimes have to be pushed to dance. The women will say, "We're wasting our songs." This means that we want to dance, but the men won't join in. We tell them that it would be good for the village if they dance more often. We need to dance to maintain our health and vitality. The women love to dance. The problem is getting the men to dance enough!

Women talk to themselves about how the men don't keep their ropes strong through dancing more often. Trickster knows how to deceive men easier than women. The men don't keep their nails strong. This has always been true, even when some of us were small girls. When the women start singing, it only takes one song for us to get our nails strong.

Women are the strongest healers; they are now and they were

---

*Healers throughout the world have reported their entry into healing being precipitated by a family member's sickness that does not respond to any local treatment, followed by a visionary experience calling them to heal their relative (see Keeney 2003a).

when the first anthropologists came here. It's strange because most of the anthropologists thought that the men were stronger and that the women didn't know much about healing. We didn't show them anything. We would privately conduct the g!oah dance and we kept almost everything about it secret.

Perhaps anthropologists never found out that women are the strongest healers because the men they interviewed would brag and tell them that women are weak. The women would be quiet and not say anything. Know this: when it comes to the dance, the women usually stand first, leaving the men behind. Today the women are always ready to dance.

Giving birth brings one deeply inside the workings of first creation. Here new life is brought into the world, as it is each time we move ourselves into first creation. Whether you are a woman or a man, we all give birth to the whole of creation each time n|om is heated by heartfelt song and dance. Follow the wisdom of the strongest women who sing with all their hearts. This is what changes the world and enables all of creation to dance.

Editors' Commentary

12.1. On healing in women's dances

The women's g!oah dance was unknown to the Marshalls during their fieldwork during the 1950s in the Nyae Nyae area (Lee 2012, 148). Lee wrote that "no healing of the kind commonly seen in the Giraffe Dance occurs in the Women's Dance. This is a major difference between the two forms" (Lee 2012, 176). On the contrary, we have never *not* seen women nlom-kxaosi healing like men heal, with their trembling hands, during an intense women's g!oah dance. While there are variations across all healers, the placement of trembling hands on other people's bodies is found in all Bushman healing dances if a nlom-kxao has sufficiently heated nlom.

13

N|OM SONGS

We have many healing songs. These include songs from the gemsbock, giraffe, leaf, millipede, eland, buffalo, and wildebeest. These songs carry the n|om of these animals, insects, and plants when we sing them with all our heart. When a dancer gets hot with n|om, he will be dancing one of these songs. A particular kind of n|om comes into his body, and then he can slip into first creation. This is when an animal we love can enter the healer's body to help get the sickness out of others.*

When we sing these songs, the animals come to the village to help us. Sometimes a healer must go into first creation and fully own the animal before healing can happen. This only happens for a moment. After a healer goes into first creation, he must soon come right back.†

The wild animals were tamed in second creation and kept like domestic cattle are today. When an animal was named in second creation, it was automatically tamed and made available. The first animals tamed are those who gave us their song. This enables us to have a rope

---

*More accurately, it is an animal's n|om that comes into the healer's body.
†Staying too long in first creation risks coming out of it in a changed form that is not desired for second creation. As a Bushman storyteller healer might tease about this situation, a healer could come out of first creation talking like a hippo, walking like a giraffe, and making love like a lion.

with them, a means of contacting them. For example, healers may dance to go into first creation to attract an animal. The animal's nǀom helps us heal and it also brings us some meat to eat.

When a healer is very hot and strong in a dance, he can stand and dance on his toes. This indicates an entry into first creation, where our feet become like that of an animal. We walk and move like the animal. It's an extraordinary experience. When the women see this, they are happy because they know this brings a good hunt. The next day when we go out to the bush to look for that animal, we can easily get it. This is how we survive. We are thrilled when someone dances on his toes. This brings us a great hunt the next day.

It is important to emphasize that each nǀom song of an animal carries the nǀom of that particular animal. If a healer is strong, a song will enter his heart, enabling him to enter into first creation. The animal comes the next day because the animal has felt the rope pull him toward the healer. The healer's experience of identification with the animal inside first creation arises from nǀom-inspired feelings. While a healer won't see himself as the animal, at the same time he won't see himself as different from the animal. He will properly see the song that rises out of his heart and feel it in the way it is correctly associated with the animal. The most important changes take place through how feelings change, which in turn transforms how we see, hear, and smell. (See editors' commentary 13.1 on page 96.)

When we are hot and owning the song of an animal, we can climb its rope. We are able to climb the rope of the animal because its arrows have cooked us and are circulating within our body. There is a way in which we become the animal, but it is not how some people think we do it. For instance, when we climb the eland's rope we do not outwardly look like an eland. If you photograph us, we will still look human. We become the nǀom-feeling of the animal. When we see properly, we are the holder of the animal's nǀom; this is the equivalent of saying that we own the song and the rope of the animal.

When we enter first creation through the feeling of a gemsbock, giraffe, or eland, among others, we can climb their ropes. We can climb the giraffe rope during the time we feel we are a giraffe. This is because our heart is rising to its song and we use this rising feeling to climb that particular rope. We also dance in the way of the giraffe. Or we can walk as an ostrich if a person has the ostrich song. A healer can dance like an ostrich if she owns its song.

When we go into first creation and become a giraffe, an eland, or another animal, we definitely feel as though we are related to the same animal that we are familiar with today. We don't become like the original ancestors, but we become the animal we know. We dance for the animal—that is, we dance for the feeling we have caught. When healers are in first creation, their heart becomes like the animal. The community is then asked to sing for the animal. This is how we dance and sing its medicine.*

Editors' Commentary

13.1. On synesthesia and ecstatic shamanism

A key to understanding ecstatic shamanism, healing, and spirituality is underscoring the role of awakened feelings, rather than giving too much importance to visionary events. Outside scholars, who typically value visual experience over other sensory modalities (see Ong 1982), tend to prioritize visionary accounts and minimize how another culture may value other forms of sensory experience and description as equally or more important. Hence, scholarly reports on shamanism lean toward providing details of visions while commenting less on how practitioners feel or make different kinds of sound. The so-called "shamanic journey," for example, is portrayed more like a visual sequence of events, where the drama unfolds as the practitioner watches it play out in a dream-like vision. For

---

*Since Bushman medicine is about handling the ropes, it is relational medicine that bridges one living thing to another. Having community present in a healing ceremony accentuates and nurtures the importance of relationship, another way of helping the ropes get strong.

ecstatic shamans and other practitioners, it's the arousal of intense feelings that lead to song, movement, and synesthetic experience that marks the authenticity of a spiritual voyage. For the Bushmen, a visual display without these experiences would be regarded as a distraction produced by trickster, resulting in little more than seducing the recipient into believing that she had acquired power.

14

THE HEART
OF THE SPEARS

Each of our strongest healers is referred to as a heart of the spears, a *g≠aqba-n!a'an*. A heart of the spears is given the most n|om from God.* The nails from God keep coming to a heart of the spears, and everyone benefits from this. There are times when we drink n|om—great healers can hold up a cup or tortoise shell and receive n|om as a liquid to drink. This drink is God's urine. |Ae-N≠unhn is the name of the ancestor who gives us this drink of water from the Sky God. This special water is called *!Xu g!u*.

Strong healers, especially a heart of the spears, sometimes find that a vibration spontaneously comes into our head when we lie down

---

*Prior to this work, no scholar or anthropologist had heard about a "heart of the spears," the highest designation for a Bushman n|om-kxao. It was assumed that all n|om-kxaosi were the equal in ability and attainment. As we have learned, there are actually four categories of n|om-kxao: (1) a beginner who learns to feel n|om, (2) a pulling healing doctor, (3) a transmitter of n|om, and (4) a heart of the spears who is an elder teacher and source of heightened n|om for other n|om-kxaosi. The more advanced healers are the least likely to share information about n|om, knowing the futility of trying to explain that which must be experienced to those who have not felt its presence.

to rest.* Such a vibration is a kind of kabi where our ancestors come to wake us up and renew our mind and body. It's a very fast vibration; it can feel as though somebody is pouring n|om inside our body that flows all the way down from our head, making us feel warm and tingly inside. It feels very similar to receiving God's water. We call this experience *mi-n|ai-dci,* meaning "my head is wet from God's water." Afterward we begin to shake, and it feels very good and refreshing. This only happens to the strongest healers.†

N!ae G≠kau had a kabi where she met her late husband, |Kunta |Ai!ae, who was a great healer. He gave her some of God's n|om water and she started shivering and shaking. He told her to sing. That's when she started feeling the vibrations on her head that brought her renewal when she needed it. Her husband wanted to make her strong so she could become a good healer. She is becoming the strongest woman healer among the Bushmen today.

Beginning n|om-kxaosi may be so excited and surprised by their introductory experiences with n|om that they believe they are experiencing all the gifts n|om has to offer. However, as they mature and grow, they will later find out that there is no end to what is possible

---

*A n|om-kxao never knows when this experience will take place. It is always desired and when it happens, the n|om-kxao considers it a special gift and is deeply appreciative. We can note, however, that it is most likely to occur after a lot of n|om activity has taken place and left one physically tired. When the n|om-kxao then lies down to rest, the already present vibrations in his body may trigger a high-frequency vibration to come on his head, usually localized in the uppermost cervical vertebrae. The vibration can play itself out in seconds or minutes, depending on both the need for revitalization and how free of noninterfering conscious reflection the recipient is while the frequency is being received. In other words, the n|om-kxao must be empty of distraction and already pulsing with n|om, ready for a higher frequency to entrain, inspire, and lift already present somatic rhythms.

†To someone not familiar with this experience, it is more than a vibration. It is not uncommon for anyone to experience ongoing trembling and shaking after exposure to a Bushman healing dance. What is unique about this vibratory experience is the amplified current of n|om that flows inside one's body, bringing instant renewal and inspiration.

with n|om and that they were usually only receiving a small taste in the beginning.

As we get stronger, we want to be in thara most of the time. This is when we begin to have no fear of n|om. We are always hunting for it. If we are strong, we want to keep standing as long as we can in a dance. Weak healers always fall—they are unable to hold a lot of n|om. Yet those who are strong may occasionally fall when they get too hot with n|om. The people in the village catch us when this happens. When we start to fall they make sure we don't hurt ourselves falling. Usually the people who love us the most, like our family, will come quickly and hold us if they see us wobbling. When an advanced n|om-kxao falls, the ancestors will visit and see how he is doing.

When we fall and are lying on the ground we aren't actually dead, although it may look like it. This is a time when the ancestors take care of us.* They take us out of our body and enable our soul to travel, providing us with whatever important teaching or spiritual gift they want us to receive. This doesn't always happen when we are dancing; it often happens after the dance, when we fall asleep. The ancestors may come at that time and reveal things in a kabi.

In the dance, we mostly feel these other places; in the kabi we actually see them. We can see what is happening in another village and then we tell the people that another village is having some difficulties. A healer can feel this in a dance or see it in a kabi. Of course, we can sometimes see it in a dance as well as feel it in a kabi. We are speaking about how it usually is experienced.

We remember the time that Bo danced all night, and then the next morning when the sun came up he asked who were the twelve women in green dresses who suddenly showed up in the village. Bo said they

---

*The strongest healers seldom fall, but when they do, the ancestors typically teach and renew them. While this takes place, other healers in the dance will cool the fallen healer and help bring his or her soul back from its ecstatic flight. Keep in mind that a n|om-kxao does not want to fall like this and have a flight of his soul. It is too dangerous and not necessary for healing. It is better to stand and keep dancing as n|om circulates and heats.

were staring at him. Only a strong healer can see this sort of thing. Those women were the ancestors and they were checking him out. They looked like real people who were very serious, but they didn't talk; instead they stared in a very intense manner. Their eyes had bright light shining out of them. They were able to shoot arrows of nǀom if you looked at them. Most people would be scared of those ancestors, but Bo stared back. That's another reason we say that he is a brave heart of the spears. We say that he is like someone from the past, like our grandparents who lived the old ways. Those ancestors came to give Bo their strongest nǀom.

When an ancestral relative comes to the dance, he or she may hold us. Other ancestors, especially the old ones from the distant past, just stare. They watch how we become reborn in !aia. They don't come to the inexperienced healers who think that !aia is death. Those healers are too scared to see deeply into the invisible world. When beginners say that they are dying it's a kind of lie. They know they likely won't die— but fear that it will be painful and may bring them close to death and, if unlucky, might actually bring it about. The older healers will look at a young healer and tease, "Why is this one so afraid?" The inexperienced ones say these things because they are scared, while at the same time they are courageously showing that they are facing something that is very powerful, strong enough to bring you near actual death or a death-like experience. If they were truly scared they'd run away from the village and never return. Instead, they're showing that they are both scared and desiring nǀom at the same time.*

Nǃae Gǂkau had a kabi in which she experienced herself dancing

---

*Similarly, an experienced nǀom-kxao holds contradictory attitudes about nǀom. While professing an unwavering desire to experience nǀom, she is well aware of its transformative power and that there is nothing she can do to control its presence or how it will change her. While this is a bit disconcerting, the desire for nǀom outweighs any nervousness about the way it can overtake one's life. Ultimately, the strongest nǀom-kxaosi will discern no difference between the most cooked form of nǀom and the presence of the Sky God, the source of creation. Surrendering to this nǀom is akin to a full spiritual surrender and humbling before the Sky God, who is trusted as a supreme parental figure.

with Bo. "When we shake together, the rope between us gets bigger and stronger. This rope comes out of the right side of our bodies. It is a very big rope between us and the nails quickly travel back and forth. His needles are very clean. We say that he is a heart of the spears."

There are usually only a few healers in a village, though many people will acquire a healthy relationship with nlom. Most of the time it's fear that stops someone from feeling and receiving more nlom. If our heart is right and absent of worry, we will be soft enough for nlom. That's when God is able to make us an owner of nlom, or possibly even a healer. It partly depends on braveness—that is, how brave a person is to experience nlom and healing.* During a dance God can see someone being brave and feel compassion for that person. If God sees us dancing with our heart and getting hot with nlom, he might say, "Let me give this one a gift."

The more sincere we are, the better chance we have of God gifting us. We can't say, "I am going to become a healer, I am going to be brave, and I'm going to make it happen." It doesn't work that way. Some people God chooses. He just makes them a healer without the person asking.

The strongest healers are made by God; they are not trained by a father, grandfather, mother, grandmother, or some other teacher. When God makes a healer, he comes to her in a kabi or meets her in the bush and directly sends the nails of nlom. This is how the strongest healer is made. This healer can train another healer whose heart is open, but that next healer will typically never be as strong as the one that God made. It's still God's nails, but they come through someone else. However, some healers who have been taught by others might later receive nails directly from God, making them as strong as anyone.

The issue of who is the strongest nlom-kxao is irrelevant because no nlom-kxao is separate from the whole community. Yes, some healers are

---

*The other likely candidate is someone who has existentially hit bottom. In this emptiness they are without purpose, ready for any opportunity that offers genuine transformation.

stronger than others, but this is another way of saying that everyone is different and we need all kinds of people to make the strongest village. For example, a weak healer actually helps a strong healer become stronger because when nails are given, both healers become stronger.

God made Bo a heart of the spears so he can accurately and wisely convey the powerful truth that is here and so that we can leave this wisdom for all people. We have spoken these words while our nails of nlom are hot. To those who own nlom, these words will help make them hot and clean. The words we are saying are able to transmit nails and arrows of nlom.* To those with no relationship to nlom, perhaps these words will make them laugh, fall asleep, soften, or die in a good way, helping them prepare to receive a nail and God's love in the future.

---

*A story or literary exposition spoken or written while one is in nlom holds the changes that may evoke transformation in another.

15

THE OLD WAYS

For n|om and life to exist, we must have first creation and second creation going back and forth. In first creation, nothing was sick and nothing died because everything was changing all the time. When things were named and sorted out, a problem arose.

When living beings step outside of first creation, they get sick and die. We essentially need one foot in first creation and another foot in second creation in order to keep things both stable and alive with change. This happens in the most transformative way when a healer is in thara. (See editors' commentary 15.1 on page 107.)

We sometimes refer to the movement between first and second creation as similar to breathing. As we go back and forth in this way, life is breathing us. |Kunta Boo remembers the first time he was given medicine cuts when he became a man. "It was a time when I went into first creation as part of the process of moving from a boy to a man. It took place when I hunted my first big animal. They made the cut and put a medicine from the animal on it. When the pot was cooking the animal's meat, foam came to the top. They took that foam and placed it on my cut. It was a way of placing first creation into me. It gave me a stronger rope with the animal. This made me lucky whenever I hunted the animal again. When I went out in the bush, I could more easily sense this animal."

A boy becomes a man when he goes out on a big hunt for the first time. The healers will cut his arm and put some medicine powder on it. They will mix some medicine plants with sinew from the animal's arm and the back of its neck, along with some fat and the ear of the animal. All of this will be crushed and mixed with a stick and then cooked together. The sinew makes the rope stronger with the animal. It helps the animal not run away when he gets close to it. This rope also helps him make a perfect shot with the arrow. The ear from the animal makes the ear of the animals hear the music and the dance and bring it closer to him in the future. It also helps the animal not run away if they hear the hunter in the bush.*

Healers must first know that everything changes and that sickness arises when people get stuck in second creation. They have to be shaken up in order to free the changes to take place. This is why we dance. We step into first creation and help things move around the circle.

When a girl starts to bleed and become a woman, we cover the girl with a blanket and put her in a hut. We then tell others to go dance for her. They will feed her and dance for five days. During this time the girl is likely to have a special kabi. The dancing during her initiation helps the girl have this kabi. On the sixth day they take her out of the hut. This is a strong dance. The women have a special feeling during this time and can dance a whole day without food.

The young girl entering womanhood must be kept separate from the men because she might inadvertently bring bad luck to them when she's menstruating. Her bleeding takes her into first creation, where she can turn into a hunter and hunt the men, perhaps shooting them for their meat. She must also eat a certain kind of food during this time and become very thin. Since everyone is going into first creation

---

*Whenever blood appears, there is an opening to first creation. As animal parts and medicines mix with the blood inside this mythic domain, the rope connecting the hunter and animal is empowered. A new relationship with the animal, one that is felt and seen when awakened by nlom, is brought into the initiate's life.

during the dance, if she has any extra fat on her she could be mistaken for an eland, whose fat is desired as meat.

There is a special kind of kabi that we want her to have. Her nails need to be cleaned for this to happen. She must be opened to nǀom. We place a bit of a root around her neck that she has to eat. This medicine helps her have a kabi, and it will help her to have a baby in the future.

The ancestors will tell her that they've given her this menstruation. They may say, "We are the ones giving you this blood." They will tell her that this is the way they are teaching her and that she should move toward the ancestor's way, entering first creation with them. At this time, she must not speak to men because her blood has such strong nǀom that it could hurt someone. Her blood can actually kill a man if he becomes hunted in first creation. When her bleeding is finished, then it's alright to be physically near her. However, she cannot do anything with the people until the bleeding is finished.

This is how healers talked in the old days. They rarely talk this way today. Talking like this helps wake up nǀom and contributes to making our dance stronger. When these teaching are shared in this way we are able to more fully participate in moving with the circular changes brought forth by first and second creation.

Women have a tortoise shell, a ǁ'ora, that they keep a medicine in. The men also have a tortoise shell, called a *xurua o nǀom ga,* that holds the medicine for hunting and dancing. In addition, the women carry a bag for their perfume; this bag is called a *san ǃauah.* The perfume, made of ground leaves from a tree called nǁoaqǃ'ae, is used in a dance to cool a nǀom-kxao. It's also used for other purposes—if you are dizzy with nǀom, this powder can help calm the spinning.

The men's turtle shell holds a medicine made of animal fat. It can be the fat of an eland, giraffe, or another animal. The fat is mixed with a medicine stick that comes from a special bush named ≠ang. We put a hot coal in the shell and make it turn to a smoke to help treat sickness. If ancestors are causing the sickness, the smoke pushes the ancestors out of the body and makes them go away.

Bushmen sometimes have a small horn that is filled with a medicine and used to bring good luck. The medicine, called *g!oan,* is found in the north. It's from the roots of a bush called Rhodesian teak. We grind it and draw a vertical line of the red powder between the eyes and around the upper arms for good luck in a hunt.

Of course, the most powerful medicine is God's water. It is a gift from God, and we are very fortunate if we ever receive it. The next most powerful medicine is the love we have for each other. After that medicine is the love we have for the animals, followed by the plants. If we had no love for the plants, then we wouldn't be able to receive their roots to make medicines. A healer's sweat, *tco-tcaq,* is also a medicine. We smear it on a person to give nails.

All of our medicines are ways of delivering nǀom—which means that nǀom is really the only medicine, and it can be given through different means. The old ways never depart from nǀom. It is found, awakened, and heated by song, expressed through vibratory voice and body, and when dispersed along the ropes, is able to permeate all aspects of vitalized living. The old Bushman way is always a hunt for nǀom. It pulls us toward that which hunts us, the longing of creation for deeper involvement with its creating. The changing of first creation is its original procreative action, felt most deeply in the heart that inspires our bodies to tremble as we participate in the rebirth of ancestral time and place. The oldest truth and mystery of our way is summarized with one word: *love.* We are hunters of God's love and, when found, we share it so that it becomes large enough to embrace the entire world.

Editors' Commentary

15.1. On the continuous renewal of first creation and second creation

The relationship between first and second creation is less a back-and-forth movement and more a circular process, where first and second creation emerge out of one another in a continuous recursive manner. The dynamism of Bushman healing and spirituality is in the constant changing of first creation, which, in turn, feeds the development of second creation, the ongoing generation of new interpretations and meanings. The distinction between first and second creation does not simply constitute a dualism in which things simply go afoul in the world of indication and then require therapeutic healing in first creation. Instead, both worlds are mutually embracing one another with a necessity for continual entries and exits to and from both in order to serve the changing that gives vitality to life, which is experienced as nlom. Rather than a back and forth between first and second creation, and more than the embeddedness of second creation inside first creation, we are talking about the reentry of creation into creation, a recursive operation in which creation acts on itself, redistinguishing, reindicating, reframing, and renewing itself without end.

16

THE IDEAL BUSHMAN LIFE

We learn songs and stories from our elders, but when we express those stories and songs, nǀom can change the details. This is what helps make them more alive. While the song and story are generally the same, the variations bring it into first creation.* This wakes the nǀom. When a story has an unexpected change it helps us laugh together. Laughing is another way of cleaning our nails. It is important for families to laugh together.

The ideal Bushman family life consists of a mother and father who are both healers. They are always cleaning their nails and giving them to the children. The parents teach their children to dance and to have no fear of the nails. They always tease each other and tell stories that make them laugh. The best families are always laughing, singing, dancing, touching one another, telling stories, and giving each other clean nails and arrows. This is as good as Bushman life can be!

Please remember that one of the best ways of using words is to make each other laugh. We should be most serious about thara and the least

---

*The part of the story that remains the same can be understood as what stands in second creation, while the alterations in the story reside in first creation. The storyteller can never know what he will change when he tells the story. The change must happen spontaneously, the sign that first creation has entered the story and the storyteller.

serious about what we say. Language should serve teasing and telling funny stories. Let dancing and shaking rather than words express the most important truths. (See editors' commentary 16.1 below.)

The Sky God gave us songs to lift our heart and gave us our body so we can enter thara. Music and shaking enable us to learn from God. Words were given to us to help us laugh and tell entertaining stories, though when used properly, they can also shoot arrows and nails of nlom.

If a person is too serious, it's hard to make them laugh. This tells us that they are not following a good rope. By this we mean they can't wake up their feelings and have their hearts adequately rise. We don't trust anyone who acts too seriously. If they can't easily laugh, they can never be soft enough to experience nlom.

Words don't teach. Nlom-filled singing and dancing are the teachers. We can determine what people know about nlom by seeing how they shake in a dance, how they laugh in the everyday, whether they sing with the appropriate vibration, how they move with a story, and how they interact with us. What words they utter isn't very important. What matters is whether there is any evidence that they are ready for nlom or in relationship with it.

Editors' Commentary

16.1. On activating nlom in conversation

Anthropologists (e.g., Lee 2012, 143) have noted that Bushmen do not spend much time engaging in abstract philosophical discussions of their healing and spirituality because they are more interested in everyday concrete practicalities. It is more accurate to say that Bushmen value talk that helps awaken nlom, whether it takes place while discussing nlom, telling stories, or provoking humor. Strong healers enjoy having philosophical discussions about their ways if the conversational participants have a highly developed relationship with nlom and the discussions are able to weave back and forth between reflection and activating nlom.

17

EVERYONE IS INVITED TO DANCE WITH GOD

People all over the world need to start dancing, singing, and receiving the nails and arrows of nlom. Everyone is invited to dance with God. Each human being was created by the Mother God and Father God, and God's family wants us to dance with them. Everyone should dance with the Mother God and Father God and be ready to step into their hearts, allowing our bodies to be danced by them. We want all the people in the world to dance and make themselves soft so they can know God like we do. Then they can receive nlom and learn to sing. It doesn't matter whether you are black or white or red, it doesn't matter where you come from. We are all invited to come together in the dance that awakens nlom.

IKunta Boo speaks for the Bushman elders when he says, "We want the world to know what we learned from our ancestors. This book holds our oldest and most enduring truths. God thinks that these things we are doing are right and good. Perhaps the most important teaching is for people to never stop loving God, and to never stop raising their hearts so as to make contact with him.

"We want the missionaries and Christians to know that if Jesus is in your heart, then you, too, will love the dance. If you love the dance, you will love all of God's family. We also want anthropologists, educators, medical doctors, outside helpers, politicians, and others to dance more often so their hearts may be opened to deeper learning about our ways."

If you want to understand and experience God, you must receive nails and arrows of nǀom. If you want to help people, you must be filled with nǀom.

The Sky God is the supreme nǀom-kxao who never ceases practicing thuru. First he appears as the stable Sky God and as the always-changing trickster gods. Next he creates the lesser forms, the ancestors who shift between being malevolent and benevolent entities and forces. And finally, on the human level he creates the Bushman nǀom-kxao. When we are dancing on God's rope we may shift into any form as we enter first creation. As a nǀom-kxao, we are able to experience all of life and participate in the whole of creation. We are the caretakers of the ropes that hold the world together. When the ropes of nature—including our relationships with the plants, animals, land, water, and one another—are broken, we are there to repair them. Most importantly, we sing and dance in order to keep all the ropes to God strong. We are maintaining, servicing, and empowering the way human beings and God are able to reach and touch one another. In this way, we serve all of creation. We are hunting to bring back the meat that keeps the community alive. We are also hunting to catch the songs and nǀom that can fill all hearts with God's love. In this way, we are the hunters of and for the whole of creation.

You are invited to make yourself soft and get ready for nǀom. Listen less to the words of trickster and allow your heart to be touched by the sacred songs. Climb into God's pot and get cooked. Anything less leaves you standing still with no way up the rope. The Sky God is waiting for you to make the truest journey. Walk toward the rope. Sing it into being there for you. Be touched by the ancestors so that the ropes will get stronger and bring renewed life, as you fully participate in the ongoing rebirth of creation. Dance with us on the rope to God.

PART TWO

THE ELDERS SPEAK:
REMEMBRANCES

18

N!AE G≠KAU

"I was born and raised in Dobe, Botswana, near Tsodilo Hills, where my grandmother was born. I remember the first time I met |Kunta |Ai!ae. I was still a girl, too young to marry. When I first met him he was putting on his loincloth and getting ready for a hunt. He said, 'You must grow up quickly so that we can marry.' He knew we would marry. He was also a great hunter and always brought back the meat. I was thrilled to marry him when I grew up.

"|Kunta was a healer when I met him. He knew everything about healing and he danced all the songs for the animals. The community would sing all night at his place. They would often dance throughout the night. |Kunta would want to heal them. Some people were scared of him because he was so strong when he stood and shook. I sat with the women and sang when I watched him dance for the first time. He danced with another healer. I remember that they gave each other nails.

"|Kunta was very fortunate. He received his first nails from the Sky God. His father and brother were with him when it happened. They were at home together, and while |Kunta was sleeping in the night he had a special kabi and was told to sing; the songs immediately came through him. He picked up his n|om songs that way. He learned the giraffe song and started dancing it. In his kabi he was dancing the giraffe dance and then God gave him the nails.

"After he received the giraffe medicine, the giraffe would always come to him. IKunta had a very special kabi where he dreamed he was riding a giraffe. He got very hot and was trembling so strongly that he started to cry. He woke up and started singing very hard. He was in first creation.

"In another kabi, God threw him inside a giraffe's intestine. He discovered that this is where the dancing comes from. He went through the anus of the giraffe from behind and found himself dancing with the ancestors. IKunta believed that this was his most powerful and important kabi. Sometimes people cook and eat the large intestines of an animal in order to help awaken their nlom. But whenever a giraffe was slaughtered, my husband didn't want the intestine to be cooked for him to eat because he owned the giraffe dance and he had to respect that organ and animal by not eating it.

"I was living with IKunta when he had that kabi. Later I became very sick and the other healers and elders told him that he must sing and heal his wife. Another healer had given me some nails of nlom that nearly killed me. They weren't correctly aligned so they hurt too much.* My husband had to heal me and he did.

---

*Nails and arrows of nlom are believed to require appropriate alignment on the body: they need to be lying horizontally on the side of the lower abdomen when they sleep and then stand up vertically when they awaken with heated nlom. As N!ae explains, "If a needle goes straight up when we are resting, it gets out of alignment. A bad diet, especially worms from the trees, will cause them to stand straight when they should be resting horizontally. Also, some fruit must only be eaten when it is ripe or it can misalign our needles. We adjust our nails by rubbing our abdomen and moving them in place. If they are not lined up correctly, we will have a pain in our gut."

She further explains: "When the needles are heated and stand up, they head toward the center of our belly. They are ready to pump up and down with further heat from nlom songs. This can cause a cramp if we are not careful. We know how to massage them and pull them to the right side of our body when it is time for them to rest. When they wake up, they always stand straight up. There are different needles that rest and wake up in various places in our body. G!oah nails, for instance, rest in the stomach and kidneys and when activated move along the chest and spine to the cervical vertebrae. They cause these parts of the body to shake when they come to life."

"|Kunta |Ai!ae now lives in the village in the sky. The stars are the eyes of the ancestors. There are some stars that are his eyes. Recently he came down and danced with us. I saw him above Bo during the dance. He thanked Bo for what he is doing. He is very happy as he watches Bo work as a heart of the spears.

"The gifts from the Sky God and ancestors must be graciously accepted. They come because God opens his heart to us. This is why we accept these gifts without hesitation. We don't know what to say about why this happens other than God loves us and wants to share his gifts."

"God's greatest gift is his ostrich egg. |Kunta never told me about God's ostrich egg until after I saw it myself. He only talked about what I was ready to hear. (See editors' commentary 18.1 on page 118.) It's rare for that egg to be given to someone. However, you don't need to see it in order to receive the giraffe dance or any other kind of dance. The dance, along with its song, can come to you. You can own a dance without being an owner of the egg."

The first time N!ae G≠kau saw the ostrich egg was in a kabi. "I saw Bo with me by the egg. Bo was in front of me on the rope. I was behind him and we were dancing together. When I woke up I was shivering and shaking. That kabi was for both of us, to help wake us up and make our hearts rise.

"Now the people want Bo and me together in a dance. They worry when the dance isn't strong. They want their nails to be kept clean and strong. The egg made Bo reborn and it enables him to receive songs in a kabi. He brings them to us and we are renewed. We are together in the egg, sharing its ropes, songs, and nails of n!om. In my kabis, I see us inside the egg and in each dance I also experience us inside this egg.

"When I was younger and received a lot of needles, I used to feel dizzy and fall. I wondered, 'What is happening?' Now I am strong. Bo and I are as strong as the strongest healers we knew as children. That's why we like spending many hours together in thara.* In the old days, people would do that more often than today. When we do this, it can be so strong that it takes us to the sky village.

"When I was shown the egg in a kabi, it was very big. A rope was next to it going straight to the sky. Bo was on the rope and the egg was to his right. There were many ancestors inside the egg dancing. I recognized them as family members from the past. They were my ancestors and Bo's ancestors. This experience gave us clean nails and brought an amazing happiness.

"In another kabi the ancestors took me to the sky village. There I was shown a special waterhole, but I didn't go near it. I stared at it from a distance. The primary classrooms are both high in the sky and in that particular waterhole.† There we continue to learn and receive more nlom."

"I remember that, when I was a young girl, the women used a dancing stick made from the gloah tree, called a *!'hana,‡* to help attract nlom in a dance. It would often be carved and painted. A dancer would have a kabi of a dance stick and that entitled her to own it. We can use that stick to heal, shaking it at somebody when we are full of nlom. A healer would hold it on the ground and shake it. Then she touched the bottom of her own back with it or held the stick near the back of someone else. She would also use it to pass over the back of a sick person. It could heal the disease.

"The first time we hold the dance stick we have to tilt our body while holding it, saying out loud, 'This is my stick.' Only the owner

---

*When two strong healers shake together during the day it can last for hours or even all day, sometimes bringing forth a healing dance for the entire community. This immersion in shaking and dancing is a good way for healers to give each other many nails and arrows of nlom. (See editors' commentary 18.2.)

†Bushman healers differ on their opinion as to whether the waterhole is a classroom to be avoided or not. Those who have been to it and learned important lessons there also express concern about the trickster nature of its inhabitants.

‡Both men and women may have a dance stick or *!'hana.*

will touch it to her body. The person being healed is not touched—it just goes near that person's body. We point it at them. When we use it on ourselves, it stays on our back. We leave it there during the dance. It acts like a rope that the needles can climb.

"The men also use a dancing stick and point it at others to transmit a nail or arrow. In addition, that stick helps keep them from falling over in a dance, as it is used to keep their balance.

"We used to dance more often in the old days. Then we would more likely dance all night. Now an all-night dance only happens rarely. The community's feelings have to be awakened and intense enough for it to go all night."

N!ae remembers when she was a girl and became a woman. "When I started to bleed, I slept through the morning. The people were worried and they came to ask what was going on. They went out to make a hut and when they came back they made some noises. Soon they started to sing and my grandfathers came. The grandfathers and the women undressed and were naked. The women put on headbands and wore bead necklaces and aprons. This is when the eland dance begins. This dance is for a girl entering womanhood.

"They danced and would sometimes stop to eat. The only men who were there were my grandfathers. They are the only ones allowed to dance for the granddaughter. They dance naked for the granddaughter, though my eyes were covered so I could not see them. After they finished the eland dance, they took me out of the hut. That's when I knew I had become a woman."

Editors' Commentary

18.1. On talking about God's divine egg

Bushman nlom-kxaosi seldom discuss God's ostrich egg unless the person they are talking with has experienced it. This is why no anthropologist ever heard about it. Our Bushman interpreters also had not heard about it. It was only discussed among healers who had received it. After reading Brad Keeney's report on this experience, anthropologist Megan Biesele visited some of the Bushman healers we have known and asked them about Brad's reports on God's ostrich egg. She received confirmation that this was one of the Bushmen's most important experiences.

18.2. On different ways of talking about the reception of nails

Bushmen often use the terms *nail* and *arrow* interchangeably. When asked to differentiate, they explain that although all nlom comes from the Sky God, they can specify when it is delivered directly from God versus through an intermediary animal or plant. When nlom comes directly from the Sky God, they call this a nail, needle, or thorn of nlom (llauhsi). They also refer to a "nail" of nlom that is received in the women's !goah dance, though this kind of nail is more accurately called g!oahnaqnisi.

When a Bushman receives nlom directly from the Sky God, she usually says, "I received a nail (llauhsi) from God." When a nail is received during a !goah dance, she typically says, "I received a nail (llauhsi) last night in the dance" without specifying it as the specific nail from !goah. If pressed to differentiate this nail, the more specific name may be mentioned (g!oahnaqnisi) or a more general comment may point out that everything comes from the Sky God, implying there is no need to differentiate names. The latter response is more from a first creation perspective, while the differentiation of names belongs to second creation.

The "arrows" of nlom (tchisi) come from animals like the giraffe, eland, and the elephant. While they have a specific name for each of these different sources of nlom, this does not imply that nails are stronger than arrows or that some animal arrows are stronger than other animal arrows. All sources of nlom are equal in importance and strength.

It is likely that nlom from animals is called an "arrow" because Bushmen hunt animals with arrows. The way they shoot an arrow into an animal is reciprocated in the spiritual world where an animal can shoot an arrow of nlom into them (or the Sky God shoots the animal's arrow). For a plant, the most common everyday way they experience a plant crossing the boundary of their skin is when pierced by a thorn. Though these thorns are not part of all plants, by association this is the plant-like equivalent of an arrow. The name "thorn" is also the oldest name for the conveyor of God's nlom and only more recently did they start calling this a nail or needle, likely because these objects are more recent associations with the skin-piercing quality of a thorn.

Animal forms of nlom are generally called *n!ang tchisis,* the nlom of !goah is *g!oah nloma,* and so forth, with each having a respect name. For example, *≠oah naqnisi* is the name of an arrow of nlom from the giraffe and its respect name is *≠oah tchisi.* Nlom in general also has a respect name of *tco.* When the Bushmen feel nlom awakened and heated in an arrow or nail, they then shift to using the respect name. When this name is used, it tells others that the nlom is hot and they need to act appropriately in such a situation. Note that a respect name is the name used when one begins entry into first creation. Using this altered name indicates the contextual shift along with differentiating and emphasizing the now active and empowered nlom.

Animal arrows and !goah nails can be transmitted by a strong nlom-kxao who owns them. Or the Sky God can throw a nail directly and make a healer. The ancestors can also bring a healer nails and arrows. They can give a nail either during a kabi when the healer is sleeping or during a dance.

19

N!ae Kxao

"When a father finds out that his daughter is having her first menstruation, he won't say a word. As soon as a young girl starts bleeding, the men must keep quiet. They must sit in the shadow. When it happened to me, the women didn't notice at first that something was happening. I had to throw my digging stick toward them to help them notice. They went away and told my mother that I did not return with them.

"My mother decided that she and the women must go look and they found me sitting under a tree. They talked to each other as they brought some blankets to cover me. They then went back and roasted some beans for me to eat. They washed and smeared my body with animal fat. The old woman put me on her back and carried me to her house. I slept alone there while several men went hunting for an oryx. The people kept washing me and at sunset they came from the west side to bring in the oryx meat. I would bend down my head and not look at anyone.

"My mother told me to hide my eyes from the men who went to hunt an oryx. If a girl looks at the people during this time, she feels very scared. At first I didn't listen and I looked a little. But after doing that I became very scared and embarrassed to talk to them again. I listened to her instructions and stopped looking. During this time my flesh was shaking from fear. I feared being hunted by the men. When someone brought me food, he would come by the side of the hut while I wasn't looking and leave it there. When he left, I took the food to eat while bending my head. People came to take the turtle shell dish away when I finished eating. I was told that I must not eat all the food. It is also a ritual requirement that the girl must not take any food with her hand. I had to use special sticks to eat with. The sticks are sharpened on the end to help grab the food. I couldn't touch anything. In addition, my feet were not allowed to touch the ground. I was given sandals made from the skin of the eland. I wore them so my feet did not touch the ground.

"During this time I could only sit on the bed. I could not communicate with a baby or else people might curse me or say bad things. I was forbidden from talking to any young child. I was not even allowed to look at the shit of a baby or child and was forbidden from saying the word *shit*. This is the way it has always been for our people. As soon as a girl starts menstruating for the first time, she is covered with blankets and the ritual begins.

"When I went inside the hut, the people said I needed to hide and avoid being seen by others. This was preparation for the eland dance. If there are only old women around, they can't do the eland dance. There must be more people—men and women—to dance around the hut. They dance naked without any clothes. Everyone danced for me, including the old people and men. The people undressed themselves in order to avoid my making them blind. They took off their clothes to protect themselves as they went into first creation.* There the culture of the ancestors was revealed. Both old and young men danced naked for me, though I had heard that in some villages only the old men would dance. Everyone danced in order to bring the animal nearby so we could have its meat.

---

*Being naked is an indication of presence in first creation whereas wearing clothes marks the identity of second creation. Entering first creation while we are identified in a second creation form is dangerous and can lead to blindness. We must be in first creation while in the form of first creation.

"When the men flirted with me, they didn't talk. They flirted with their dance movements, though I wasn't looking. No one talked to me during this time because they were scared. I sat inside listening, as I was covered. The men danced as if they were competing for me. I held my husband's bow that he had killed an eland with in a previous hunt. I did this because I needed to be ready to hunt for an eland in first creation.

"Whenever someone in the dance went into !aia, our elder healer cut that person's ear tips. Scratches were made on the tip of the ear. The blood from the dancer's ear and my blood made us equal—we were all like a hunted eland in first creation. The dance and ceremony came to an end when I no longer bled. That's when the blanket was lifted and I was brought out. The people accompanied me with singing and dancing as they brought me to the house where I would live with my husband. At that time everyone was wearing clothes again. We all reentered second creation.

"The top of my head was still covered and I only looked at the heels of the person in front of me and followed them. People in the village said that I was finished and would now be able to live. While I was in the hut they brought me gifts. This included jewelry for my neck, hands, head, and waist. My sisters and mother made me gifts. When I came out I was introduced to everyone as if I was new and everyone acted like this was the first time I had received my name.

"The girl typically has a kabi when she's inside the hut during this rite. I dreamed about a lion. The lion came and sat next to me. I was lucky and didn't scream. I wondered whether I spoke or not during the kabi. The next day I waited for people to come and tell me that I was talking during the night. I waited and no one said they had heard anything. That made me happy. I thought that I might never close my eyes again to sleep. Perhaps that's why people covered me. It's a risky time when anything can happen.

"The first blood of a woman is a very strong entry into first creation. Once she's become a woman and comes out of the hut, there are some special things she can do. For instance, the next day she can touch a man's weapons, blow on them, or spit on them. When a weapon receives this contact it makes the weapon strong. This is because the girl has recently been inside first creation and her fluid, breath, and touch helps their weapons be connected to the animals. It also makes the poison on the arrows stronger.

"During this time, the people teach the girl different things, like how to collect wild foods. The old women teach her all the things she needs to know about being a woman. They will dig up wild roots in order for her to hold them. She places them behind her back in the skin blanket. They keep digging different plants in order to let her hold all the important plants. This is how she learns about them. Sometimes they don't get to the seeds, roots, or the edible parts. They just dig and bring a part of it, leaving the rest for later when it is ready to eat.

"The elders also teach her about making and tending a fire and cooking because when she is taken home she will roast all those collected foods and serve the family. During the ritual they have her hold the things that will be cooked. For example, sweet potatoes are good when they are roasted. The same is done for the meat. Later when she first cooks the meat, the people will all have a taste of her first meal for them."

20

Tɪǃ'AE ≠OMA

"Let me tell you about the eland dance that took place when I became a woman. We were still in the village in Botswana where a lot of Herero people also lived. When I began to bleed the people immediately cared for me and brought food. At first I was separated until a special hut could be set up. Then I was brought back into the village and placed in the covered area where I received milk to drink. My grandmother came by to provide meals and sit with me in the hut.

"The eland dance began as soon as I followed the women inside the house. That night the elders taught me things. When the sun came up the next day, the people put up a special hut for me and I was placed inside it. During this time everyone was undressed and naked like they were in first creation. The women and an old man were there to dance—the old man can be your grandfather or an elder. In my dance it was my grandfather. He knew the dance and joined the women to dance for the eland. He held the eland horns, using his fingers.* He would show the eland with his fingers while the women danced naked. The dance went into the middle of the night and then it stopped.

"The old woman healer made a small cut on the dancers' ears so

---

*In the old days the dancers used actual eland horns held over their heads.

they bled with me. This happened when they went into !aia. It is done to the old dancers too, but only during the eland dance.

"When an eland dancer enters !aia, he crosses into first creation and feels the eland. His blood is the blood of the eland, and his ear is cut in order to own the feeling for the eland. The girl who is being initiated finds that her blood is connected with the blood of the eland and the people in !aia. They are all in first creation. The people come together for her eland stage.

"When a girl is alone out in the bush and starts to have her first menstruation, she will just stay there and wait. When the blood starts we must be separated from others until a covered place is made for us in the community. It is dangerous for men to be near us at this time because we are in first creation. We could change into a hunter and the men could change into an eland. That's when we might hurt them with a first creation arrow. People look for a girl starting this change and when they find her they feel like crying. They take her home and make a bed inside a covered hut for her to lie her down. The people then click together the iron tips of the axes, making the clicking sound of the eland. They do this around the young woman.

"An old woman puts an apron on the young woman. It is the only thing she wears and it is just in front of her. They are celebrating her because she has entered the eland stage. The people are happy.

"As I mentioned, a small cut is made on the ear of an eland dancer during the dance and the blood flows a little along the ear and then stops. When they say 'someone is stranded,'* a cut must be made on the ear. We cut the tip of the ear for the people from the past. In other words, we bleed with the young woman and our blood enables us to enter first creation and be with all the people there, both the girl and our ancestors from the past. During this time our hearts burst. The mother will be very worried, asking what her daughter is eating. The

---

*Saying "someone is stranded" is an indication that a girl has entered first creation and is stranded there until the rest of the community can prepare themselves to also enter first creation.

people will talk and ask why this child knows so much now. They will make her a bed, place her on it, and dance around her hut. It is very powerful.

"Like all great dances, we enter first creation. The girl will feel very close to the eland. She will sometimes feel like the eland and know that she is about to enter the eland house. In first creation, we become the eland. Similarly, in the giraffe dance, we enter first creation and the strong dancers become the giraffe. The heart of the giraffe comes into your heart. As we like to say it, we catch the feeling of the giraffe.

"The eland was chosen for the girls' dance and it is for a woman who has just entered the hut. The name of the dance is 'running an eland'—this means running after the eland's heart. The people celebrate, saying that the little girl has shot an eland. This is what we say when she menstruates. It is a way of commenting on her entry into first creation. We are happy for the dance when she enters the hut. (See editors' commentary 20.1 on page 135.)

"It's like a part of her becomes an eland in first creation that has been shot, but then she reenters second creation where she is bleeding like the one she shot in first creation. Here we go back and forth between first and second creation. This is why we only cut the ear during this dance. Everyone bleeds so they can go back and forth between being the hunter, the hunted (the shot eland), and a human being as they continuously cross and re-cross first and second creation.

"When we catch the feeling of the eland, we will only be thinking about the girl who is going through this. This lifts our heart and we start going into !aia. As we undress to be fully in first creation, we start dancing for the eland. We try to catch the eland to celebrate the girl who is becoming a woman. The eland is a special choice of animal because it is beautiful and it has a lot of fat that is the part of the meat that we like.

"Again, when a girl starts menstruating, the elders say that she has shot an eland. That's how they start the eland dance. After she moves into first creation, she is amid the changing of first creation and can change into any form at any time, sometimes being the eland or meat for the men to hunt. She becomes both hunter and hunted in this interchange. Since the eland is one of the most desired meats, being an eland is desirable to men. This awareness is also part of what she feels.

"Part of the puberty rite involves covering the girl with a blanket. This is done to hide her from the men who are hunting. Otherwise she might immediately be shot when she is an eland. She is also covered because she cannot look at anyone. She is able to change and be like the hunter and this makes her dangerous, for she could kill someone.

"During this time the girl is scared of people so no one can stare at her. The women must take special care of her. She isn't allowed to light a fire. People bring her gifts and decorate her with things and she is given what she needs as a woman, including a special necklace. The women also shave her hair. Meat is brought to her, along with rolled sinew. The men cut some animal skins and make something for her to wear on her arm. It's usually kudu skin, especially the part from the forehead. Keep in mind that the people didn't have clothes in the past like they do today.

"The most important understanding of the eland dance and all of our ceremonies is that they serve going back and forth between first and second creation. This going back and forth is the power behind the shaking. The movement takes place because God's heart has so much love that it makes things move back and forth. It is like the beat of God's heart and it's the most beautiful thing in the world. Talking about these things makes us want to weep."

Ti!'ae sometimes plays the thumb piano [mbira] when she feels an emotional heaviness. "I was given the gift of playing this musical instrument. When I was asleep in bed at night, the ancestors came and woke me up, giving me a thumb piano to play. In a kabi we can be given such a gift. When I play the thumb piano I go into thara, as do the people listening to my music. The ancestors come and stand by me. I can see them enjoying the music."

Ti!'ae knows, as all healers have experienced, that she must listen to n|om-inspired music as a means of doctoring her heart.* It is true for the ancestors as well. They may wake her up because their aching hearts need to hear her music. "It's good for them and it's good for us. It helps us keep our ropes strong."

Ti!'ae's ancestral mother wakes her up the most. Her mother also played the thumb piano when she was alive. God came and asked her to play in the same way he did with Ti!'ae. There are times when Ti!'ae feels like her mother is actually playing through her fingers; there are also special moments when it feels like the Sky God is playing and comes through her flesh. This is when her heart and God's or her ancestor's heart are one.

"When this happens it makes us feel so happy that we want to cry out of happiness. It's a very special healing and uplifting experience. When the ancestors wake us during our sleep, we are so happy to see them that we want to cry with joy and start playing music. This is what happens to the strongest healers. It takes place with the thumb piano and also in the dance.

"Several months ago I was playing the thumb piano and my deceased husband and his friend came. They stood together right next to me. I was startled; they looked the same as they did when they were alive. I also found that I could change into an animal or a bat while I am playing the music. I play it when the moon is showing. Sometimes I have to stop playing and put the instrument away because so many strange people from the past come to me. It only happens when the moon is out. I hear them talking, 'Why is she doing this? It is so nice.' I play it as long as it feels good, but when too many strange things happen, I put the instrument away.

"We can only see these unusual things when our feelings are awakened and our heart rises. This is what music does—it helps us go into

---

*Transforming suffering into spiritual joy is also the alchemy underlying other great wisdom traditions.

!aia. When that happens, the ancestors are ready to come. They can also be quickly transported to a distant dance. Whenever there is a song drifting through the air from a faraway village, the ancestors will hear it and join the dance and music. Our nǀom-kxaosi can do the same. We go where the music and dancing is being held. If we want the ancestors to join us, we need to start clapping our hands and singing the nǀom songs that they enjoy.

"When people are learning to enter !aia, they're sometimes over-whelmed by their strong emotions. When I play the thumb piano, I hold on to these feelings and allow them to rise until they become a medicine ready to share with others. This medicine is held inside me and lives there. It is something that races my heart.

"If I tune the thumb piano well, it will feel like I am not touching it when I am playing. As nǀom gets hotter my fingers will feel like they are making the sounds, doing so without the thumb piano. It feels like nǀom is moving my fingers. This is one of the best ways to raise my heart and cook the nǀom. It is as good as being in the gǃoah dance.

"I once had a kabi where I had a drum in my belly. I was pregnant with the drum, and it was beating inside, causing me to shake and sing. That's how I came to own the drum. I woke up singing and the people came to sing with me. With this sound I can awaken nǀom to heal myself. Healing is accomplished by receiving the vibrations from the drum inside of me. It inspires me to express a big shout and then I start singing. This is how nǀom can catch us.*

"Such things happen if we are on the right rope to the Sky God and ancestors. Heated nǀom, awakened by our nǀom songs, enables our heart to rise and it helps us stand until the end of a dance. Nǀom makes the voice shake, and when this sound is expressed fully nǀom gets the strongest. As we continuously say to one another, we must remember to sing in this special way to get fully cooked. Nǀom also

---

*We could hypothesize that vibration per se is the agent of transformation, and nǀom is a metaphor for its felt presence.

comes into my thumb piano as its music sends the vibrations of n!om into others.

"Bo and I have had similar experiences. They say we are the strongest healers and I love dancing with him. Other men healers are afraid of me because my n!om is so strong. But Bo and I are equal in our strength with n!om. His voice is very good and when he sings it follows the right tracks.* We've taught him and now he knows. Some men pretend and they will not open themselves. We are happy that Bo is always open and that he can come sing and dance. He owns n!om. Today I follow his songs. What we love most is climbing the ropes with him. It's wonderful.

"We have been dancing with Bo exchanging n!om needles for many years. When he visits, I watch him and say to myself, 'Why does he know so much? Why is it that we are at the same place in our knowledge?' That's how I see him. All the other Bushmen people also ask, 'Why does he know so much?' He and the other strong healers are on the same track. That's why they like dancing all night when he comes.

"God brought Bo to us. We have the same heart. We haven't ever heard of anyone coming here and doing this. No one has come from the outside that knew how to sing, dance, and heal in our way before. It is amazing that he is the same as our ancestors. This is why he is so strong. When we are together, our dances are like they used to be in the old days. Bo gives us nails and arrows of n!om. This makes our ancestors happy and they want to join us again. They are happiest when we live the old ways.

"The ancestors enjoy hearing the songs and they come from above to watch. In our strongest dances, we turn to water because we are so hot inside that our n!om becomes steam. I get a very fast vibration on my head and then God's water spills inside of me, flowing down my body."

---

*To his surprise, Bo found that he spontaneously sang Bushman songs when he was immersed in the women's dance.

❖

"I had a kabi in which I was given the beads I wear around my head. After I saw my ancestral parents holding the beads, I woke up and made them. I am frequently visited in this way. Some people have been tricked into thinking that they went to a classroom, but they were only having a regular dream. If we seek power, trickster will come and take us to a false place. We need to tell highly respected healers about our experiences so they can help us determine whether it was a trickster dream or an authentic kabi.* (See editors' commentary 20.2.)

"I was young when I had my first kabi. My mother was a healer and she gave me nails when I was young, so I grew up with this. I still receive nails from the ancestors. This is how healers can keep getting stronger even as they get older."

Ti!'ae ≠Oma started dancing when she was young and has grown old with it. Like all of us who were taught these things, she was told that the strongest healers are those who were given nails by God when they were young. She grew up in Botswana and lived there when the Marshall family was filming. She was a young woman at that time. "I had already been through my eland dance of initiation before they came. I also have seen most of the anthropologists who came later. I am not sure how much they understand about our healing ways.

"I recall when a woman anthropologist came to dance and started crying and shaking. After that experience she left and went someplace else. At another time she asked for a dance and we did it so she could take our photos. She was scared because she was afraid of the nails. She said g!oah was very painful and it made her cry. After that she stopped and didn't want any more nails. I think that is why she started working in the schools. She loves the people and we love her, but she is too scared to move from her head to her heart in the way

---

*Arguably all spiritual seekers need an ordained spiritual teacher to help them discern the nature of their experiences. Otherwise, they risk being led all over the place by trickster persuasion.

that we do it. Maybe she is ready to learn now. It would make me happy to see her in a dance again.*

"The dance will always be strong for the Bushman healers as long as we can see the stars. God and the ancestors come in the kabis and do the teaching. This is their job. We follow their teaching. We dance and get wet with nǀom as the ancestors pour God's water on us.

"God chose the gǃoah tree to be special because that tree has great strength. The gǃoah dance is danced by our sisters. It's as old as our ancestors. In the old days we used to make a stick that we would wear on our neck to help the needles go into our body. It was made from the gǃoah tree and is called a gǃoah dancing stick. We would decorate it by putting different colors on it. This took place back when we were young women. We would touch the ground with it and sing. After touching the ground we'd take the tip of it and touch our back. It helped bring the needles from the earth to our back.

"We rarely use those dancing sticks anymore. There are old ways that are being forgotten. For example, it a very special thing when a man and woman who are both strong healers work together in a close way, though this is not happening as much as it used to during the time of our grandparents. This practice of intensely shaking together takes place when Bo is with either Nǃae or me. When this happens, we say that we follow each other, that is, we are on the same track, walking the same rope. We have the same vibration and it gets stronger when we are together. If two healers hug each other and exchange nails, everybody's heart is made clean. Nobody is jealous when this takes place because it makes us all feel good about one another. This embrace helps make a happy dance.†

---

*A similar experience happened to Richard Lee who writes about his attempt to enter ǃaia in a dance (2012, 173): "The state is painful, as I discovered on my one attempt to enter ǃkia. . . . It seems there is both a psychological and physiological barrier, on the one hand involving maximal physical exertion and on the other an acute fear of loss of control."

†This practice requires that both people be nǀom-kxaosi and it is best when at least one person is a heart of the spears. While any two people can shake together, what we are discussing here is a unique and highly integrated form of sharing vibrations that few are able to accomplish. It requires sufficient preparation in handling nǀom.

"When we met Bo long ago, we already knew he was an owner of nlom even before he danced. We could feel it. The old healer who was alive then, |Kunta |Ai!ae, said he felt it in his flesh. |Kunta could also smell the scent of nlom in him.

"All healers must learn that it is dangerous if someone asks to receive a nail when their heart isn't soft. We must be careful about giving nails. We should not give them to someone who is not open or someone whose heart does not feel ready. If we do so, we will experience pain.*

"On the other hand, we are able to notice when someone is ready for nlom. We feel the desire to give them a nail. It is mutual attraction for both the person giving it and the person receiving it. When we give a nail or arrow of nlom it honors and shares God's love. It helps our relationships be healed and strengthened in a good way. We are talking about our relations to all things, including our neighbors, ancestors, animals, plants, and God."

"When we are asleep the ancestors can visit and show us places. They can give more training about the dance. They may provide specific instructions and we find that suddenly we are able to do it. When I was in the sky village, nails were put into my neck. They were put in the bone on the back of my neck. Both the Mother God and Father God gave them to me. They came to me and spoke. This was when the nails went into me. I woke up shaking.

"I discovered that I had a new nail and that they healed me. The gods said, 'Wake up and stand. We want to watch you dance now.' In some of the kabis we only look. In other kabis we only hear something. Or we may hear, see, and feel something. In this kabi I experienced everything.

"Recently Bo had a wonderful kabi. He heard the ancestors singing as he saw a golden flower. Then with a burst of light all these bees came

---

*It is both naive and risky to give nlom to anyone who asks for it. Healers must use discretion in dispensing their ecstatic medicine, making sure that the person is sufficiently soft and ready to receive an arrow or nail of nlom.

out and danced around the flower. They became the ancestors letting him dance with them. That is our bee dance. It used to be danced by our grandparents. It's wonderful hearing about it again.

"I know these bees and I felt them that same night too. Those bees were coming to bring us a message. They want to dance again. They are showing their dance. The ancestors are always dancing around us."

Editors' Commentary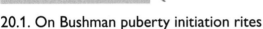

20.1. On Bushman puberty initiation rites

The Bushman puberty initiation rites for girls and boys have remained mysterious because few, if any, investigators have seen a complete ceremony, and even those who have seen any portion at all are still uncertain about aspects of its meaning. For the Jul'hoan Bushmen, what remains consistent in the girls' puberty rite is that the first sign of bleeding signals a time for immediate community action. The girl is covered with a blanket and placed inside a small hut so no one can touch or be touched by her. Elder women bring her plates of food, but no one can look into her eyes, nor can she touch the ground.

Meanwhile, the community prepares for an enthusiastic eland dance. Some anthropologists have reported that a few elders dance naked, but according to most of the Bushmen we interviewed, it was not uncommon in the past for most elder adult members of the community to take their clothes off in the dance. It depended on the village's own adaptation of these customs, the number of elders available, and those overseeing the dance. The community sings eland songs as the old men hold eland horns over their heads. (The latter is less common today than it was in the past because of limited access to elands.) The young woman having her first menstruation is unquestionably regarded as strong enough to bring negative consequences to others, should they make contact with her. She is regarded as especially dangerous to men because their hunting could be negatively affected, including an animal becoming harmful.

Lorna Marshall never witnessed a menarchal rite, but she was told that menstrual blood, while not believed to be unclean, was said to be strong, meaning that it has strong n|om. She admitted, "I was left to think about the mystery of blood" (1999, 188–89). David Lewis-Williams and David Pearce (2004, 160), whose theory largely relies upon other ethnographic reports and nineteenth-century interviews of imprisoned IXam Bushmen conducted by Wilhelm Bleek and Lucy Lloyd, hypothesized that the rites of "new maidens," the early IXam Bushman name for girls at puberty, did not necessarily involve altered states of consciousness. Lewis-Williams and Pearce noted that the hut of the new maiden was described as "!kouken-kallnein" (2004, 162), the first word referring both to "trembling" and to "be ill." While assuming that "the association of !kouken with a girl at puberty does not mean that the IXam believed new maidens to be in trance" (2004, 163), they proposed that a menstruating girl's blood is related to the potency that is associated with the "magic power of rain." They interpreted the old men dancing like old eland bulls as an effort to attract a spirit eland to the dance. All of these confluences of myth and potentiated power, Lewis-Williams and Pearce concluded, result in a moment when the community believes that staring at the girl can, following a Lucy Lloyd interview excerpt, "turn a man into a tree" (Lewis-Williams and Pearce 2004, 162).

Guenther (1999), who conducted interviews with Nharo (or Naro) Bushmen in the Ghanzi District of Botswana, heard that most of the eland dancers are old women, with a few old men joining in. They expose bare buttocks and dance around the girl's hut. According to his account, the dance includes mock male fighting, followed by the women teaching the girl womanly tasks and responsibilities. At the conclusion of the rite, she is formally introduced to each member of the community as if she were just born or reborn.

Silberbauer (1963) worked with the Glwi Bushmen of the central Kalahari of Botswana and found the same restrictions and fear associated with people coming into contact with the girl's menstrual blood. He also reported that both the young woman and her husband were given tattoo incisions during this time, and their blood was mixed to unite them as man and wife, suggesting that the puberty rite was the final ceremony of marriage for a young couple who had been chosen for a trial marriage. Silberbauer reported that "rain" refers to the emotions of the community members, as a symbolic "rainstorm" and "getting wet" are indications of the excitement expressed through shouting and laughter.

Lewis-Williams (1981, 51–52) also interpreted early Xlam Bushman interviews to mean that a new maiden is regarded as a source of nlom. Regarding her as metaphorically linked to hunting, he proposed that the girl's status is paradoxical—that is, "she is spoken of as if she were a hunter and as if she were an eland." Guenther (1999, 175) hypothesized that this is less a metaphor than an association with the themes of "women as meat, meat eating as sex, and hunting as marriage." For him, these themes suggested that the puberty rite is a symbol of Bushman cosmology. He added that the eland dance is so intense that they may experience a transformation of moving from human to antelope. Silberbauer (1963) also found that the eland hunting theme permeated a girl's identity during the Glwi puberty rite, but no dance was performed in the ritual he witnessed, though the girl was run "in a circle" (1963, 21).

For two decades we have conducted interviews with Bushman elders across Botswana and Namibia, including the central Kalahari. Based on reports of elders who resided in the Nyae Nyae area of Namibia (Keeney 1999, 2003b), we found that the most important contextual frame for the puberty rite is the distinction between first and second creation. The first appearance of the girl's menstrual blood is interpreted as an opening to first creation. During this time she is regarded as existing inside first creation. There she is capable of constantly changing her form, and this changing is what fills her with strong nlom. It is her presence inside first creation that makes the situation highly charged, not her blood per se.

The girl's first menstruation (and often the next few menstruation periods as well) opens the door to first creation for all members of the community. They dance naked because this is a sign of being in first creation, a time when people did not wear clothes. The men do not dance as an eland simply in order to attract a spirit eland; they dance as an eland because they feel they have a rope to the eland people, the form of the original ancestors. They expect the ancestors to return to the here and now of ongoing second creation because first creation is eternal, bringing past, present, and future into simultaneous participation. In this situation, all members of the community can change at any time. The young girl can experience herself being an old woman. She can also transform gender and become a boy or man as well as an animal or hybrid form. The same is true for all other villagers who are inside the dance.

To help make everyone more like the girl, small cuts are made on each person's ear. An elder nlom-kxao administers these cuts, and it is regarded as a sacred act. IKunta Boo has often performed this ceremonial duty. This results in blood dropping to the ground and deepening each person's own entry into—and identity with the girl who has entered— first creation. Everyone bleeds during the ceremony; the situation is dangerous because the girl may suddenly become a strong male hunter while a man can become an eland, resulting in the possibility that she will hunt and kill him. Similarly, a male Jul'hoan will not hunt when his wife menstruates because he might get hunted by carnivores.

In the girl's initiation rite, she may be symbolically or literally given a bow and arrow as elders ready themselves to announce that she "has shot an eland." In the changing forms of first creation, the young maiden shapeshifts between being a hunter and being the hunted animal. The ritualistic behavior that governs a girl's relation to the eland during the puberty rite is circumscribed to respect the girl's shifting identity with the eland. For example, she isn't allowed to eat eland meat, and the design painted on her cheeks and forehead typically resembles the eland's red tufted forelock. More important, she cannot utter the name of the eland but can only use the respect name while she is smeared with eland fat. Her own fat is seen as comparable to the eland bull's fat (the eland bull is believed to have the most fat of all antelopes)—again, a gender shift takes place. Biesele (1993, 86) suggests that eating fat is a Jul'hoan euphemism for sex. It may more generally refer to the transformation that sex implies, in both the act of creation as well as the birthing of another being. In Bushman epistemology, polyphony and transmutation are always valued and implicit in their discourse and ritualistic performance.

IKunta Boo reported that "everyone must bleed in order to enter first creation." He explained that when each person bleeds like the girl, they have no fear because they, too, are like her, and the changing makes them as strong with nlom. The danger is being stuck in the form of the hunted animal, for then one may attract a hunter and his arrow. Bushman elders also make the point that nlom is the feeling for the changing that takes place in first creation. Creation is literally "changing," or n!o'an-kal'ae. When you step inside first creation you feel this changing viscerally, and it makes you tremble. Nlom refers to both the changing and one's experience of feeling it, as well as to the creator god's inspiration for creating. It evokes an enhanced state of awareness accompanied by heightened ecstatic emotion.

20.2. On preserving Bushman wisdom in words

One of the reasons Bushman nlom-kxaosi don't talk about their spiritual experiences is that such descriptions can seed trickster ideas and images that sprout for others as wishful fantasies about their spiritual experiences. Traditionally, Bushmen (and other old-school healing traditions) prefer that a person report a kabi to others without knowing anything about those people's spiritual experience.

The cost of preserving the Bushman wisdom in discourse is unavoidable—this text, of course, risks feeding people's desires or psychological dreaming for specific spiritual outcomes. Yet, without any future elders to be on hand to discern the nature of what Bushman healing and spirituality is about, we risk losing its important truths. Therefore, the Bushman elders have sanctioned this book so that their most closely held teachings and truths can be shared with willing listeners.

21

ǀUı Nǃaʾan

"After we first see the rope in a kabi, we subsequently feel it whenever our nails get hot enough. We know it's available for us to climb as long as we have sufficient nǀom. We can climb when our dance turns into a stomp and we breathe heavily, making the rhythmical sound of ǁxoan. Some inexperienced nǀom-kxaosi get scared when they first feel this pumping action and when the sounds come out of their mouths. They think they might choke or be unable to breathe. They must learn that it is a good thing and that it won't hurt them.

"We climb the rope as our belly is pumping. This is when we feel a fire inside us called *nǀom-daʾa*. The stronger and hotter we get, the more ecstatic the sound of nǀom that comes out of us. This is when we are going up the rope. It's not possible to talk. We can only make nǀom sounds. When we are so full of nǀom that we can no longer speak words, it is called *ju ka gǂom*. At this time the ancestors make strange sounds through us called *nǂoahn.** This is when we feel our truest self. We are fully awake and our heart feels like it might burst with joy because we're so completely alive and strong.

---

*These sounds are capable of transmitting arrows and nails of nǀom and are therefore considered more valuable than recognized words and speech.

"There are different classrooms for learning things. I have been taken to rocky places, desert areas, plains areas, as well as dwelling places where the ancestors live. I also went to a mountain and the ocean. I went underwater once to a place called *!'han-n!ang*.

"We should always move away from the power of the fire to the love of the heart, but be warned that people may find that, as they get stronger with the fire, they will go sideways into thuru. We should keep going along the purest way of the heart. There are some men who will say that when other healers are jealous of them, they try to hurt those healers as protection. They might send themselves as a snake to hurt the ill-intentioned healers. This is not a good thing and no healer should do this. What they say is caused by them being deceived by trickster. The best and strongest healer only wants to feel nothing but love in his heart, and that makes him shake the strongest and feel the best.*

"If our heart is strong and we keep going up the rope, it cleans everything and it scares trickster. Then we don't have to worry about getting lost and doing bad things. When we first get our power we can feel the bad spirits, that is, the bad feelings of g||aoansi, but as we climb the rope they go away. (See editors' commentary 21.1 on page 142.) The only way we can come fully into our heart and go all the way up the rope is to sing as strongly as we can. The singing puts a vibration in our whole body that makes us as hot as we can possibly be. If we keep those songs singing in our head all day, then we will always be clean and have no worries. This is a secret to being a strong healer.†

"Being a strong doctor is all about love and loving God. This lifts us

---

*There are situations when even a heart of the spears decides there is no other course of action for protection than to blow a special nlom wind or use other nlom-filled ways to block an enemy's harmful attacks, especially when those attacks are intended for his family.

†We have never met a strong healer, especially a heart of the spears, who did not imagine hearing music most of the time and who was likely to sing or hum frequently throughout the waking day and dreaming night. No music, no nlom—and the stronger the music, the stronger the nlom.

high and makes God and the ancestors happy. They then give us more love, nails, and songs. It keeps getting stronger. I had a kabi recently. The ancestors asked me why I was sleeping so much and not dancing more with them. The ancestors want me to dance. It is important that we dance often and keep our nails hot and clean.

"The other hearts of the spears, from the past and present, are always around today's hearts of the spears. They are listening to us talk right now. Our ropes are all connected. We all know about God's ostrich egg. We are the same. We dance to keep each other strong."

Editors' Commentary

21.1. On power and defense

If we stay stuck in power all we will see in the world are battles of power. This is as true for the Bushman nlom-kxaosi as it is for the anthropologists studying them and the public reading or hearing about all of this. On the other hand, when our heart rises high enough we will only see love and the good inside all living things, including our enemies. Even when we have to defend ourselves from harm, we do so without malice. In the same way we can remove sickness without anger or attack, doing so while owning the feeling for that which raises our heart.

22

≠OMA DAHM

"In the old days some n|om-kxaosi used to fight more with the bad healers, especially the ones who wanted to kill us. However, the good healers were always willing to intervene. They would try to stop those who were jealous and trying to cause harm. The healers would use their awakened feelings to see who was exercising harm. We would keep our heart high as we did this, not wanting to inflict harm. We just watched what the bad healers were trying to do.

"When |Kunta Boo says that in the old days we would shoot each other with poison arrows when we were threatened, this was not true for everyone. Similarly, when he mentions that today he sends a feeling into a snake to go bite another person, many of us think he does this when trickster is in him. This is not how a good healer works. Yes, some healers will do these things when they are tired and weary of troubles. That's when he might make plans to turn himself into something else like a snake, doing so for protection.

"Other healers like me, however, say, 'We never do that. We should always raise our hearts and try to make everything clean.' When our heart is high, it is the best protection. We think |Kunta Boo may spend too much time in the waterhole, a classroom where trickster can visit.

It's easy for some people to get tempted by the power of the fire. It is always better to go high in the heart."

When ≠Oma first received his nails and began to heal, it scared him. As he grew and became more experienced, he learned to enjoy this work. "I am no longer scared. It's the best feeling. I had to get past thinking it was about power—being told this wasn't enough. I had to allow my heart to move past the temptation of power. Here I learned the importance of the songs. The lines are the songs. The song that we hear is the line we see. After a dance, we can go home and lie down. That's when we might see the lines more clearly and be taken to a special place where the ancestors teach us. This is when I learn new songs from God or my ancestral father.

"My father usually teaches me when I go up the rope. When I see him, my heart is opened and I start crying. I may later wake up crying because it is so strong. Among other things, I learned how to use an animal tail to take out disease. I can brush a person's body with it and it can attract the dirty arrows to come out. When the dirty arrows and nails come out, we usually make a shouting sound. It helps push them out.*

"When the ancestors come to a dance, they may sit and watch or stand right next to us. When I get very hot, I float above the dance. The people look like ants. Everything in the dark looks like it is daylight. I see animals in the bush, including the jackals. The trees are upside down. The roots will be up and the branches down. After the dance, when I am cooling down, the ancestors will say that they are now going to rest. They will say good-bye to the people, and I say to them, 'You go be well, too.'

"We can't emphasize enough that the ancestors who try to hurt us are only missing us. They can get selfish and find that they, too, need to

---

*It cannot be emphasized enough how important ecstatic sound is to intensifying nlom and spontaneous body movement. Again, it cannot be purposefully voiced but must spontaneously arise without intention.

dance to keep their nails clean. Whether in living people or ancestors, bad feelings—selfishness, jealousy, or anger—cause sickness. All of us, from the past and present, must dance often to keep ourselves clean.

"We shake because of the ropes. They make us shake when we see or feel them. We start shaking in the healer's way when the ropes are attached to us. If a person is always calm and does not shake, then she does not have a rope. If she doesn't shake during the singing or dance it is because she has no rope. (See editors' commentary 22.1 on page 148.)

"We learn about ecstatic healing and spirituality in the spiritual classrooms. I used to go down the waterhole. I would be scared so I had to keep myself strong. There were some important teachings there. The ancestors gave me songs and arrows. There's no fear when I go up the rope, but it's scary when I travel down it. If I have the courage to go down deep it makes me stronger so I don't have fear when I do this work. That's the most important lesson of the classroom in the waterhole.*

"We love to ride the animals in our kabis. It's a very special experience. I once saw a gemsbok walking by and I tried to shoot it with my bow and arrow. I missed. I shot and missed again, wondering how could I miss a gemsbok that was so near. It started to run, but then it stopped. As I prepared my arrows, it came back again. It came toward me and though I wanted to shoot, I felt scared. I didn't shoot it. That night I had a kabi. I heard the voice of an ancestor who came to tell me, 'You must go find a real gemsbok to shoot, not the one you saw today. Tomorrow go in the other direction and find a gemsbok you can shoot.'

"It happened like that the next day. That morning I went out in the other direction and found a gemsbok that I killed. The ancestor taught me that there are two different kinds of animals. One is for hunting

*The Shakers of St. Vincent have a similar spiritual classroom where it is understood that going deep into the ocean gives courage and conquers fear, thereby developing a deeper trust of spontaneous spirited expression. Sometimes a Shaker receives the spiritual gift of a weight or vest of weights whose weight helps him sink all the way to the bottom of the ocean floor.

and eating. The other is for spiritual matters. They teach and bring us nǀom." (See editors' commentary 22.2.)

Because everything is always changing in the continual dance between first and second creation, nǀom-kxaosi may see the ropes to God in different colors.* ≠Oma Dahm would see two ropes going to God. "One is white and the other is green. They are both equal in size and they both belong to God. These two lines are always together. For me, the red line is the path to trickster. If I want to meet God, I follow the green or white lines. I use both of these ropes, but I usually go up the white one. I also use the white rope to visit another village. I can travel along it to see what is happening in another place. Some of the healers see two ropes while others see only one rope."

≠Oma's father told him to not be worried about the different ropes. "He advised that we should only be concerned with one rope. Only use the rope to God, which for him was the green rope, not the red rope or the black rope. The green rope was his path to other places, especially to God. It is the size of a finger. It is always next to the white rope. When I climb that rope to the sky village, there are ancestors I can visit. They teach me how to sing different songs.

"When I am climbing the rope during a dance I can see other healers climbing. We climb the ropes together. There are times when a rope or line breaks. God is the owner of the ropes and he is able to repair them. They break when someone dies. When this takes place, God sends his children to repair the ropes.† Every time a person dies,

---

*The color of the ropes leading to God can be reported as different from one person to another. One can argue that the different colors and ropes that nǀom-kxaosi see is a consequence of what they were observing the moment they reentered second creation, the time when language returns to name their experience. In first creation the colors are changing, but it stops at the moment of reentry into language-based second creation. At the same time, white is usually the most preferred rope (as it is the emanation of all colors in the light spectrum).

†Other ecstatic traditions also see the ropes and believe that they must be repaired. Brad found an elder, Mother Samuel in St. Vincent, who had visions of herself fixing the spiritual ropes.

the rope is repaired and it gets longer. The rope is the spirit of every-one who has died. We sometimes say that all the ancestors are dancing while holding each other's back.

"I have seen God's children repairing a rope. The ropes are very beautiful and they shine. There are green ropes that go from our bellies to the bellies of others. They are all the same size, about the diameter of my finger. When a healer feels close to somebody, the rope or line feels tight. When it's real tight we can send messages to each other. We have to be in !aia to send these messages. We must place a lot of feeling into the rope in order to send a message. The healers feel this with other healers when they dance or are in !aia."

On a journey to God's sky village ≠Oma saw God and was surprised to see "that he had a beard. God told me what to do. He also touched me and gave some very strong nails. I saw God's wife and children. God has eleven children—five males and six females.* The children sang and danced for him. God's children also touched me. It was a very special experience and it only happens once in your life."

≠Oma also reported on one of the sons of God. "He has many arms and hands. I went up to him and all his hands touched me. My father also had this happen to him." Here we learn that there are many ways of touching people as a means of giving n|om. In all cases, our n|om must be very hot in order for this to happen.

≠Oma believed that "the rope is actually God's finger. It sometimes looks like a stairs or a ladder. When I get near it I fly up. It takes us to the sky where God lives. Sometimes it takes us to the earliest village where the original ancestors live. They, too, can give us nails and teach us important lessons."

The first time a healer gave ≠Oma a nail, "he touched my stomach and it made me very sick. I felt like I would throw up and I thought I was dying. This was a long time ago. It can be difficult when we first

*Many Bushman n|om-kxaosi report meeting God's wife and children, though the num-ber of children they see varies.

learn. It takes many years to learn to enjoy the arrows and nails of nǀom. As we like to say, !aia for a new healer is death, while for a strong healer it is new life.

"The stronger a healer becomes, the more he learns to only pay attention to his good feelings and inspire them to get stronger.* When we talk about being a healer, the most important words are love, God, and awakened feelings or !aia. These are the things that make one a healer. If somebody isn't emphasizing these things, they don't know what they're talking about. The greatest healers have the biggest hearts, hearts that get so large that they feel like they're going to burst with good feelings."

Before he died, ≠Oma Dahm's final words to Bo were, "My father and grandfather are very proud of the kind of healer I became. They helped me stay alive all these years. Now I will soon die, but we will always dance together because our rope is strong."

Editors' Commentary

22.1. On ecstatic spirituality, somatic experience, and discourse

To cultures that value discourse over somatic experience, ecstatic spirituality is arguably the least familiar form of transformative practice. For cultures for whom the written and spoken word is dominant, spiritual practices and healing most often emphasize understanding, relaxation, and stillness—all of which diminish body movement or regard it as secondary. As a result, the "body dictionary" familiar to such cultures as the Bushmen is unknown or forgotten, along with awareness and expertise concerning the automatisms that are initiated by spontaneous movement and the natural healing responses associated with heightened emotional arousal.

---

*It is more accurate to say that a strong healer pays attention to all of his feelings, while only feeding those that are resourceful and not feeding those that dirty his arrows.

22.2. On spirit connection with animals

Brad has had numerous unexplainable (outside the knowing of Bushman epistemology) encounters with animals, from eagles to crocodiles, snakes, elephants, lions, and leopards, among others. He has faced leopards several times while walking through the bush, during both daytime and evening, staring into the leopards' eyes as life and death were held in uncertainty, only to watch the leopard slowly turn and walk away in the midst of a shower of nlom that inspired empowered trembling and sponta-neous ecstatic singing. Among the Zulu, Brad was named Ingwe to honor his rope or relationship with the leopard.

23
G‖AQ'O KAQECE

"I was born and lived my whole life in the same village. I learned about n‖om from my uncle and grandfather. They were from the same place. They first taught me about ‖'ai *djxani,* the grass dance. They later taught me to dance the giraffe dance.

"I saw God's ostrich egg and know others who saw it too. God was holding it in my kabi. The needles, nails, and arrows of n‖om are contained inside that egg. When I first saw the egg, it didn't crack open for me. My grandfather was the one who gave me the needles. After I saw the egg crack open, I was able to climb the ropes. When I get hot enough my heavy breathing delivers the drum sounds and helps me climb with a stomping motion. I have to push and pull on that sound.* I went to many classrooms, including the deep waterhole, the original village, the yellow flower that is filled with many bees, and inside the beehive. I received special teachings in these places. When I returned, I knew many things.

"I have had to protect myself from attacks. I turned myself into something else in order to fight back. I have turned into a lion as well

---

*This mention of having to "push and pull on that sound" is significant, for it shows the interaction between body movement and ecstatic sound production that occurs during the experience of climbing a rope.

as other animals.* I was once one of five men who drank the greenish liquid of an eland's liver. After we drank it, we became an eland. I could not sleep. I felt I was in the fire. My mother saw what was happening and told everyone in the village, 'Do not criticize him, but go set up a fire for a dance.' In the dance, I could turn into other animals. I would stare into the fire and see the animal and then I would become it. It jumped and swallowed me and then I turned into it.

"The giraffe is good to us. I rode it in a kabi. There are different giraffes—some are used for the meat and others are found in kabis. This is also true for the elands. Some we ride and some we eat. I have also ridden an eland and a gemsbock. All these animals gave me their song. As I rode them, I was hearing and singing their song. We love the animals we ride. We catch the feeling for them and our hearts become one with their hearts. It makes our rope strong with them. When we have a kabi of riding an animal, the next morning that animal will come close to the village.

"Sometimes we make love with an animal in a kabi. I have had special kabis where I made love with the eland, duika, gemsbok, and giraffe. Their songs enable me to own the feeling for them. When I am in a kabi with a special animal, I hold it close to me as I would my wife. We become like husband and wife because the song makes our hearts one.† It's the strongest love. When we love an animal it is like we are married to it. We shake very strongly.

"When I hold the feeling for an animal, I can go touch it while others are dancing. The animal will be present at the dance. I will greet and welcome the ancestors, then go down to the animal, hold it, and even massage it. I'll be looking at the animal while I am dancing. After the

---

*Brad has known numerous Bushmen who turned into lions in both Botswana and Namibia and has experienced this visionary occurrence himself. There are different means for making this transformation. See Keeney, *Kalahari Bushman Healers* (1999), for more information on this topic.

†The nlom-kxao's kabi experience of intimacy with animals is simple, like the way it might be portrayed in a children's story, and serves to deepen love, empowerment, and relational involvement with the whole of life.

dance, I inform the animal that it must return later so that I can ride on it. In a kabi, you enter first creation where everything can change. I can love an animal inside first creation and even kiss it.

"It would be impossible to believe what happens to us if we hadn't experienced it for ourselves. It takes courage to be a true nlom-kxao. Bo and I are the bravest. We can dance with our ancestors, drink God's water, ride the animals, and become a lion, among many other wonderful experiences.

"My uncle and grandfather usually teach me in the classrooms. They taught me how to approach a lion and sleep next to it. I watched them make a lion smaller and me bigger so we were equal in size. The lion looked at me and stretched itself. That woke me up. This all happened while the ancestors watched. I caught the lion's heart as it wrapped its tail around my waist. That's when I received a tail and owned the lion. The lion can throw me. He grabs my tail and throws me. I can do the same with the lion. I grab its tail and throw it. We throw each other. After that we both stand up and shake each other's hands. We do this in first creation. In this way I am made a stronger healer because my rope with the lion gets stronger. I own the lion.

"The ancestors tell me when there is a lion far away or nearby. They will say that a lion is coming. There are different kinds of live lions. Some will attack us and are dangerous. Others are the lions of the ancestors. They enable us to turn into them and throw them. They are the special ones for the healers.

"The same is true for other animals, including various snakes. The ancestors can make us belong to a snake. If a nlom-kxao hates another person, he might turn himself into a snake and be able to bite his enemy. These things can happen. Once I threw myself into a mongoose. I wasn't dreaming about it or visiting it. I was watching it through my feelings. I could see what it saw from far away.

"I have seen the original ancestors, the people with human bodies and animal heads. My grandfather first told me about those people. They still exist. A strong healer like me can go back and know the original ancestors through my feelings. They exist between us at the border of first and second creation.* They are traveling to all places.

"When a healer shakes, he is going back and forth between first and second creation. When we shake very hard, it's like slipping out of our skin so we can become something else. As all strong healers know, it's not physically being the other animal. It's becoming the feeling of the other animal and following its rope and song. A strong healer can close his physical eyes and ears and awaken the strong feelings of the heart. This is when our second eyes and ears open, and when our senses of taste and smell become altered.

"Being a strong healer requires concentrating on one strong feeling that escalates. We must hold on to it and not let it throw us to the ground or scare us. Simply hold on to this huge feeling. We have to sing strongly because the singing makes the body shake more and gets us hotter, enabling us to stay on course, remaining inside the feeling without any bending of the rope.

"When healers shake, we also catch the feelings of each other. This makes all our ropes stronger. It helps keep everything aligned. If we don't do this the ropes get bent and break. Because all the ropes are connected with each other, healing helps save everything, including the animals, trees, bees, and humans. As we go back and forth between first and second creation, all the ropes get stronger.

"Good teasing and laughter help the world stay loose and ready for change. When we tell the old stories about first and second creation, the stories must change. These stories also help keep the world changing. The stories are medicine. (See editors' commentary 23.1 on page 156.) Our healers know these things. They are aware that the stories, the laughing, and the teasing keep things moving, alive, and healthy.

"God has a pot. He can throw you in it and cook you. This is how

---

*The boundary between first and second creation appears in other cosmologies, in Africa and elsewhere. It is the place for spiritual crossings, symbols of which include the image of the cross and what has been popularized in the blues musical tradition as "the crossroads."

the strongest healers are made. This pot is used to impart teaching—you get cooked with nǀom rather than taught words. We are put in the pot to be remade as vessels for holding and sharing nǀom.

"All hearts of the spears have received the sacred water from God. It feels like God is pouring a liquid inside our head that flows down our body. This water comes from inside a tree trunk in God's village. When we fly past the stars and see that single tree in the sand, we see God's tree. The nǀom water is inside the trunk of that tree.

"There is a story about the first time a man saw a woman's sex organ. It took place when a woman went up the sky to get some water from God's tree. The man looked up and saw her special part. The woman noticed him looking and shouted back, 'Now that you know about it, you can stop putting your penis in my ear.' The man then climbed up the rope and had sex with her. After they finished they fell back to the ground together. This is why there are heaps of sand all around the desert—they were first created when that man pulled the woman back to the ground. It made the heaps on the earth.

"That's when men learned the right place for having sex with a woman. Men no longer had sex in the ears of a woman ever since that woman showed her vagina. That same woman went to pull up the grass and clean herself when she bled. It is now called the grass for the vagina. Thereafter people started to marry each other and have children. That's how marriage started and why we are able to give birth to children.

"God's tree is where man and woman first had sex. It happened because water was taken from it. The tree is very important. It is in the middle of God's place. In a kabi we can climb the tree in order to drink from its trunk. This is a moment when we own God. We say, *!Xu-kxao,* 'I am an owner of God.' As we can catch the feeling of an ancestor we love and then step into him to become the ancestor; we can also feel like we've become one and the same with God. We become one person by stepping into him.

"People need to be x-rayed by a nǀom-kxao who sees properly before they are sent to a classroom. When a person is ready and is sent to an ancestral teacher, she can learn everything, including what food to eat, what clothes to wear, and what songs to sing. We are taught to follow the way that takes us to the home of God. In the beginning there was only one road leading to God, but later it separated. There is now a fork in the road and we must choose the direction we will follow. Because people get selfish and ignorant they may want power. The power of the fire makes them forget that they should go past it and head for the heart of God. Trickster, who the Christians call Satan, holds the fire. His way is ignorant. We must lift our heart to follow the best way to God.

"When a healer gets on a bad rope, he will be taken to dangerous places. There is a cave where the tunnels are separated. When a healer is inside the cave, he can be taken in a direction where he will be burned. He will cry out. 'No, let me take the other way because the good people are there.' The ancestors then warn him that he nearly got trapped in the wrong way, and that they must be allowed to cool him down. He will be sent to a special healing place so others can repair him. He will be given healing water and be made good again. They will pour God's nlom water on him.

"When we're cooked we are readied for handling nlom. We do not feel jealous and we do not easily get angry when our nails are heated. Our heart has gone to God. The ancestors have used God's water to cook us and our heart is good. Whenever our nails and arrows start to get dirty we go to the dance and allow them to cook us again. We are cooked over and over again.

"If people come to us for help, God sends a message along the ropes and our body speaks for God. We must do things together. When we hold someone and shake them, we are helping God express love to the people.

"The rope is really God's love. Since this love is expressed as a song, we say that a song is a rope. Sometimes God throws us to see whether we'll fall. But he's holding on to us. There are times in a healer's life when we are tested. We are sent to scary places and we see frightening things, but if we stay strong God will never send us to those places again. When we come out of God's pot, we are thrown back in the world. If we need to get cooked again in the future, we will be thrown back into the pot. (See editors' commentary 23.2.) This is how God helps us keep on track. With God's rope we receive all the gifts and happiness anyone could be looking for.

"When people come to us for help we will sometimes tease them. If a couple is fighting, we might tease them saying that they must leave each other and let us sleep. Teasing is a good medicine. It prepares people to receive nlom.

"The women teach the men how to move past the fire and raise their heart. There are a lot of men who show off and never raise their heart, but when they do so they're very strong. The elephant dance can also lift our heart if we are clean and our hearts have risen. Some people say it is bad because they are scared that it might bring them pain. It can be very strong or it can lead one astray. It can go either way. All the dances can lead to either power or God's love. Always choose the right rope."

Editors' Commentary

23.1. On Bushman storytelling as a doorway to first creation

The art of Jul'hoansi storytelling emphasizes "great latitude for individual artistry" (Biesele 1993, 66) and is often characterized by perplexing richness and even apparent contradiction. !Unnlobe told Biesele that stories are always changing because "people use different words and names for the same things," "there are different ways to talk," and "different people have different minds" (1993, 66–67). Going further into their relationship with a god of creation, the Bushmen believe that "a direct channel may open at any time between them and this great god through inspirations" (1993, 68). Storytellers serve as interlocutors for the divine and help in the "transfer of new meaning from the other world into this one" (1993, 70).

Bushman stories emphasize transformation and shape-shifting, where a man can become a lion, an eland can turn into rain, a feather dropped into water can become a whole ostrich, or a leather sandal can become an antelope. |Kunta Boo, regarded as one of the great Bushman storytellers, states that the primary purpose of telling a story is to awaken and transmit nlom. As |Kunta Boo explained, it is one of the mediums in which a doctor or nlom-kxao can perform the activity of "shooting an arrow of nlom" into others. As such, it is a specific way of doctoring and revitalizing the community.

The dramatic enactment of a story, especially the ecstatic ways in which the voice is used in its spoken deliverance, sets up the delivery of nlom. As |Kunta Boo explained, "I must enter first creation to tell a story. Here the story will change and have nlom." Like a nlom-charged song, a nlom-charged story can transmit nlom, but "if the story is not told by someone who is full of nlom, it will be dead." It must be spoken with nlom and that performance helps take others inside first creation. Similar to the puberty rites and healing dance, a nlom-filled story is an entrance to first creation. As |Kunta Boo stated, "When a nlom-kxao tells a story, it is like being in a dance—I can shoot an arrow of nlom into you."

This view suggests that alterations and contradictions offered by a storyteller are more than stylistic variations. They are the very purpose of the story itself. In other words, the story is a vehicle for holding a change or transformation that aims to surprise and catch the listeners (and speaker), tripping them and helping them fall inside first creation, the domain of creative changing. As |Kunta Boo articulated, the old stories that tell about first creation, in which everything changes, must be altered with each telling. The key to understanding a Bushman story is to be aware of how much change and transformation is instilled in its words and scenes.

Bushman elders believe that a written story can easily kill a relationship with nlom, for it will be stuck in the same form. For the story to be alive and serve as a deliverer of nlom, a storyteller must change it and express awakened feelings with a voice that transmits nlom with its tonal shifts, rhythmic alterations, dynamics, and musicality. An analysis of Bushman storytelling would be better served by studying how the same story is changed in different performances, doing so by noting the specifics of its contexts and the nature of the unique interactivity between story-teller and audience. Similarly, an archive of Bushman stories would ideally consist of multiple renditions of each story to assure that the importance of different deliveries is conserved.

A search for the "correct" interpretation of Bushman stories misses the point. As Biesele (1993) has argued, Bushmen give no particular significance to holding any fixed meaning or narrative. They prioritize "hunting for nǀom" and entering first creation, and this applies to storytelling as well. Stories offer a resource when they help awaken inspired emotion that brings them inside the experienced whirling of change, an indication that one is entering first creation.

Bushman stories are unambiguously about transformational change and its embodiment. This is not interpreted or conceptualized change; it is evoked change, brought about by situational improvisation with minimal concern as to whether meaning is construed. Unless scholars recognize the importance of the heightened feelings and whirling perceptions that inspire a Bushman to dance, laugh at a story, or shake during a puberty rite, a wide gap will inevitably result between a subsequent professional narrative and the Bushman experience that gives no importance to stabilized naming. The alternative to attempted captures of Bushman experience through representational means (whether discourse or visual image) is to underscore the ambiguity, circularity, change, and sudden shifts in the Bushman performance, trying to do so in a way that recursively enacts its form. In other words, the organization of an explanatory discourse should match the form (but not necessarily the semantic content) of the discourse being studied. In the case of the Bushmen, a theoretical analysis that values coherence, consistency, and lineal causality is at odds with what Bushmen value and prioritize in storytelling.

As was noted by Lorna Marshall (1999), the Bushmen have "respect names" for important words, including those with religious significance. If a Bushman feels nǀom "cooking" inside him- or herself, then no one in the vicinity will say the word *nǀom* or any other word that is associated with it. Marshall (1999, 59) recorded the respect word for nǀom as *shibi*.

Biesele (1993) noted that the hundreds of respect words practically form a second language. Though they can "enhance the politeness, prudence, or delicacy of any utterance" (Biesele 1993, 24), they may also point to the importance of not being overly attached to the name, for its vitality in first creation is in part derived from being freed of a name. It is problematic to speak of nlom when it is present, not only because nlom is strong and dangerous, but because naming is the antithesis of being in first creation. Here secondary naming is used to loosen the choking grip that any primary name might have on the transformative power the word is indicating.

When a Bushman story mentions a body organ, it will typically emphasize the organ that embodies the most transformation. The best example is the intestine, an organ the Bushmen regard as having the most nlom. IKunta IAi!ae was regarded as a strong doctor because he had a vision of the Sky God throwing him up a giraffe's anus, where he danced in the animal's intestines. His transformative dance was situated inside an organ that emphasizes transformation, thereby evoking more change. If the story of his vision is performed, one can assume that exaggerated motions will indicate how a dance in an intestine is truly capable of delivering further evocations of change.

One classic form of a Bushman story involves a hungry wife telling her lazy husband to go on a hunt. When he returns with some eland meat, she is so hungry that she eats her husband. Later in the story she finds herself shitting out her husband who, in turn, eats her. Although the story dances across many levels, including sexual hunger and exchanges of who is hunting whom, the most important aspect of the story is to deliver the kind of change that helps the listener feel the nlom that underlies all changing forms.

Bushman storytelling asks a storyteller both to deliver the story with nlom and to use the story as a way of receiving nlom. The latter is as true for the teller of the story as it is for the listener. As a story is told, the speaker's emotions become amplified and the story starts to come alive. It seems to have a mind of its own and is improvised beyond any previously designed expectations and control of the performer. It is the surprise of improvisation and the way it feeds emotional awakening that helps the storyteller feel nlom. As nlom continues to embrace both story and performer, the context is invigorated and the emotional intensity of an ecstatic performance spreads to all. In this climate of energized immediacy and creative possibility, everyone is given an opportunity to feel more alive and be transformed by any sudden, unexpected change that is delivered by a voice moved by the situational truth of its own spontaneity.

A Bushman storyteller begins with a story that is recognized by all. The emotional delivery of the story helps make its telling be more than mere repetition. It brings life to the story, which in turn inspires the story to become improvised and changed in the telling. Of course, a storyteller may already come to the story full of nlom, in which case the story immediately starts inside nlom and first creation. Furthermore, as the audience becomes emotionally excited, this also fires up the performance. Story, storyteller, and audience all interact in ways that help bring forth awakened emotions that serve the deliverance of nlom. In this ecstatic theater, everyone aims to enter first creation, the source of renewal and healing. We move from a changing story to a charged storyteller and a transformed audience.

Perhaps we could say that a story must be "cut" with the knife of a newly drawn distinction so it can bleed, marking entry into first creation. When the story reenters life, it revitalizes the storyteller, who now is feeling the nlom associated with this changing. The community, captivated by his performance and the sounds of nlom that deliver it, is also recharged as all members enter the creation of a changing story and altered storyteller, doing so while crossing into the life of a newly reemerged world.

23.2. On the cyclic process of becoming a Bushman nlom-kxao

Bushman healing and spirituality emphasize cyclical process more than developmental growth. However, this cyclical nature of learning is not held as one side of a duality—the other side being the lineal progression of a developing nlom-kxao. Instead, the lineal progression is considered to be recursively emergent from the cycles. At the same time, each identified stage of development is regarded as a trickster artifact of conceptual "punctuation" that hides the constant movement within the whole cycle of learning throughout a nlom-kxao's career. A more advanced nlom-kxao is able to more quickly traverse the stages of a recycled progression, sometimes doing so in a single dance, whereas a beginner may have to wait years for the first cycle (and its marked progression) to complete itself.

24

N!ANI G|AQ'O

"I dance the elephant dance. In it I use a horn to shoot a nail. Before the dance I make a mixture of cow fat with plants that have been burned and crushed. I then take the mixture and put it on different spots of my fingers. My fingers are shaking when I dip it into the medicine. When I shake my hand and point, it shoots an arrow.

"In the g!oah dance, we shoot a female and male nail so they can make other nails of n|om. This is the medicine for the g!oah leaf. We may give the male nail first and the female nail afterward. Or we may do it the opposite way, as long as both come together.* We do so in order to see whether a person will shake.

"When the nails sleep they move to our side. When they get hot and wake up, they come to our belly. The people must sing very hard for the nails to wake up. When the nails wake up they stand straight and climb our spine.

"The first time we are shot with a nail, it might knock us down to

---

*Bushmen provide no detailed or consistent description of what differentiates a male from a female nail of n|om other than assuming that the stronger n|om nail is the female form because it is believed to be strong enough to give birth to more n|om. It is simply assumed that some nails are male and others female in order for offspring to later appear, mirroring the rest of nature.

the ground. That's when the ancestors watch very carefully. The people will leave us while we sleep. They come back to look at us from time to time, making sure that we eventually wake up.*

"I had a kabi in which the oldest ancestor of the elephant dance came to me. He told me that I must not be scared because he was only visiting. He was an elephant. He told me that I was to inform the people that he was coming, but that he would not hurt the village. He would safely pass through. I went to inform the village. They were scared and wanted to run, but I told them not to and immediately they saw the elephant come. The elephant came with two daughters and I heard it speak, 'Let us pass so we can go back home.' People again wanted to run away, but I stopped them. After the elephants were on their way and at a distance away from the people, the elephant sent me a message. The elephant gave me its medicine. That's why I own the elephant dance.

"When the tourists and anthropologists are here we do not show our power. We give them a dance for show. The elephant told me that we should not do a real dance with these outsiders. We keep on singing and dancing when they are not around. This makes the elephant ancestor happy. (See editors' commentary 24.1 on page 165.)

"When elephant dancers go out in the bush, we might see a falling tree that is white. We go over to it and rub ourselves with its dried leaves. It's good to rub our feet with it. This helps keep the nails in the right position. We should also shake some dry leaves to make a sound that frightens the leaves so that they won't take our nails.†

---

*Quite literally, a strong nail of nlom can make one fall to the ground and enter a deep sleep or unconscious state. Or it can make the initiate physically ill, instantly draining him of energy, action, and thought, and he will feel like he may die. The person receiving such a nail will be taken to his hut and later brought to a healing dance. This is part of the education of a Bushman nlom-kxao.

†Any living form with which a Bushman has a nlom relationship may either receive or transmit nlom. For example, a giraffe may give arrows of nlom or take a Bushman's giraffe arrows (if the Bushman owns those arrows). Similarly, the spouse of a nlom-kxao may receive arrows and nails of nlom from the other spouse during sleep. This is one of the reasons Bushmen value marrying a nlom-kxao.

"If we see a mouse hole in the ground we cover it up. Otherwise our nails might stay there. Our stomach will feel an ache if a nail departs. We don't cover up other kind of holes in the ground. The mouse hole is the one we have to look out for as we walk around the bush. It is shallow and should always be covered.

"All the dances come from one source. They just get split into different paths. When we dance and get very hot, the nails turn to steam and rise to our head. That steam will come out of a hole in our head. It then falls to the ground and gets cool, turning back into a nail. When we dance, it comes in our feet and moves up our body.

"When we shake in a dance, the ancestors come to watch. As we start dancing we can see the ancestors as well. They are moving about. In the beginning of the dance, we'll only see them for a second. We'll see those who have bad feelings. As we get strong, they run away. As we get even stronger, the ancestors with good feelings will arrive because they want to be happy, which is what happens as they see us as good healers. The bad feelings look very ugly and stink, while the good feelings are very attractive and smell sweet.

"Sometimes the needles inside us battle. The elephant and giraffe needles may fight each other. This is why some people are afraid of different needles. If we're dancing one, we don't want to dance the other because they will fight. But when we are fully cooked we can take all the needles. God and the ancestors serve us nlom with many different kinds of nails, arrows, and needles when we are a heart of the spears. At this stage there is no longer any good versus bad in our lives. Everything is transformed into nlom."*

---

*From the perspective of a heart of spears, there is only one kind of nail, rope, and song. The stronger one becomes, the less need there is to indicate different kinds of nails, ropes, songs, medicines, dances, gods, ancestors. There is only nlom. A person not fully cooked can be said to have more trickster inside of him, and trickster requires more talk, distinctions, and explanations. A fully cooked nlom-kxao has no need to know or explain. She is nlom.

Editors' Commentary

24.1. On dancing for outsiders

It is typically the case that dances for outsiders, including anthropologists, are staged performances. Healing may be impersonated rather than authentically conveyed if it has been asked for by the observers. This is not because the Bushmen are trying to deceive but because it is very difficult to open one's heart when the discerning eyes of second creation are casting judgment and naming upon a first creation process. It is also believed that strong nlom is dangerous for those not familiar with it, as it is dangerous for strong nlom-kxao to open themselves when people are not appropriately soft. Observers may believe they have witnessed a strong healing dance even when the Bushmen would not regard one as having taken place.

25

Tci!xo !Ui

"We travel on the ropes. Sometimes we feel like we are upside down with our feet in the air and our head down. When we go up to the sky village we see our parents, grandparents, other relatives, or friends and talk with them. It happens as soon as we walk toward the rope. Take one step toward the rope and you can start going up. It is a smooth and even motion that gets us up. It's not jerky and it's not too fast. It happens easily and gently, but it takes only a few seconds to get up to the sky village."

Tci!xo !Ui was a young woman when she first saw the white rope going to the sky. "It took place in a dance and I walked over to it and immediately went up. I saw the Sky God and the son of God. God touched me because he wanted me to be a great healer."

The lines or ropes of Bushman n|om-kxaosi are described as red, white, green, or black in color. There are a lot of horizontal lines that are connected to the healers. Only the healers are connected to all the ropes because they use them to visit other healers. For Tci!xo, "the black line goes to the son of God and it can be used by a healer for traveling. The green and white lines are God's lines. The red line takes us to a bad place whereas the green line takes us to the good place. If we ask God for an animal, he can take the white rope and connect us to it, enabling a successful hunt.

"Both my father and mother were healers. My father once followed a rope to a special waterhole because he was a strong doctor. He said that place had very dangerous animals like lions and leopards. He was not scared because he was the owner of other animals that helped him. He used their nǀom and abilities. He would see the animal in a dance and catch the feeling for becoming it.

"My father is now an ancestral spirit who visits me. He once woke me up in the night and told me to take the lion's soul. He said I could use it to treat myself when I was sick. He continues to teach me many things.

"The rope to the sky normally looks white. There are two lines going up to the sky. The other one is green. Last night we all saw Bo walking up the rope to visit God. Some healers use the white line and some use the green rope. Last night Bo was only walking on the white rope.

"The lines and ropes go in many different directions. Sometimes they look like a giant spider's web.* Before we get fully cooked by nǀom, we see the lines as a spider's web. As we get stronger, we see there are two ropes that go straight up. In addition, there is a red rope that goes to a bad place. Of course the straight ropes can bend when we get weak as we are climbing up. A nǀom-kxao must stay strong to keep the white and green lines straight. Finally, when we become the strongest healer, we no longer see the red rope. When we're really powerful, we usually only see the white rope to God. This is when the rope is strongly connected to our head. The rope

---

*A nǀom-kxao reported a kabi in which he witnessed his own birth. He was in the sky and it was a cloudy night. When he looked below he saw many different white lines going in all directions. It looked like a spider web, and only a few lines went straight down rather than sideways. A voice told him to choose the right line and travel on it on his way to earth.

is always above us. Whenever we dance we will see and feel the rope. Every strong doctor has a rope from his or her head that is felt in the dance."*

---

*When a person first receives a nail of nlom, a rope is attached to the top of his head and other parts of the body. Some Bushmen will have a kabi of this taking place after the dance in which they first receive a strong nail.

26

KAQECE |KAECE

Kaqece was born in the village of Makuri. When he grew up, his father was the only nǀom-kxao there. "He taught me about curing and hunting. He would tell me about the ropes. When I first went up a rope I told him and we discussed climbing them. There are two ropes—one is thin and the other is thick. The thick one takes us up quickly to the sky where we are taught what we need to know about nǀom.

"The first time I saw the big rope was in a kabi. I floated up the rope and saw the ancestors. They danced and sang for me. After that they would come to me and visit, saying, 'Hello, my friend. I want you to go hunt something.' They would help me hunt. Sometimes they would simply visit and say, 'Good-bye, I'll come to you tomorrow.'

"Though my father told me about the ancestors, I discovered them myself. The first time I went up the rope they danced with me a lot. They put me in the fire and I felt burned throughout. I still have the burn marks.

"At times, my body has felt like a cloud, or a fire, or wind whenever I am hot with nǀom. The ancestors are always there to help me. I have seen the rope to God three times. It is not something we see often, though we will feel it in each dance after we have seen it. After I saw it, I owned the feeling for it. The rope became my own thing.

"When many of us first received an arrow of nǀom it hurt. Then later the nǀom-kxao would come back and take it out so we'd feel better. A strong healer can keep doing this over and over until it no longer hurts. Those arrows can come from the giraffe, eland, oryx, or other sources."

Kaqece's father was always singing and dancing the giraffe, oryx, and eland songs. He also owned the honey song. His songs were given to him from God. When he received a song during the night he'd start singing it and the people would wake up and learn it that evening. Kaqece remembers this happening when he was a boy. He and his family would wake up and listen to their father's song and then start singing with him. Sometimes it turned into a big dance.

It happened to Kaqece later when he became an adult. "For example, my ancestral father once gave me a song in a kabi. My family woke up and sang it with me. Now our whole family owns the song. We are better with that song. When we all sing together, we also dance together as a family. We make a small fire and there we sing and dance, celebrating the newly arrived song."

Kaqece went up the rope three times. "It was like a wind taking me up. When I got to the village, I looked at the ancestors and learned from them. They gave me powerful nails. I also saw God and he gave me some nails. When I received those nails I also received knowledge and wisdom. It all happened automatically. The more nails we receive in our life, the more we know about the most important matters.

"God gave my father a nail and my father gave it to me. The nail can be passed on like this. It is delivered by a nǀom song. When such a song opens your heart it can help you receive a nail.

"The hearts of the spears teach that when we get fully cooked, we might see God's ostrich egg as we shake. This is when we feel like we are becoming a cloud. As we are able to turn into a luminous cloud, we become more like the luminous egg. The perfectly formed cloud is the egg. We return to the source from which we came."

27

ǀUi DEBE

ǀUi was regarded by his community as one of the last old time Bushman hunters. He had no interest in living any differently than his ancestors had taught him. He still made his arrows out of stone in the old way.* When there is an animal nearby in the bush, a great hunter like ǀUi feels a tapping on his arm. His heart also starts pounding and he asks, "Am I going to hunt?"

ǀUi's grandfather took him into the bush when he was very young. "That's when I learned to hunt and feel the tappings. My grandfather would ask, 'Do you feel that?' That's how I learned to feel the tappings.

"The tapping can also be along the chest or on the wrist. The tappings tell us whether it is a young or old animal, male or female. It also tells if the animal is small or large. The tapping is stronger when it is a big animal.

"If the Sky God gives us an animal, that animal will speak to our heart. Our heart will be happy, that is, it will quiver and tremble when the animal is near. God brings the animals to us. It is God who makes these things happen. God makes the animal come near us and causes our hearts to flutter with joy.

---

*Brad provided one of ǀUi's arrows for exhibition in the Origins Centre museum, Johannesburg, South Africa.

"It feels like God pulls us toward the animal and, at the same time, pulls the animal toward us. It is a pulling in both directions. The nlom-kxaosi say that God has a rope attached between the animal and the hunter. This is what God or the ancestors pull. We feel those ropes pulling us."

Whenever |Ui had a kabi of an animal, he would wake up knowing it was time to hunt. "The ancestors come to me and say, 'In the morning when you wake up, you must get up and kill this animal. But don't tell anyone. Otherwise the animal will go away.' When the animal is shown to me in a kabi, I must go and hunt alone. This is how it works for me. God or the ancestors can also tell me where the poison is—where the trees may be found with the larvae that I use on my arrows.

"God can choose a person to be a hunter of a particular animal. God gave me the kudu—that is the animal I am connected to and I am pulled toward it. God made me a kudu hunter. The kudu and I walk side by side. It's like God made a special connection between the kudu and me.

"The kudu gave me a song. When I feel its rope pulling me toward a kudu, I sing that song. I keep singing it in my heart as I am pulled toward the kudu in the hunt. I sing it during the whole hunt.

"Sometimes in a kabi, I will look into the eyes of a kudu. It makes me shake and feel nlom. I sometimes see my own eyes reflected in the kudu's eyes. That makes me really jump and feel incredibly hot. There are even times when I touch the kudu in my kabi.

"When I pull back the string of my bow and move it up and down, I am trying to find where the pull is strongest. I could close my eyes and shoot the animal because it is the pulling that aims the arrow. Shooting is more 'feeling the pull' than 'aiming with your eyes.' God makes all of this happen. I know God is present when I feel the pulling. This means that God has brought the animal to me.

"The Sky God is the hunter and I am God's bow and arrow. I feel closest to the Sky God when I feel him shooting through me. When this happens, I know the animal will die and provide meat. This makes me very happy and it makes God very happy. This is God's hunt.*

"A hunter is a special kind of nǃom-kxao doing a special kind of work for God. I am now old and my eyes are getting bad. There are only two great hunters left—my son and me. All the other great hunters have died. I still make my arrows out of bone. I will hunt until I die."

---

*This way of hunting and taking an animal's life is a way of bringing more life and nǃom into the world.

28
TCOQ'A |U|

Tcoq'a's nephew and father were n|om-kxaosi. "They told me about the lines and ropes and inspired me to become a healer. When I was a girl, they told me that those lines are special roads. Some of these lines provide a direct path to God. My father told me to always take the red road and not the green road. Red is the color of the fire that we need to survive. God gave us fire. It is a good road.* The green road can take you to trickster, where bad things can happen to you. In addition, there are lines that connect each of us. These lines are shiny.

"A bad feeling looks ugly. If I see a bad feeling it looks like a white spot on the person's flesh. If a person has clean needles, there just won't be any white spots. You see nothing on them and can say that the flesh

---

*The color red has various connotations for n|om-kxaosi because fire has different meanings. Fire is good because it enables a Bushman to stay warm at night, keep the lions away, and cook meat. It is also a bad thing for it tempts a n|om-kxao to test his power by entering it. Thus, different n|om-kxao will regard the red rope as good or bad depending upon which view of the fire they are emphasizing. Similarly, the color green can be taken as either good or bad. When it is seen as symbolic of life (the green plants are associated with life), it is good. At the same time, all of life is changing and this gives it a trickster connotation, making the color a bad rope if you view it this way.

Most n|om-kxao regard the green rope as good and the bad rope as red. The view reported here is an exception.

of this person does not have bad feelings." Tcoq'a believes that "the nee-dles of the elephant dance often look ugly in the flesh. That's a dance I don't want to be around."*

Tcoq'a recalls when a medical doctor came to visit the Ju|'hoan Bushmen. "He brought a group of tourists with him. He asked us about the nails and mentioned that he wanted to receive one. We didn't know what was wrong with that man because he said strange things. He claimed he didn't want to shake and that he did not want to dance. He demanded that we give him a nail. He then said he would teach us how to be a healer by just holding hands. He was very mixed up. He didn't know how to shake and tried to tell us that it was not necessary to shake. He was very lost, arrogant, and ignorant.

"He had a group of people and they sat in a circle holding hands. He asked me to sit with them and he held my hand. Then he asked, 'How can I renew my nails?' I said, 'You can only renew them if there is a big dance. That's where you will start to shake.' The man still didn't understand and asked, 'You mean you must shake in order to give me a nail?' I responded, 'It is you who must shake if you want to be a healer.' He remained quiet for a long time and refused to shake or believe it was important. Then he announced, 'I don't shake, but I have a better way of doing it.' We left him at that point. He sat there with the other tourists and they all held hands.

"After he departed we said to ourselves, 'What is wrong with him? What's that man doing? He doesn't understand healing at all. He

---

*Other nlom-kxaosi regard elephant nails differently. In recent years, this has become the main controversy among nlom-kxaosi in the Nyae Nyae area—whether the ele-phant dance is good or should be guarded against. Local critics of the dance point to the use of elephant nails to inflict harm on others in addition to using them for healing. Proponents of the dance believe that both ways of sending nlom are necessary depend-ing upon whether the purpose at hand is protection or promotion of health. This lat-ter way of thinking, critics add, is evidence of the manner in which trickster works as he promotes both good and bad deeds as appropriate when some are best avoided. Whatever the case, the strongest healers typically only use dances that serve love and are not tempted by any form where trickster can more easily bend the ropes.

believed that holding hands could renew the nails. He said, 'Go ahead and give me a nail. I am holding your hand. Go ahead and give me one.' We could not stop laughing. He was a pretender who only listened to trickster. No one can ask for a nail as if asking for a piece of meat or candy. God decides whether you will be a healer."

Tcoq'a's grandmother and mother gave her nails. When she was young her mother told her to keep going to the dance because there was a pot waiting for her. "I was told to drink from this pot. In the evening the people made a fire and called the girls to come and have a drink from it. While we were drinking around that fire, the healers would put a nail into us. We would cry out. They would tell us to be strong and dance hard, but not fall over. They put a nail into the back of my neck and pulled it apart so it spread across my tongue."

Tcoq'a's grandmother was a very strong nǀom-kxao. She taught Tcoq'a to be near the fire. There the trembling starts in her legs and is soon caught by her back. It moves up and down her body. After a dance she'd fall asleep and be awakened by the ancestors who would say something like, "Wake up. Why are you sleeping like this? Stand up. Let's do this dance together."

Her grandmother gave her two nails. "She told me that I must use them after she died. It was painful when I received them. Her advice was to go near the fire to help my nails get strong and wake up. The fire pushed the nails deeper into me. The fire was also important because that is the best place for the ancestors to see me. After she died I started going near the fire. I could then see my grandmother who would say, 'You are dancing like this. Now go to this side and then go to that side. Don't go into the fire, but go near it.'"

29

|XOAN |KUN

"I like remembering my grandmother because she had that special tortoise shell that she used to collect God's water. It did not appear to be any different than any other tortoise shell that the women healers use. But when her nails of n|om were hot, when she held up her shell during a dance she would receive this special water. The sky would rain a fluid into her shell. Not a drop fell anywhere else. When we drank it, n|om flowed down the inside our body. It was stronger than the touch of any healer.

"When she first gave me a drink of God's water it instantly gave me powerful nails. It is a powerful medicine. It first tastes like cool water, but it makes you hot inside. If we drink it we become a strong healer—we then no longer have a choice about healing. When I drank that water I was forced to become a healer. The water simply made me do it because it gave me a medicine that was meant for sharing. It is the strongest medicine." All the healers would drink God's water when it was available in her tortoise shell. "It seems that all the people who drank it became very kind and wanted to help others. It changed our lives when we drank it."

|Xoan's brother would even wash himself with this water. Perhaps only the Bushmen are aware of this kind of healing water and how it

is possible for a shell or cup to be filled with it if the owner is strong enough.

When |Xoan's grandmother passed away they buried the tortoise shell with her. |Xoan says, "After my grandmother passed away, she still brought me the water in my kabis—I am still able to drink the water; it tastes the same as it always did. God gave her this special gift and it changed my life. If someone was sick, she would remove the sickness from the body and put it in her hand to show the person. I was only starting to learn from her when she died.

"When she was alive my grandmother traveled to the sky on a very soft rope; she would tiptoe on it. Now she comes to me at night and we ride a horse that goes up to the sky. We go up God's rope on a horse— she travels like the wind going up to the sky.

"Once we rode away on that horse until we came to a pool of water. She told me to wash with that water and to pour it over the middle of my head. This was not God's water, but a special water from rain. She said that this would keep me from catching malaria. Everyone was suffering from that disease, but I never got sick. I have never caught malaria after washing with it. I never go the clinic because my grandmother takes care of me. She lifts me above all sickness."

|Xoan's grandmother taught that we should only use the white rope. It is the strongest and most direct rope to God. There is no need to work with the other ropes. As |Xoan remembers what her grandmother taught, "Leave the green and red ropes alone, and only handle the white rope. If we follow the green rope we may easily get lost and might disappear. It's not as strong and pure as the white rope, which means that it can bend too easily and therefore keep us from going to the sky village. While the green rope can take us to the sky village, it is riskier than the white rope. There is no need to use it over the white rope. My grandmother only used the white rope and climbed it to visit God. If we're sick we can hold on to that rope and treat ourselves with our hands. I saw her do it. She touched her head, chest, and stomach.

"There is a white rope attached to my hip. It brought me up to meet the Sky God. He touched me and gave me the strongest nails of nǀom. When God touches a person, she is turned into a specially empowered healer. I also met God's children and was touched by them. I usually meet my grandmother in the sky village. She teaches me new songs and continues to give me more nails.

"Whenever I become ill, my grandmother always visits and pours me a little of God's water. When I meet her in a kabi she usually tells me that I need to get a little bit of that water and then she pours it on the middle of my head. This is how my grandmother is still teaching me. She will wake me up in the night and tell me to get up because she has something to give me. She also tells me when Bo is coming. That's when I tell everyone that he is going to arrive so we can prepare to dance and receive some new nails from him."

"I dance today, but I miss my grandmother. She was going to teach me more about the way she dances and lifts up her arm with the tortoise shell. When she lifted up the shell, her body was shaking a lot. In the past, the old people used to tie these shells on their sides, but nowadays they are not used.

"Bo is like my grandmother and we see that he receives God's water. It's great when he dances all night and never falls. We have seen him bring and deliver this water. The ancestors and God give it to him. It means that he is clean and there is nothing bad in his heart. His nails are the hottest. He has a lot of giraffe and gǃoah nails inside of him and they are all clean needles.

"Recently I had a kabi in which the ancestors told me that Bo was coming and that they want to dance with him. They reported that he is able to see what is happening around the world. God brought him here. We are happy that Bo was given the drum. It was put in his belly so he could give birth to it. This is the old way of receiving the drum. He owns it. This is how God told him that he must play the drum. He must also use the music of the piano to wake up nails. (See editors' commentary 29.1 on page 182.) We have experienced his healing and have received nails of nǀom from him in our communities.

"Sometimes a person decides on his own that he wants to become a healer, but if he is not soft enough and his heart is not open, God will not allow him to become a healer no matter what he tries. When our heart is ready, it will rise easily and open us. That's when trickster gets out of the way and we are able to accept whatever God wants us to do."

ǀXoan's mother was a good nǀom-kxao and healer. She had the dream of the ostrich egg that cracks open. ǀXoan also had that dream. "It was in front of my face as if floating in the air and then it cracked open into two halves showing the red and green ropes on one half and the white rope on the other half. I normally only use the white rope.

"When we are standing on the rope, our voice gets lighter, higher, and stronger. This is when we can move on the rope. When we fall to the ground, it's because we're too hot and need to be cooled down or we have not learned to hold nǀom in the correct manner. It can be dangerous when we fall on the ground if we go to sleep, especially if we are inexperienced with nǀom. Our soul is at risk of being taken by the ancestors, but we don't know it when it happens. That's when the other healers have to try to bring our soul back. It is always good when we are awake while climbing the rope. You remember everything and are better able to climb safely. A strong healer must stay awake and climb the ropes. We need each other to keep us standing and going straight up.

"It's risky to fall. Walking on the rope with others is the best. When we are with another strong healer as we stand on the rope, the original Father God or the original Mother God can come into our flesh, using our bodies. This experience makes us very awake with the strongest nǀom. When the gods enter us they remove every dead part in our flesh in order to clean our nails. It's a wonderful experience. There's nothing like it. It is impossible to explain this unless one has experienced it. All of our strong healers love doing this with Bo. This is why we want him to be here all the time. (See editors' commentary 29.2.)

"After a good dance, a strong healer might stay with the other healers—usually the women healers—while the rest of the people go home. The women who are strong like to remain with a strong male healer so they will continue shaking together while the rest of the community goes to sleep. We normally do this. We come together this way after dancing. In addition, we blow a special medicine powder on each other so it can dispel any bad dreams in order to have a good sleep.

"It's important for us to be on the right ropes. We are happy when we see properly and experience all the things that can be received from God. Most people are hunting power. They have not learned how to make their heart rise. They might say they have, but if they are not singing and dancing in a strong way, then they are being misled by trickster. They are stuck in the belly; that is, they are unable to leave power behind. Without a n|om song there can be no high spiritual ascension. (See editors' commentary 29.3.)

"This is how most of the rest of the world becomes lost. Trickster convinces false spiritual teachers that they are clever enough to preach and that there is no need for them to wake up their feelings, sense differently, sing with a vibratory voice, and move spontaneously. They mislead everyone into remaining asleep and being vulnerable to all kinds of deception. The world must wake up and learn about n|om. Without a song and dance, there is no rope and no access to n|om.

"The last time Bo was here he healed me. I was in the cave and no one could lift me up. But he is strong and can ride the ropes in a good way. He brought me back. It is very natural dancing with him. He is like my grandmother."

"We have not been allowed to tell anybody about that ostrich egg because it's been our secret. For the first time, we are telling the world about the egg. It is time for the truth to be told. (See editors' commentary 29.4.) Trickster has made too many people get lost. Without the egg, you are always going to be misled by trickster or by those impersonators of teaching who are pulled by trickster and power.

"We were very surprised when Bo received God's ostrich egg. This is when we knew that it was time for the world to know about our secrets. My mother and grandmother taught me about all these things. My grandmother was one of the greatest healers, which is why she was able to receive water directly from God."

Editors' Commentary

29.1. On receiving the drum

When a person spiritually receives a drum or musical instrument, it does not matter whether he has had any previous musical training—he will be able to play the instrument spontaneously whenever his nlom is hot. This same spontaneous acquisition of musical ability has been reported in the history of the sanctified black church, where parishioners have received a vision in which they were given an instrument and found that the next day they could play. For instance, a young African-American woman who sang in a well-known choir in Minneapolis once dreamed that Jesus held her hands and walked her over a gigantic piano keyboard in the clouds. The next day she was able to play the piano.

29.2. On spiritual community

The strongest nlom arises inside interaction with others. Bushman spirituality prefers community not because of any idealistic belief about the social importance of the collective whole, but because nlom is stronger when sharing it with others. It's simply a practical matter that more people, as long as they are singing and dancing together, are able to bring forth hotter nlom that is more easily available to everyone.

29.3. On ecstasy and nlom singing

We find that some participants in ecstatic spiritual traditions (and other traditions as well) are able to feel great joy in an ecstatic ceremony, but afterward they feel discouraged because they are unable to maintain the ecstasy, joy, and energy in their everyday lives. Some may even feel depressed when they are not around other ecstatics. This is an indication of being stuck in the station of power. These ecstatic practitioners almost always are found to not have a song and do not sing throughout the day. Without a song it is very difficult to remain on the ropes to God. Climbing the rope—moving from power to love—typically requires nlom singing to keep one on track.

29.4. On telling the world about God's divine egg

In other reports on Bushman spirituality and healing (e.g., Bleek and Lloyd; Marshall; Katz; Katz, Biesele, and St. Denis, Guenther, Lewis-Williams and Pearce), the authors have hypothesized how fragments of interviews, often taken from other historical accounts, might fit together to form a cohesive view. Over these years of study and exchange with the Jul'hoan Bushmen we created a dictionary of the words that Bushman nlom-kxaosi use to discuss their healing and spiritual ways (see the appendix). The majority of these terms are not present in other published accounts on Bushman healing and religion. In other words, in these previous accounts most of the knowledge of the Bushman spiritual universe has been missed.

30

ǀKUNTA BOO

"The people have abandoned the old ways and are not using them as much today. In the past, a Bushman young man was a hunter when he married because he had to feed his family and provide animal skins for his wife. The woman used to be given by her parents to a young man. In the beginning of their marriage she was so young that her breasts were not out yet. When the sun went down every night, the young woman would make a fire at their house. When her husband went hunting with the bow and arrow, she was alone. She would isolate herself with her grandmother and wait until her husband came back.

"That's how it was in our parents' time. A young woman was protected and her husband worked for her. He went out and got the meat.* She built a fire and cooked for him. We would sit together and share the food. Following a meal, we sat by the fire and shared news. We told each other stories before we went to sleep.

"In the old days, a girl was always covered when she first menstruated and this was taken seriously. She would not look at anyone, especially the people who are dancing naked around her hut. The old men acted like eland bucks, trying to flirt and court. She wouldn't see them,

---

*Some Bushman married couples hunt together. (See Biesele and Barclay 2001.)

but she could hear them talk. The blanket never came off in the ceremony except when they had to wash her. She was afraid to look at anyone. After she finishes bleeding and is brought back into the community, she feels she has become a woman. This is the moment she feels all grown up.

"The same is true for a boy becoming a man. They make him a loincloth after his first hunt and when he shows the animal he has killed, the elders make a cut on him so that he bleeds. The old people will make a cut on his arm. This makes him a hunter for the rest of his life. It is the only cut like this he will receive for hunting. It happens only once after his first kill. In addition, they take ash from a fire and rub it on his chest. He is also told to eat the medicine parts of the animal he successfully hunted. The oldest people, especially the boy's grandfather and grandfather-in-law, eat the animal's heart. Then the other organs and meat are served to everyone else.*

"The women also used to make cuts on the sides of their face. They used the thorn of a berry to make the cut. They made an additional cut along the leg and smeared ash on it. When we are cut and the blood comes, this signals we're going into first creation and becoming the hunted. First and second creation, through dancing and cutting, are constantly being reentered. In the case of the male initiation, the young boy, the men, and the animals end up constantly exchanging roles as they traverse first and second creation. The hunter is the meat and the hunted is the hunter. It goes back and forth. The animal is the hunter and the animal is the meat. They reverse positions as they go between

---

*When the men see that a boy is starting to behave like a man and is ready to hunt, they begin an initiation. Here they must arrange for the boy to bleed so there is entry to first creation, similar to what happens with a menstruating girl. They make cuts on the boy's forehead. When he bleeds, the people are also forbidden to look at him. He enters first creation, and all the dangers found in the girl's initiation also apply to what happens to the boy. For both initiation rites, the nlom-kxaosi will wait for a sacred dream, called a kabi, or visitation with the ancestors. When this takes place, it is announced that the ancestors have joined the community, another indication that they are inside first creation.

the two creations." (See editors' commentary 30.1 on page 203.)

"Thuru is another way of transitioning back and forth between first and second creation. For instance, T!aia's mother-in-law was a person who turned herself into a lion. She was the owner of that kind of thuru and used the rope for changing into a lion. It started during a long walk when she went out to a lion. She announced that she was going to go and be with the lions. She came back with that ability and started singing as she kneeled. She owned the lion's song.

"My mother-in-law would walk like a person, but sometimes she would say, 'Today I am going to see my relatives.' She knew the lions were near and she could see what they were seeing. She had caught the feeling of the lion. Her body felt them when they were near. She could stay at home and still see them. When she caught the feeling of the lion and her heart held the lion, she could say, 'I am the owner of that lion,' meaning that she had a rope with the lion. At a dance the people would sing her song as she danced it. All the people then joined her and created the lion dance.

"There are different kinds of lions and you have to be careful which one you are dealing with. For example, there was a time when there were a lot of lions. ≠Oma was still alive at the time. Once a lion came nearby when we were sleeping and we thought it would try to kill us, but it just sat there for a while. Then the lion jumped and took our dog, running away with it. After he finished the dog, he came back to attack us. ≠Oma took a stone and threw it at the lion. He hit it and then chased it with a stick of fire. The lion went to attack the next village. This kind of lion is very skinny and has a greenish color. It is called a *n!hai !oqru*."

When |Kunta Boo was a boy, his grandfather taught him about the medicine of n|om. "My grandfather was deceased before John Marshall arrived. He gave me the medicine and then he died. After that my father took over the teaching. My grandfather also began visiting me in kabis. Whenever I saw him in a kabi, it made my heart open so much that I wept. He asked me how I was doing and whether I was waking up. He might say, 'Here you are. You grew up. Are you waking up? Here you are today with the medicine.'

"The people say that my grandfather first sang the song for the eland that is danced today. I was too young to hear him talk about the ostrich egg, but my father told me about the egg and how it is our source of life. My father was the greatest healer. He taught and cared for me. He was in the film that John Marshall made of our healing dance. He was the best nǀom kxao in those days.

"He taught me that we come from God's ostrich egg.* We are born out of it. Life comes from this egg. It holds all the needles, ropes, dances, and songs. It gave birth to all those things and then distributed them, making them available to people. My father told me that he saw that ostrich egg. He explained that all of us are getting life from the ostrich egg. The egg came to him and it cracked open. He said that other Bushmen from the past had the same experience. His elders told him this. My father mentioned that he knew others who had witnessed the egg like him.

"My father used to sing and dance often, even before a hunt. When an eland was killed we'd be very happy and sing the eland song he received. He danced twice a week. The village would dance all night after they killed an eland. There were times when we danced all week.

"When we dance all night, it is special when the sun first comes up in the morning.† This is when we feel the strongest. We feel like

---

*Some Bushmen are taught about God's ostrich egg from their nǀom-kxao parent or grandparent who is overseeing their early training; others may overhear private conversations about it. However, most Bushmen never know about God's egg unless they experience it or enter into conversations as a nǀom-kxao.

†All Bushmen agree that the strongest moment in a dance is when the sun comes up in the morning. The dance cycles throughout the night, hitting peaks of arousal and then moving into less intense expression, but sunrise always brings a sudden burst of maximal intensity. The singing becomes most enthusiastic and the energy reaches its height. We have seen Bushman nǀom-kxaosi get so strong at this time that they lift other people off the ground.

we're bursting. We might jump straight up into the air without any effort at all! The n|om medicine lifts us up. We feel like we are floating on top of the people who dance. We experience our own authority from high above. It may make us feel that we are alone in the dance.

"When I first met John Marshall and his family, I was beginning to learn about the medicine. I was starting to be a healer. While we were singing and dancing, he kept on filming us. The people told me I was becoming a great healer. They would say, 'You are learning something. Today you are becoming a big healer.' My father also said this. He'd add, 'You must keep going. When you heal a sick person, do not get afraid. Don't be scared all day long. Go ahead and heal so we can keep watching you.' When I healed a person who was dying, they thanked me very much, saying, 'That is what we want you to do.'

"My first successful healing of another person didn't take place during a dance. It took place with a few people sitting around the fire and singing very quietly. A baby boy was dying near the fire. Some people said he was already dead. We sang the healing songs. When I was told that he was dying, I immediately went to meet him and lifted him up. My nails of n|om immediately woke up. The people covered him with a blanket, thinking he was dead. He was rolled up in a blanket. I told the people to unfold him so I could feel how he was doing. People were sitting and crying so I warned them not to cry. 'You must wait until I can get the medicine.' I started healing and laying my hands on him. When I took him, he cried out. The people were surprised. I blew on the baby as I touched him. He came back to life.

"My father and grandfather would be very surprised to know that a white man knows so much about our healing. They would be very thankful that Bo is full of wisdom and is with me. God shows us that anything is possible and this gives us hope. It's a wonderful thing.

"We went to a missionary's church where some of the black people were shaking. They weren't very strong because they kept falling over.

They were not able to stand firm and climb the rope. It appeared they were scared to wake up their feelings and see properly. They were like new beginners with n|om—when the medicine caught them, they had no control. It might be a good thing if we could show the people in the Christian church how to be strong and go all the way with n|om. (See editors' commentary 30.2.)

"In the same way that we forage and gather the plants, we also forage things about God, dances, and music. If we go to another part of the country and find a group of people who have a different religion, we can also gather its gifts and include it within our own. (See editors' commentary 30.3.) We did this with the drum dances. Our healing and spirituality are always evolving and we learn one thing after another. It always comes full circle. The original ancestors danced the drum dance. Then they forgot it, while other Africans started it again, followed by us relearning from them. Sometimes it works this way.

"This is actually another example of first creation at work. A Bushman dance jumps to another culture and then it jumps back to the Bushmen. The original ancestors also knew everything about Jesus, the son of the Father and Mother Gods. He was with the Bushmen in the beginning, then the knowledge of him jumped to other cultures, and finally it came back here. All things that are true were always inside God's ostrich egg in the beginning with the first Bushmen. When they get lost or forgotten, they come back later. When a strong healer hears a story from another religion and his heart feels good about it, then he knows this has always been a part of the people.

"It's hard to teach this to ministers because trickster is too often inside of them. There's no way one's heart can be open to God and not feel good about our dance. That's not possible. If others say that our dance is bad then this means there is no God in their heart.

"Once a man was dying, but the people from a so-called 'love and ministry' church refused to let our dancers heal the person. They said that they themselves would pray for the person. They kept on saying that until the person was dead. They should have let him be healed by the healers. Though they spoke of loving God, they had neither love nor God in their hearts.*

"However, there was one missionary from Canada who came here with a good heart. He went around praying for the people and he was able to lift the sick. He trembled and shook in a good way and we could see that God was in his heart. The moment he laid a hand on a person he would shake. He was a good healer. A good preacher will understand that the love of God lives in the Bushmen's heart. If a preacher's nails are clean, he will immediately see that singing and dancing are big gifts from God.

"The big ostrich egg of the Sky God holds the truths of all religions. Everything that is true is inside the egg. If a preacher comes here with a very big heart that is filled with God, he would want to learn from the n!om-kxaosi. Then we would come together and all our hearts would get bigger. They would learn what we know: Jesus was a n!om-kxao who also loved the dance. What others call the 'Jesus power' is n!om. It comes from the egg."

!Kunta Boo visited Botswana a long time ago. That's when he met Elizabeth Marshall, who was working there. "John Marshall, the son, came and found me later, after he heard about me. John was just a boy then. He and his family spent years living here. Then he came back after his father died. Several years ago he came to visit for the last time. He said he thought he might die soon. He died shortly after that trip. He wanted a statue or monument made for him out here. It is here.

"The Marshalls were the first white people that we met. We were scared when we first saw them. We hunted a lot back then and wore animal skins. John Marshall gave me coffee for the first time. At first

---

*One missionary from Tsumkwe, now retired, confessed to Brad that he had not been able to convert a single Bushman in his entire career, which lasted for decades. He concluded, however, that "in spite of the fact that they give the Bible little importance, they are not lost souls, for it seems that God etched the ten commandments on their hearts."

we couldn't drink it, but when they added sugar it was fine. We became friends.

"When young John Marshall made the film of me dancing, we would talk about the dance and healing. I was serious about wanting him to understand. He questioned about how we got our nlom medicine. He tried to dance with us. We also tried to give him some nails of nlom. He started shaking and it scared him. He fell to the ground. When he stood, he'd fall again. He became very scared and stopped dancing. He would sit and watch after that experience. He'd say, 'No, I can't dance because I'm working behind the camera.'

"When John Marshall was an older man he brought a doctor with him who had a famous reputation as a strong Chinese healer. We were excited and gave him some nails. He passed out and remained in a coma for four days. When he woke up he said he was very sick because he felt pain in his belly. We told him he was not sick, but he was scared of nlom. He was John Marshall's friend. He didn't dance with us again after that. He was too scared.

"No one else in the Marshall family tried to dance or receive needles. They just photographed and talked. Years later a well-known anthropologist tried to be in the g!oah dance and it made her cry. The women in Botswana tried to give her g!oah needles. She was too scared. We haven't tried to give her needles since then. Perhaps God didn't want her to do this kind of work but chose her to help us in other ways.

"When John Marshall last came to Tsumkwe and said he was dying, he didn't talk about God or healing. He simply announced that we would not see him again. He said that he would soon pass away. After his early attempt to dance as a young man, he no longer wanted to know about God and nlom. He only talked about the film and projects he was doing. He was always more interested in hunting and filming. He helped us and was responsible for setting up boreholes for our villages so we could have water. He was generous and gave us what we needed during a difficult period in our history, the time when we could no longer move freely about the land and hunt as we did when I was younger.

"The Bushmen have suffered greatly over the years and John Marshall learned what we went through. It made him angry and likely affected his health. His criticism of the country's politics and treatment of Bushmen got him kicked out of South-West Africa,* because he did his best to change the atrocities going on here. The interpreter used by the Marshall family was a Heiǁom man named Nǁami. He became a close friend to John. That man could speak a lot of languages.† Nǁami told John what had happened to his family when he was a boy. It made quite an impression on John and it changed how he saw what was happening out here.

"Nǁami's family was massacred because they hunted an eland [during the late 1920s or early 30s]. The Bushmen used to be hunted in the not-so-distant past. There was widespread extermination; they shot us while we were on horseback, gunned us down at waterholes, or shipped us off to the mines as slave laborers. A law had been passed called the Bow and Arrow Act‡ that made it a criminal offense for a Bushman to possess a bow and arrow. We weren't supposed to hunt. This is why a commando group of farmers gunned down Nǁami's mother and siblings when they were hunting and dragged his father with a rope around his neck that was attached to a camel. Nǁami was caught and placed in a burlap bag and the commando farmers raised him as a pet.

"As he traveled with his master across the country he picked up the ability to speak many languages. One day somebody played a joke on him and had him drink a glass of lye. That made his voice sound sort of funny. After John met Nǁami, heard his story, and found how useful his language skills were, Nǁami became his interpreter and was with him for many years. Finally (in the early 1970s), after John

---

*South-West Africa is the former name of Namibia.

†Nǁami spoke fluent Juǀ'hoan, English, Ambo, German, Herero, and Africaans, and could conversationally handle many other African languages.

‡The Bow and Arrow Act was passed in 1927.

Marshall had been kicked out of the country, N‖ami died of malnutrition and tuberculosis when he was found in a burlap bag on the yard of a Grootfontein hospital.

"All this made John angry and he should have learned to dance to clean his nails. A human being can't handle this kind of anger and upset on one's own. We have no choice but to dance. Otherwise we would lose all hope and get sick. The Bushmen have suffered greatly, yet God has given us the most amazing way to heal ourselves. I wish John were still alive. I'm still ready to give him a nail of n‖om even after all these years.

"We also knew John Marshall's mother and sister. They mostly talked with the older people. They especially talked to the women about their affairs, wanting to know how they did things according to our tradition. The Marshalls did not talk to my father about the medicine. The strongest healers were always in the bush and didn't see the Marshalls very often. I don't think that the Marshalls ever really talked to the strong healers because the men were always hunting. That's why they didn't learn much about our healing. (See editors' commentary 30.4.)

"John Marshall brought things for us like blankets, kettles, and other practical things. He also brought us clothes. That's when we started wearing them. We were happy to receive his gifts. It was a special day when we first had clothes. After we abandoned our ways of covering ourselves with animal skins, we started using modern blankets.

"Now I wish that the children would learn to hunt again and make the old clothing. (See editors' commentary 30.5.) We need the old ways. A lot of our tradition will disappear, but maybe the dance can still remain alive. Perhaps a different kind of people will live in the modern world and keep the dance alive. If the dance survives, we can accept that everything else changes. The healing dance is the most important thing. But I am worried the dance cannot survive without our people. This is why we are grateful for Bo and N!ae. We thank them for helping keep our wisdom alive. Our grandchildren and their children will be able to learn from this work. When they hear these words, it may plant a seed in their heart and then the ancestors may come visit and teach them with nǀom."

"My sister Beh first received the giraffe song. She was my older sister. There were some men hunting many years ago and one of them killed an eland. The other men went home to get the women so they could help bring back the meat. As the women were walking toward the hunt site, two giraffes came from the south. Though they didn't know it at the time, these animals were bringing the giraffe medicine. At that moment a wind suddenly came and frightened the people. They had to run, but one of the women looked in the direction of the giraffes. She instantly caught the feeling for them and started to run like they were running. She imitated their movement.

"The giraffes passed the women as they continued to run until they reached the eland meat. When they arrived at the hunt site, the woman continued to imitate the giraffe. The men who had remained behind said, 'Hey! Why are you doing this? What are you starting?' The other women replied, 'We were on our way here and we met the tall animals. That's when these things started with her.' After the group mixed the meat with the eland fat, they ate. However, the woman did not eat. She kept shaking for the giraffe that had been given to her.

"That night her husband was awakened by her singing. He asked her, 'What is it that you are doing?' Once she started singing everyone was confused because they didn't know the song. She sang for the whole night and day until falling asleep. Some people in the village were upset by her constant singing. Most of them had learned other songs and the men were accustomed to singing the grass song. The wife said to her husband, 'You must leave that grass song. Instead, you must let us sing the giraffe song that was brought to us.' She taught her husband how to sing it and told him that he must inherit it because it is a song for the men. She said, 'You'll be getting the song, so sing, dance, and heal with it. I will be singing it for you.'

"They started singing it together and their singing became louder. The husband then told the other people, 'This song was given to me. Why not learn it with us?' The people were confused and worried whether they were being tricked. But the couple taught the people who began singing and dancing with it more often. The husband, who was a strong healer, even sang it to heal his wife, the woman who had caught the song. The people eventually accepted the song and it became the main song for the men's dance.

"Beh was given the animal nǀom of the giraffe and this is why she could bring forth its movement. When she went to sleep she experienced a kabi where the ancestors gave her the song. When she saw the giraffe running, its rope made a connection with her and initiated her going into its motion. She was full of the giraffe's nǀom as she went to sleep that night. This made her ready for the ancestors to come and bring the gift of the giraffe song.

"This happened when I was a young boy. I remember everyone talking about it. They would say, 'She got this song from the giraffe.' People kept talking about how Beh had brought us a new song. She first sang it here where we are sitting now. She was a very good healer. She would tell me, 'I received this song from the giraffe.' Beh had earlier received a needle of nǀom in her neck that made her shake very hard as a woman nǀom-kxao. She was so strong with nǀom that she was able to receive the giraffe song and give it to the men for their dance."

"The Sky God lives in the eastern sky, while trickster lives in the western sky where the sun goes down. They both have wives and children, but the Sky God has a lot more children.

"Recall that when a person is born, if the weather is a certain way, then the gǁaoansi will give her a spirit like that weather. If it's a beautiful and perfect day, the newborn's spirit will be like that. The nicer the weather, the luckier a person is in terms of the received spirit. It is very good if one is born on a rainy day. That's the best condition. Beh was very lucky. She was born on such a good day and it helped her bring us a very special nǀom song.

"If a person is born during the rain, she will be asked when she grows up to throw a powder made from the bloodwood tree into the fire to help it rain. She will then take a piece of her hair and throw it into the fire. Its smoke will go up and help bring down the rain. When such a person is born we say, 'You are rain.'

"To own nǀom you must have a nǀom song. You can be touched by nǀom, even deeply shaken by it or knocked out by its impact, but you cannot own it without a nǀom song in your heart that is sung without inhibition or restraint. Nǀom emerges with the raised feeling that comes when the heart receives and expresses a song from God's creation.* This is why bees, honey, water, and rain all have nǀom. They each have a song. The nǀom from the bee (zo) is particularly strong. Size does not matter—a bee can deliver more nǀom than an elephant if you own the deepest feeling for it. Good luck, joy, and true spiritual prosperity come to you when you own nǀom.

"It is very important to understand that when a girl first menstruates she goes back and forth between first and second creation. It's dangerous to be next to someone like that because it could start to pull you back into first creation. Anything that swings between life and death, a big changing, is very dangerous to be around because it can pull us into first creation.

"Similarly, we wouldn't want to eat something while standing next to a healer who is awake with very strong nails. That could also be dangerous. The same is true being near someone who just had a baby. Even when we're at a dance and the music is strong, we would not say the

---

*Although Bushman researchers have long recognized the importance of nǀom, they did not report how its expression took place inside a more encompassing contextual frame. Defined as "spiritual energy or power" by Katz, Biesele, and St. Denis (1997, 202) and "medicine" by others (e.g., Lee 1984, 103), for a Bushman the most highly charged nǀom paradoxically goes past the experience of power. It is a move away from power, in its earliest inception, to the awakening of one's heart at its fullest development (Keeney 2003b) that brings forth music.

name of that song, because at that moment it's too dangerous. It's too powerful. If we said the name of the song, we might get an unexpected nail. We don't even say the word *nlom* at such a time. This is when we have to use the respect name for nlom, *tco*. If we are feeling a giraffe arrow, tchisi, we must only say its respect name, ≠*oah tchisi*. Similarly, when we feel the Sky God, we cannot say his name, !Xun!a'an. We have to say his respect name, G≠kao N!a'an.*

"When we tell a story about first creation and the first ancestors, the story must change all the time to maintain the changing that expresses nlom. When we're telling the story, our voice must also change. When we give the story, it must have nlom or we are wasting our time telling it. If someone tries to explain what it means, they will drain the nlom out of it. If we tell a story well enough, providing unexpected changes and keeping it clear of explanation, it will have so much nlom that someone can actually receive a needle.

"We call the first ancestors the original grandparents. They had special nlom and abilities. There was a man named Glla'inkodin who could just stare at something and it would move. The first people knew everything, and even today when we open our hearts they are still able to give us what they know. They teach us how to change our voice when it has nlom. They teach us how to see properly, hunt, make poison arrows, sing, and dance, among other things.

"The great Sky God created everything. He gave gifts to the people who had to pass on their knowledge to the next generation. The original grandparents are still teaching today. It's not just the close relatives who help us. The original ones are also active in our lives. They tell our ancestors what we need to know. Our family ancestors carry the messages from the original ancestors.

"In the sky is God's village. When we go into the waterhole

---

*Uttering the name of something that has nlom is a dangerous thing to do, as it risks the consequence of throwing first creation into second creation, thereby eliminating its nlom. Or first creation may not allow this transition and strike down (or change) the name and he who is naming.

classroom, there's a world that's underground and it also holds God's village. When we go above into the sky, it's not scary. The sky village is in both places. At each end of God's rope is found his home—one above and one below. But when we go below we have to conquer our fear. Loving God takes us up, but trusting God takes us down. When we go up, we feel love. When we go down and follow the good rope, we feel and say, 'I trust you God.' This is an advanced lesson. After we feel the big love for God, then we have to conquer fear. To be fully cooked, we must get past fear. This is why we may be sent under the ground into the deep waterhole.

"God's village is very beautiful and splendid. Its special healing water is found there and a drink of it can instantly heal and completely transform a person's life. However, God can meet us in different places and give us the nǀom water anywhere. He lives in many different places. It is even possible to find God in the ocean. He can take us to all kinds of places. In addition to the main camel thorn tree in his sky village there is also a big tree that has fruits, called ǁkaquh din. It is his tree for food. However, the oldest and most important tree is the camel thorn.

"God lives in the heart while trickster dwells in the mind. Trickster might say, 'You shouldn't pay attention to the heart because the heart is for children. You should grow up and listen to all the clever things that I am going to teach your mind.' That's the way trickster tries to get us to not pay attention to the god in our heart. God always aims straight for the heart. Trickster never gets into the heart, just the mind. When we catch the feeling of God, our heart rises above our mind and fills it with God's thoughts. When we have trickster in our head and it oversees our heart, we will feel all mixed up and frustrated. We must lift our heart so that it holds our mind, rather than drop our heart so that trickster can put mind on top. When our heart is full of God, all our thoughts and feelings will walk together in a good way.

"We look and see whether a person knows God by seeing whether they have nails and arrows of nǀom inside them. A person who has no nǀom but talks a lot about God is definitely under the influence of trickster. If we want to find out who's a trickster and who owns the feeling for God, we start singing the nǀom songs and see whether they tremble and shake. We also tell the old stories that keep changing and see how they react. This is when we can see who has nǀom and can be trusted to speak about God.

"Trickster can influence even our everyday decisions. Once I found my mother cooking flies. She asked me if I wanted to eat them and she was serious. She asked me to choose the food I would eat. I chose meat and she asked again if I wanted to eat the flies. She was testing me to make sure I remained wise."*

ǀKunta Boo reminds us of what his grandfather taught him: "Trickster is also important. Sometimes he helps us and sometimes he doesn't help. God tells trickster what to do. God is the one who can tell him to trick us. The same is true of the ancestors. They can tell us where to go, including indicating where to find an animal. They are all like a guide. The gǁaoansi sometimes will say, 'This is where the animal is,' and it's true. Or if you are lost, they might say, 'This where the village is,' and it's true. At other times they may trick us. Trickster can say, 'Go there,' and it's not true. He can either help or cause harm. He can do three things that are dangerous: steal our arrows, make them dirty, and get us lost."

As ǀKunta Boo was taught, "First we must ask help from God. If God tells trickster to tell us exactly where the animal is, it is smart to follow. Essentially, the big Sky God gives orders to the little god or teaches the little god how to help. He also gives the orders to the gǁaoansi."

When ǀKunta Boo was learning to be a healer he would follow a white rope that took him to an underground place. "It also has a village where the first people live. When I arrived there they taught me

---

*Her absurd question not only reminded ǀKunta to be wise, but it also demonstrated how absurd and astray from wisdom he can find himself should he be influenced by trickster and fail to walk on the right ropes.

what to do. They gave me some important nǀom songs. I also traveled up to God and learned similar things in the sky village. We learn the same things whether we go up or below. When we go up, we bring the sky village down so others can feel it. When we go down, we bring that village up. It's the same rope and either direction brings the same thing."

ǀKunta Boo's teacher in the spiritual classrooms is an ancestral spirit. "He was my brother-in-law. We were good friends when he was alive. He was older than me and now I visit him in the spirit hole. That's the ancestor I meet when I go down the rope. There I receive nails. There's another ancestor, an old woman, who also gives me strong nails. Her nails make my legs tremble, and then after it comes up my body it makes my head pulse.

"I always have dreams about Bo where I watch him dancing. We have never seen a white person dancing as a healer. We are surprised that a white person is a heart of the spears and knows everything about nǀom. Other people in different villages really want to see how he dances. We are thankful that is he is like the healers from the old days.

"When I was a boy, I knew I would be a man when the tapping started. It started when I was ready to hunt. If it tapped on my left arm, it meant that there was a female animal I would hunt. When I felt it on the right side, it was a male animal. It's a light tapping. If it was felt high on my arm near the shoulder, it meant that the animal would take a long time to catch. All this started to happen the first time I killed an animal in a hunt. I felt a pulling toward the animal and manhood.

"When I was a boy I asked my father to give me a nail. In the old days, they called them thorns. He told me that he was putting an ancestor into my body. The first time he did this, it was painful. I wanted to fall to the ground. He kept giving me nails and I became stronger."

ǀKunta Boo believes it is important for the Bushman people to know that it is fine for a nǀom-kxao to have elephant, giraffe, and gǃoah needles, among others, if they are fully cooked. "I, ǀKunta Boo, can handle all the arrows and nails. When a nǃom-kxao holds multiple forms of nǃom it is called *nǃom-tzisi*. For those holding only one kind of nǃom it is called *nǃom-tzi*. It can be dangerous for someone who is not strong and hasn't been fully cooked to have different nails. For them to have both elephant and giraffe arrows would be dangerous because the arrows might compete. When that happens, a strong healer must separate the arrows and nails. They pull out one kind and leave in the other kind. People who dance the giraffe are scared about the elephant because they're afraid they'll mix. Those who know the elephant can be scared of getting giraffe.* It goes both ways.

"A heart of the spears can handle everything and tries to learn all there is to know. I also dance the grass dance. It was like the gǃoah dance. I was still young when the grass dance was around. Later I learned the giraffe dance and most recently the elephant dance. All the dances awaken my nǃom and bring me close to God. (See editors' commentary 30.6.)

"I learned about the ropes in my visions. The good and bad spirits have different ropes. The best ropes are the ones that take us to God. The next best ropes go to the ancestors;† some of them are good and others are bad. Then come the ropes or strings to living people that help us be aware that someone is coming. After that are the ropes to the animals. Before a hunt you feel it pulling on you. Finally, when you need a medicine plant, there is a rope from the plant that can bring you to it. The world of the nǃom-kxao is a world made of many ropes.

---

*However, most people who own the elephant dance have no fear of the giraffe dance or gǃoah dance. Fear is typically associated with adding the elephant dance to their repertoire.

†Some Bushman nǃom-kxaosi who speak about having a rope to an ancestor also mention that this ancestor's spirit lives inside of them. From a Bushman perspective there is little difference between having an ancestral spirit inside and having an ancestral rope. The ancestor is sometimes regarded as a "little god." When either is awakened—the little god or the ancestral rope—it brings forth owning the ancestor and the ancestor's presence is immediately felt as having influence on whatever is taking place.

"A healer must keep his arrows and nails clean so his body can feel the pulling of the strings. White people and black people outside our villages, in other parts of the world, have broken many ropes. When people break ropes, it is dangerous for all living things. It pulls us apart. Only the ropes can bring us back together.

"Life is held inside the strings and ropes that make the lines of relationship. Anything that breaks the ropes and strings brings death and sickness. When the ropes are broken the heart cannot function well. When people do wrong things, like steal or try to hurt somebody, this makes the strings weak. We are shocked that most people in the world do not know about the ropes. They are spiritually blind; they don't see the ropes and don't realize that as they break them, they are putting the whole world at great risk. This ignorance is dangerous and threatening to life.

"It's very important for the young people and the future to never forget the ropes and strings. They must dance to make the good ropes stronger. This dancing along with the work of our n!om-kxaosi keeps the world alive and healthy by helping the ropes and strings become strong.* God made us the first people and our job has been to serve life by keeping the ropes strong. Now others must help us because our way of life is being threatened."

When |Kunta Boo traveled through the stars and God took him to the beginning, there was a tree that only had little bit of green on it. "This suggested to me that right now life is barely alive. The strings and ropes need to be made strong for life to flourish. The ropes we love must come fully alive and awakened again, so that the bodies of people and our land can thrive."

---

*The Bushman ecological view concerns the ropes that connect living forms and the ways we make them weak or strong. N!om-kxaosi have a responsibility to sing and dance with n!om in order to make the ropes strong, and in so doing, contribute to the well-being of the whole ecology.

Editors' Commentary

30.1. On continual reentering of first and second creation in initiation rites

In the girl's initiation rite, blood marks an entry to first creation. In the beginning act of the ritual, those not bleeding remain outside first creation and are vulnerable to being harmed. However, when they bleed and "catch the feeling for the changing," they now enter inside first creation— the second act of the ritual.

In the reentry into first creation, feelings of identification with animals, shifting forms, and identity with ancestral eland people are all encountered. The songs and dance maintain the intensity of this contextual shift. In the girl's initiation rite, when her bleeding stops, the final act of the initiation—reentry into second creation—occurs. This is why a naming ceremony takes place, as the girl is introduced to each community member as if she were meeting them for the first time.

The subsequent reentry into second creation, following an immersion inside the changing of first creation and the experience of its nlom, results in a revitalization, healing, and rebirth for the entire community. Not only are everyone's weapons recharged for more successful hunting, the doctor's capacity for healing is fine-tuned and amplified. The ritual helps the entire community, soothing any existing tensions and giving new hope for the future. It also gives new life to the surrounding environment, including the soil and the sky, possibly attracting rain.

The cycle of renewal includes a reentry into first creation followed by a reentry into second creation. Bushman epistemology carries the implicit recognition that it is neither first nor second creation that is preferred but the never-ending reentry or crossing from one to the other. Nlom is found in this passage, and every girl or boy who becomes an adult helps the entire community reenter the circularities of change that infuse nlom into their everyday existence by embodying the changing that underlies creation. Inside the n!o'an-kal'ae, or changing, is the possibility for reentry into the next changing. Although appearing to be another chapter or developmental stage, it is actually the circularity of the changing of creation.

30.2. On "holy ghost power" and nlom

While most Bushmen have met missionaries who have tried to convert them and who have generally been critical of the healing dance, there have been occasional visits by evangelical Christians whose charismatic way of expressing their faith is appreciated by some nlom-kxaosi. This is the case only when the nlom-kxaosi observe authentic ecstatic body movement and aroused vocal expression that hosts nlom. As lKunta Boo suggests, however, these energetic ministers are beginners with nlom (or the "holy ghost power") and do not know what to do with it. They are unable to withstand escalating the energy and allowing the nlom to initiate natural healing responses, such as the pulling familiar to Bushman nlom-kxaosi, nor are they able to effectively transmit nlom.

30.3. On borrowing from other spiritual traditions

For instance, today most Bushmen will often refer to trickster as Satan. Some nlom-kxaosi have had visitations to the sky village where they meet one of God's sons and describe him as "someone who can clean you." While this may appear to be identified with Christian religion, keep in mind that those same nlom-kxaosi are as likely to say that the task can be done by God's daughter or wife as well.

Spiritual traditions that borrow from multiple religions are common throughout the world. Consider the diverse Caribbean syncretic forms and the ways in which various American Indian religions were mixed with other ideas and practices as found in the presence of Christian beliefs in the Ghost Dance and peyote rite.

30.4. On outsiders learning about Bushman healing

In more than twenty years of working with the Bushmen, Brad has not heard about any other visitors who were accepted as a nlom-kxao other than he and Hillary Keeney. Most others were either regarded as pretending, not soft enough to receive a nail, or not strong enough to hold the medicine in a good way. There were several visitors who had a heart for healing and were identified as having potential for receiving nails and growing as nlom-kxaosi if they had an opportunity and community that supported it.

30.5. On gifts to the Bushmen from outsiders

Some Bushman elders and outside regional farmers who have helped the Bushmen over the years have said that beginning with the arrival of the Marshalls, "the anthropologists and other visitors ruined Bushman culture with kindness." By this they mean that gifting the Bushmen with clothes, food, sugar, coffee, tea, tobacco, and the like removed some of the necessity to hunt and maintain the old ways. Of course, it is a double-bind situation, where the Bushmen both want and need outside gifts while regretting the long-term impact those gifts may have on disrupting their cultural traditions.

30.6. The dancing entry into first creation

All Bushman nlom dances involve entry into first creation, where the changing or n!o'an-kal'ae is embodied by a trembling ecstatic healer. Here a nlom-kxao's identity, form, or expression can constantly morph at any moment. Bushman healers first feel an emotional intensity that amplifies until they experience the world whirling, a passage across the boundary between second and first creation. As their bodies start to shake, they are more inclined to sing than speak, for the emotional intensity encourages rhapsodic forms of expression. Their singing is inspired improvisation that triggers additional body automatisms, the effortless trembling that feels as if the mind has less conscious control over one's performance. Narrating and evaluating mind give way to improvised spontaneous movements, rhythm, and music. More ecstatic engagement with others is fostered, resulting in interactions that aim to inspire healing and transformation.

First creation reentry is again used as a means of accessing nlom. Dance serves this crossing and contributes to maintaining presence inside first creation once it has been reached. Songs are sung to move bodies, while dancing brings forth more spirited singing, as healers and community try to get outside the bounded frames that habituated distinctions prescribe. When a nlom-kxao is full of nlom, or "fully cooked," he loses the capacity for speech and can only sing musical tones or make improvised sounds. This is when healing interactions are most potent. As the nlom-kxao places his trembling hands and body onto another person and sings in a spirited way, it is contagious. The other person, if ready (or "soft"), will then catch the trembling, signifying a readiness for receiving an arrow of nlom. In this way, the awakening of one person functions to share an exhilarated performance with others. Healers are like lightning rods that first catch nlom, but do so to spread it into the whole community.

Bushmen live to "hunt nlom," as Bushman nlom-kxaosi often phrase it. Puberty rites, storytelling, and healing dances all serve this hunt. Each is an opportunity to cross from second to first creation and then to return. Bleeding together is transformed into collective dancing and singing. Laughing together at a story helps awaken the body trembling that encourages entry into the changing. All provide reentries into first creation where transformation resides as it shifts stuck forms and sets up opportunities for change.

The Bushman dance stages the general paradigm for all Bushman transformative performance. The singing, dancing, laughing, and trembling of Bushman performers are all variations of the enactment of change, inspired by heightened feelings. If a giraffe suddenly runs across the horizon and a Bushman "catches the feeling for it," as it did for Beh, the nlom-kxao may receive an inspired song, which in turn is shared with the people. Hearing the story and singing the song bring forth imitated movements of the giraffe and the emergence of a giraffe dance. All serve entry into first creation, where one may become experientially indistinct from a giraffe if ecstatically inspired by the latter's movement and presence. This is done to help bring the whole community into first creation, where their relations with giraffes also participate in the invigorated healing of one another.

Bushman nlom-kxaosi sometimes claim that they own god or a giraffe—that is, they own an intense feeling for them. Such ownership requires a song that expresses the felt relationship with the other. In that relationship is found a bridge that carries the nlom-kxao to becoming undifferentiated from the other, whether experienced as a sympathetic resonance or as a fantasized morphing of identity. Though second creation always sits inside first creation, without ecstatic arousal a storyteller, singer, or dancer does not always go past a conceptualization and actually feel this inclusion. Similarly they do not always feel an identity with a giraffe, eland, or god. The entry to first creation is perhaps more accurately portrayed as an entry into a sung, danced, or ecstatically voiced relationship with the other, and in so doing emotions are heightened to feel a unity that linguistic distinctions previously distanced.

The Bushmen's hunt for nlom is always the journey of carrying a song to the other. When a hunter goes looking for a kudu, he sings a vision-given kudu song. It helps him feel a relationship with the animal, and for a strong hunter, the relationship is dreamed and later regarded as a rope connecting him to the animal. The rope refers to the song lines that connect living forms—performances of relationality and connectivity. First creation, in other words, is a way of pointing to the sanctification of relations. In first creation, all relations are strengthened and the song lines connecting living forms enable heartfelt transport to ownership of any and all possible identities. Here we transcend culture, gender, and species, in favor of being a transient, changing participant who finds life inside the acts of recursive creative change, the expression and circulation of creation.

APPENDIX

Dictionary of the Ju|'hoan Religion

Words Used by the N|om-kxaosi

Beesa Boo and Bradford Keeney

Readers can go to www.keeneyinstitute.org/judictionary.php to hear an audio recording of Beesa Boo pronouncing these words.

!aaiha: A n|om-kxao at the second station of n|om, who can now heal by pulling out sickness.

|Ae-N≠unhn: The ancestor who sends down n|om drink from God. This drink is God's urine and looks like water.

≠ahmi: Refers to Bushmen as "circle people" and the circles around the sun and moon that remind people of important things.

≠ahmia-khoe juasi: Another way of referring to the circle people and seeing everything move in circles.

!ai: Mortal death. This word has no association with !aia, the waking up of a n|om-kxao.

!aia: Waking up your strongest feelings and being reborn.

!Ai||aah: A mask of death that looks like an animal head and that, when placed on you, causes sickness.

ǁ'ai and ǁoq'm: Grass associated with the oryx and gemsbock in second creation.

ǁ'ai djxani: The grass dance.

!ai-tcia: Something dangerous and deadly, such as poison, lightning, and serious illness.

ǁan: When people hear a song from a faraway village or from the ancestors and they feel they have to go to the dance.

≠ang: A bush, which, when combined with animal fat, is used to make medicine for men's tortoise shell and used to heat a nǀom-kxao in a dance by smudging with smoke; also used to help illness leave the body.

ǀ'an-jukonaqnisi: A kabi in which you receive nails of nǀom.

ǀAqn-ǀaqnce: Sky God's wife's name, which means "Mother of Bees."

≠ara-khoe: Shaking of a nǀom-kxao's heart onto another person's heart.

are: Love, which is the most important word for a nǀom-kxao.

ǁauh: Another word for a needle of nǀom.

ǁauhsi: Sky God's needles, which hold nǀom.

ca-ca: Plant root used to protect boys and girls from dangerous nǀom associated with menstruation or following the delivery of a baby.

cunkuri: A particular kabi when you see the Sky God or ancestors.

da'a: A fire in the sky seen by nǀom-kxao when traveling along a rope or thread.

djxani: Dance.

djxani-kxao: A nǀom-kxao who is dancing.

djxani-!uhsi: Two nǀom-kxaosi shaking together.

dshau-nǃa'anaoǁxai-gǃoqma: Old woman who makes scary sound in a dance.

ega: "Something for me," the message of the body tappings.

gǃa'ama-ju: When a nǀom-kxao catches the sick feeling of an animal.

gǃa'ama-nǃausi: The second experiential station of a nǀom-kxao, where the heart rises. This is when healing can take place.

gǁabesi soahn: This means "the gǁabesi is soft," that is, ready to receive needles.

gǁabesi tuih: The waking up of the gǁabesi (abdomen) and needles; the experience may include a feeling of heat and tightness in the belly.

g≠aihg≠aing≠ani: Time when there was no speech (later called first creation).

Gǂain-gǂaingǂani: First creation.

Gǁa'inkodin: An original ancestor who stared at things and made them move.

gǁaoah da'atzi: Healing songs to quietly sing around a home fire.

gǁaoanǂ'angsi: The original ancestors.

gǁaoan ǁkoa !a'ansi: Little gǁaoansi children from long ago.

gǁaoansi: Ancestral spirits, trickster spirits, or spirit of God (singular: gǁaoan).

gǁaoansi tchi: Arrows of sickness.

gǂaqba-n!a'an: "Heart of the spears," referring to the most powerful nǀom-kxaosi.

gǁauan-nǀhai: Laughing caused by ancestral spirits.

Gauh-!o: Mother of the original ancestors.

Gǂkao N!a'an: Respect name for the Sky God.

Gǂkao Na'an: Father of the original ancestors.

G!kunǁhomdima: Woman in first creation who first blew a horn.

g!oah: Name of dance with song and nǀom from the g!oah plant.

g!oahnaqnisi: G!oah needles of nǀom.

g!oah nǀoma: Nǀom from g!oah plant.

g!oan: A plant whose roots are ground to a red powder and used by men for good luck in a hunt.

g!o'e djxani: Oryx dance.

g!oh: Steam (needles that are fully cooked are called g!oh).

gua: Beginning of !aia, when you first feel the power of the fire.

gua-gua: When the fire has big flames.

gu-tsau: The clapping that lifts the dancer's legs in a dance.

G!xa maq: Breathing out the soul.

G!xoa: Name of second creation, which means "now there is speech."

G!xoa-g!xoa koarasi: The Knee Knee None people, creatures without knees about which little is known.

!'hana: Dance stick used by nǀom-kxao to give needles to others through pointing.

ǁhannǀang: Top of head where needles can be given; the place where fully cooked needles (turned to steam) exit the body.

!'han-n!ang: Inside of the waterhole that some nǀom-kxaosi visit in a kabi.

l'hare: Being very happy while dancing in one spot.

hatce koe du kxui mi ≠'angsi: Expression for "what is making me think this way?" referring to how trickster enters the mind.

≠hoe: Pulling out sickness with your hands.

≠hoe djxani: Healing dance.

!'huhn: Name of the sound made when releasing sickness.

!hui: Rope to God.

!huijuasi: The "straight line people" who aren't Bushmen (e.g., white people).

ju ka g≠om: The moment when a nǀom-kxao is so full of nǀom that she can no longer speak but can only sing.

ju!kag!ua: The liquid around the heart caused by anger.

kaakare: The dizziness of nǀom-kxaosi after a dance—this dizziness is caused by nǀom.

kabi: A visitation or sacred vision from the Sky God or ancestors.

!kabi: When the nǀom-kxao sees first creation in the dance, experienced as a constant whirling.

!kaihn: A form of gǁaoansi nǀom, used by gǁaoansi to trick a person into following a bad direction.

kaoha-kxo: God's pot that he cooks a nǀom-kxao in.

kaqian: Gǁaoansi nǀom used to make you sick or die.

ǁkaquh din: Fruit-bearing tree in Sky God's village, referred to as "the tree of death."

!ka tsau l'an: When the heart rises.

!kau: Feeling of shock on fingertips that means that a lion is near.

kau-hariri: The actual sound made by a nǀom-kxao when illness is pulled.

!ku: God's tree that holds the medicine water.

!kunsi: Respect name for gemsbock people.

kxaetci!hun: Tapping on body that means it is time for hunting.

kxae≠xaisi: Seeing properly, or "seeing the feelings."

kxae ǀxoa: Soul (the living self with its memories).

kxao-kxaoa!kui: Ostrich feather decoration for nǀom-kxao.

maniju≠'angsi: Turning against someone.

Manisi n!a'an-n!a'an: "The great turning around," referring to the beginning of second creation.

Maq: Thread for any ancestral spirit, whether good or bad.

maqdore: The strange wind used for attack and protection by a nǀom-kxao.

Mba-n!a'an: Great Father; how Sky God is addressed in prayer.

mi-nǀai-dci: Expression meaning "my head is wet from God's water."

n≠ah: Buffalo thorn tree associated with kudu in second creation.

n≠ahn: The camel thorn tree in the Sky God's village.

n!aih-ǀho: Place where we make a fire for dancing and healing.

n!aihsi: Old word for needle of nǀom.

n≠a'mǀ'an: Tapping that ancestors and God make on the body.

n!ang djxani: The eland dance.

n!ang-nǀaisi: Eland-headed tribe.

n!angsi: Eland-headed people.

n!ang tchisi: Other animal arrows of nǀom.

n!ang !xui: Tail of an eland used by a nǀom-kxao in the dance.

n!ao: Spirit of weather conditions at birth, giving good or bad luck to the person and the community.

n!aoah-ma: Beginning healers.

n!aroh-ma: A novice nǀom-kxao.

n!aroh-ǁxam: The first experiential station of a nǀom-kxao where the power of fire is experienced, the place where you must meet and deal with fear.

n!'haam: Spider.

n!'haam-n!'haam: Spider web of nǀom that covers the head of a nǀom-kxao in an attempt to stop healing by blocking the nǀom-kxao from seeing sickness.

n!hai djxani: Lion dance.

n!hai !oqru: A very dangerous skinny green lion.

nǀhaitzi: Good feeling when laughing together with friends.

n≠hang: A red pigment from the Sky God's special plant that the Sky God rubs on a person for protection—this takes place in a kabi.

nǀhuin: Spirit (breath).

nǀhuin n'ang: Breathing in (bringing back) the soul.

n!huru: Aloe plant associated with eland in second creation.

nǀoa: Bush associated with the eland in second creation.

n≠oahn: When the ancestors make strange sounds through the nǀom-kxao.

n!o'an-kaI'ae: The original force that changes everything.

n!o'an-nIom: Deliberately throwing a dirty arrow to hurt someone through black magic.

nIIoaq!'ae: A bush used for making perfume made of ground leaves and used to cool a nIom-kxao in the dance.

nIom: Non-subtle, vibratory life force that comes directly from God, recognized by the Bushmen to animate all living beings and to be the source of all inspired energy.

nIom-da'a: The fire inside the nIom-kxao.

nIom-kxao: Owner of nIom.

nIom-tzi: Singular nIom (for example, applied to a nIom-kxao who only has giraffe arrows).

nIom-tzisi: Multiple forms of nIom (for example, a nIom-kxao who has several kinds of arrows).

n!uan-ju: Refers to the spirit of an animal standing on top of a person to help heal them.

n!uan-tso: Standing or climbing on the rope to God.

n≠u'uhan: Someone pretending to be a nIom-kxao.

n≠u'uhan-kxaosi: Those who show off or boast about their nIom.

≠oah djxani: Giraffe dance.

!'oahn: "Open up the heart" (the most important teaching for a nIom-kxao).

≠oah naqnisi: An arrow of nIom from the giraffe.

≠oah tchisi: The respect name for giraffe arrows of nIom.

II'ora: Women's tortoise shell for holding medicine.

qaqm: "To awaken," used to refer to cause of !aia—analogous to striking a match. When lit, the nIom-kxao is in gua, the first stage of !aia. The fullest !aia is thara.

sanIIae: "Sinew," the old word for thread traveled on by a nIom-kxao.

san !auah: A women's bag for holding perfume, made of animal hide.

ta'ma kaice gIaoh: Very strong feeling.

ta'msi: Feeling.

Tau: NIom string.

tchi-nIIhan: Sending a deadly animal, such as a snake, to harm someone.

tchisi: Arrow of nIom.

tci-dore: Name for trickster that is used when a person is angry with him.

Tci-nǀoa ǁah jan: Hat from Sky God that is received in a kabi.

tco: Respect name for nǀom.

tco-kxao: A nǀom-kxao powerful enough to give needles to others.

tco-tcaq: Sweat; for a nǀom-kxao who is dancing, the sweat is a medicine used to help give needles to others.

thara: Shaking caused by nǀom.

thara nǀom: The third experiential station of a nǀom-kxao, the station at which new nails of nǀom can be given.

thuru: When a nǀom-kxao changes form into an animal or anything else.

tjin-kxuisi-tsa'an-tsa'an: The scary sound made by the old woman in a dance.

tso: Thread for lion thuru; that is, for changing into a lion.

ǀ'ua-nǀom: Giving a needle to another person.

ǀ'u a ǃxui: An animal chasing its tail—a way of referring to changing circles.

ǃ'uhn: Nǀom-kxao's sound made when pulling out sickness or dirty needles.

≠umsi ǃXu: Religious beliefs about God and healing.

≠um ǃXu kokxui: Refers to the belief in God brought about by the love you feel for God.

ǃ'un: A dream.

ǃuu: Dance skirt.

≠uuma-khoe: Sharing.

waqdohm: Tortoise shell to wear in a dance that is decorated with bullet shells to scare lions and gǁaoansi away.

xaam: Respect name of the lion.

ǁxaece: When a nǀom-kxao protects himself by pushing back another person's anger.

xaro: Gift.

ǃxaua-khoe: Ignorance caused by being selfish and greedy. It is the opposite of love.

ǁxoan: The heavy breathing sound of climbing the rope to God.

ǃxo' djxani: Elephant dance.

ǃXu dsuu-nǃo: God's ostrich egg.

ǃXu gǃu: Sky God's medicine water.

ǃXu hui mi: Words of an often used prayer meaning "God help me."

!Xu-kxao: "I am an owner of God," that is, "I am the owner of the feeling of love for God."

!Xun!a'an: Sky God.

ǀxuri kxaosi: Tricksters.

xurua o nǀom ga: Man's tortoise shell for holding medicine.

!Xu tci: Gift from the Sky God.

zo: The bee, favored by Bushmen for both its sweet tasting honey and strong nǀom.

BIBLIOGRAPHY

Akstein, David. *Un Voyage a Travers la Transe: La Terpsichore Transe-Therapie.* Paris: Editions Sand, 1992.

Bateson, Gregory. *Steps to an Ecology of Mind.* New York: Ballantine, 1972.

Biesele, Megan. *Women Like Meat: The Folklore and Foraging Ideology of the Kalahari Ju'hoan.* Johannesburg, South Africa: Witwatersrand University Press, 1993.

Biesele, Megan, and Steve Barclay. "Ju'hoan Women's Tracking Knowledge and Its Contribution to Their Husband's Hunting Success." *African Study Monographs* 26 (2001): 67–84.

Biesele, Megan, and Robbie Davis-Floyd. "Dying as Medical Performance: The Oncologist as Charon." In *The Performance of Healing,* edited by Carol Laderman and Marina Roseman, 291–322. New York: Routledge, 1996.

Biesele, Megan, and Robert K. Hitchcock. *The Ju'hoan San of Nyae Nyae and Namibian Independence: Development, Democracy, and Indigenous Voices in Southern Africa.* New York: Berghahn Books, 2011.

Bleek, Wilhelm, and Lucy Lloyd. *Specimens of Bushman.* London: G. Allen, 1911.

Bleek, Wilhelm, Lucy Lloyd, and Dorothea Bleek. "The Bleek and Lloyd Archive" housed at the University of Cape Town Library, Cape Town, South Africa. Digitally accessible at http://lloydbleekcollection.cs.uct .ac.za.

Connor, Steve. "World's Most Ancient Race Traced in DNA Study." *The Independent,* May 1, 2009.

Dickens, Patrick. *English-Juǀ'hoan, Juǀ'hoan-English Dictionary*. Koln, Germany: Rudiger Koppe Verlag, 1994.

Goffman, Erving. *Frame Analysis: An Essay on the Organization of Experience*. London: Harper and Row, 1974.

Guenther, Mathias. *Tricksters and Trancers: Bushman Religion and Society*. Bloomington: Indiana University Press, 1999.

Katz, Richard. *Boiling Energy: Community Healing among the Kalahari !Kung*. Cambridge, Mass.: Harvard University Press, 1982.

Katz, Richard, Megan Biesele, and Verna St. Denis. *Healing Makes Our Hearts Happy: Spirituality and Cultural Transformation among the Kalahari Juǀ'hoansi*. Rochester, Vt.: Inner Traditions, 1997.

Keeney, Bradford. *Brazilian Hands of Faith*. Philadelphia: Ringing Rocks Press, 2003a.

———. *Bushman Shaman: Awakening the Spirit through Ecstatic Dance*. Rochester, Vt.: Destiny Books, 2005.

———. *Kalahari Bushman Healers*. Philadelphia: Ringing Rocks Press, 1999.

———. *Ropes to God: Experiencing the Bushman Spiritual Universe*. Philadelphia: Ringing Rocks Press, 2003b.

Keeney, Hillary, Bradford Keeney, and Ronald Chenail. "Recursive Frame Analysis: A Qualitative Research Method for Mapping the Movement of Change-Oriented Discourse." Special publication of *The Qualitative Report*, an online journal published by Nova Southeastern University (2015).

Lee, Richard B. *The Dobe Juǀ'hoansi*. 4th ed. Belmont, Calif.: Wadsworth, 2012.

———. *The Dobe !Kung*. New York: Holt, Rinehart and Winston, 1984.

Lewis-Williams, David. *Believing and Seeing: Symbolic Meanings in Southern San Rock Art*. New York: Academic Press, 1981.

Lewis-Williams, David, and Thomas Dowson. *Images of Power: Understanding Bushman Rock Art*. Johannesburg, South Africa: Southern Book Publishers, 1989.

Lewis-Williams, David, and David Pearce. *San Spirituality: Roots, Expressions, and Social Consequences*. Cape Town, South Africa: Double Storey Books, 2004.

Marshall, Lorna. "!Kung Bushman Religious Beliefs." *Africa* 32, no. 3 (1962): 221–52.

———. "The Medicine Dance of the !Kung Bushmen." *Africa* 39, no. 4 (1969): 347–81.

———. *Nyae Nyae !Kung Beliefs and Rites.* Cambridge, Mass.: Harvard University Press, 1999.

Maturana, Humberto, and Francisco Varela. *Tree of Knowledge: The Biological Roots of Understanding.* Boston: Shambhala, 1992.

Ong, Walter. *Orality and Literacy: The Technologizing of the World.* New York: Routledge, 1982.

Silberbauer, George B. "Marriage and the Girl's Puberty Ceremony of the G|wi Bushmen." *Africa: Journal of the African Institute* 33, no. 1 (1963): 12–24.

Spencer-Brown, George. *Laws of Form.* New York: Bantam, 1973.

Thurston, Linda. "Entopic Imagery in People and Their Art." Master's thesis, Gallatin Division of New York University, 1991.

Tishkoff, S. A. et al. "The Genetic Structure and History of Africans and African Americans." *Science* 324 (2009): 1035–44.

Index

xvi – film
xxi – Don't follow traditional shamanism
xxvi – most healing modalities are
stuck in trickster language & mind game
xxxi – All contrasts churn the wheel
pg. 18 resisting n|om
pg 42 life organized by n|om
pg 74 – trickster comes near us
pg 76 – excellent quote